Neither Cold War nor Détente?
Soviet-American Relations in the 1980s

Contributors

Seyom Brown

John Lewis Gaddis

Richard A. Melanson

Thomas W. Robinson

Myron Rush

Harry M. Scoble

Kenneth W. Thompson

Allen S. Whiting

Laurie S. Wiseberg

Alexander Yanov

Neither Cold War nor Détente?

Soviet-American Relations in the 1980s

Edited by Richard A. Melanson

University Press of Virginia

Charlottesville

THE UNIVERSITY PRESS OF VIRGINIA
Copyright © 1982 by the Rector and Visitors
of the University of Virginia

First published 1982

John Lewis Gaddis, "Containment: Its Past and Future," © 1982 by John Lewis Gaddis. Alexander Yanov, "Toward a Method to Madness: The U.S.S.R. in the 1980s," © 1982 by Alexander Yanov. Myron Rush, "The Future Soviet Leadership," © 1982 by Myron Rush. Allen S. Whiting, "Sino-Soviet Relations in the 1980s," © 1982 by Allen S. Whiting. Thomas W. Robinson, "American Policy in the Strategic Triangle," © 1982 by Thomas W. Robinson, Kenneth W. Thompson, "Human Rights and Soviet-American Relations," © 1982 by Kenneth W. Thompson. Laurie S. Wiseberg and Harry M. Scoble, "Human Rights and Soviet-American Relations: The Role of the NGOs," © 1982 by Laurie S. Wiseberg and Harry M. Scoble. Richard A. Melanson, "A *Neo-Consensus?* American Foreign Policy in the 1980s," © 1982 by Richard A. Melanson. Seyom Brown, "Power and Prudence in Dealing with the U.S.S.R.," © 1982 by Seyom Brown.

Publication of this volume is sponsored by the Kenyon College Public Affairs Conference Center, Kenyon College, Gambier, Ohio. The authors above are responsible for the opinions expressed and any policies recommended in their respective papers. The Kenyon College Public Affairs Conference Center is a nonpartisan educational program and as such takes no position on questions of public policy.

Library of Congress Cataloging in Publication Data
Main entry under title:

Neither cold war nor detente?

Background papers of a conference held at Kenyon College Public Affairs Conference Center, Gambier, Ohio, Sept. 18-20, 1980.
Includes index.
1. United States—Foreign relations—Soviet Union—Congresses. 2. Soviet Union—Foreign relations—United States—Congresses. 3. United States—Foreign relations—1981- —Congresses. 4. Soviet Union—Foreign relations—1975- —Congresses. I. Melanson, Richard A. II. Public Affairs Conference Center.
E183.8.S65N44   327.73047   81-16299
ISBN 0-8139-0924-4   AACR2

Printed in the United States of America.

Contents

Preface	vii
Containment: Its Past and Future John Lewis Gaddis	1
Toward a Method to Madness: The U.S.S.R. in the 1980s Alexander Yanov	34
The Future Soviet Leadership Myron Rush	69
Sino-Soviet Relations in the 1980s Allen S. Whiting	90
American Policy in the Strategic Triangle Thomas W. Robinson	112
Human Rights and Soviet-American Relations Kenneth W. Thompson	134
Human Rights and Soviet-American Relations: The Role of the NGOs Laurie S. Wiseberg and Harry M. Scoble	151
A *Neo-Con*sensus? American Foreign Policy in the 1980s Richard A. Melanson	186
Power and Prudence in Dealing with the U.S.S.R. Seyom Brown	215
Contributors	239
Index	241

Preface

There is no more significant theme in modern American foreign policy than our relations with the Soviet Union. Ever since the titanic ideological struggle between Lenin and Woodrow Wilson, Soviet-American relations have been characterized by an unstable blend of ignorance, distrust, enmity, and sobriety. The 1980s promise to be a decade of exceptional danger in these relations because of a host of new and continuing global, regional, domestic, and technological issues.

On September 18, 1980, about thirty distinguished men and women passionately interested in the future of Soviet-American relations gathered in Gambier, Ohio, for a three-day conference sponsored by the Kenyon College Public Affairs Conference Center. Drawn from academe, government, business, the press, and public interest groups, the conferees intensively discussed the nine essays published in this volume. The conferees represented a wide spectrum of opinion, and, not surprisingly, points of consensus emerged much less frequently from these discussions than did areas of disagreement. What this conference did, however, was to initiate a dialogue on a theme of paramount importance, to sharpen and refine perspectives, and to assist the essayists in the revision of their papers.

No volume that seeks to be accessible to the educated public can hope to deal comprehensively with every issue in the complex interactions between the United States and the Soviet Union. The reader will look in vain for essays dealing exclusively with weapons technology, arms control, economic ties, or the Persian Gulf, although several of the papers touch on aspects of these problems. Rather, these essays focus on five significant dimensions of Soviet-American relations, and do so from a variety of viewpoints. Specifically, John Lewis Gaddis examines the history of the Cold War and suggests a set of considerations that ought to guide American foreign policy during the 1980s; Alexander Yanov and Myron Rush offer provocative analyses of the Soviet succession question; Allen S. Whiting and Thomas W. Robinson consider the massive complexities of Sino-Soviet-American relations and propose two quite distinct policies for the United States during the next decade; Kenneth W. Thompson and Laurie S. Wiseberg and Harry M. Scoble look at the volatile problem of human rights in Soviet-American relations; and finally Richard A. Melanson and Seyom Brown suggest American policies toward the Soviets in the 1980s that differ both from one another and from the one offered by Gaddis.

By thus limiting the central concerns of the essays and the conference and by juxtaposing distinctive perspectives on these several themes, I have attempted to present the major options that will be available to the United States in the 1980s vis-à-vis the Soviet Union. The result, I hope, is a thoughtful and balanced volume, of interest to policymakers, university audiences, and the "attentive public."

We gratefully acknowledge our indebtedness to the Armco Foundation, the Exxon Education Foundation, B. F. Goodrich Company, Eli Lilly and Company, Marathon Oil Company, Murch and Company, Inc., Owens-Illinois Fund, and the Procter and Gamble Company, whose generosity helped to make this conference possible. I would particularly like to thank Mrs. Sheryl A. Furniss, Administrative Assistant to the Public Affairs Conference Center, William S. Reed, Vice President for Development of Kenyon College, Robert H. Horwitz, former Director of the PACC, and Mrs. Judy Sacks, for their patient, generous, and skillful assistance.

RICHARD A. MELANSON
Director, Kenyon College
Public Affairs Conference
Center

Neither Cold War nor Détente?
Soviet-American Relations in the 1980s

Containment: Its Past and Future

John Lewis Gaddis

NATIONS, like individuals, tend to be prisoners of their pasts. Rarely has this been more true than in the thirty-seven years of Soviet-American competition we know as the Cold War. That phenomenon, one of the longest-running in modern times, has appeared, more than once, to be on the verge of passing from the scene, but it never really has. Something always seems to happen to revive it—Korea, Hungary, the U-2, Vietnam, Czechoslovakia, Angola, the Carter human rights campaign, Afghanistan—just as pundits are about to consign the Cold War to those scavengers of dead issues and defunct controversies, the historians.

Why this extraordinary durability? How is it that a rivalry that arose three and a half decades ago over issues few leaders on either side today would be capable of recalling, much less discussing intelligently—how is it that such a competition can still preoccupy us today, in a world that could hardly be more different from that of 1945? And how is it that this rivalry, which, in any other age, would long ago have produced war, has not in fact done so, even though by anyone's standards there has been ample provocation? What are the prospects that this standoff between competition and caution will continue? What policies should the United States adopt in the 1980s to insure that it does?

I

The Cold War began as a direct outgrowth of the way World War II ended, with victorious powers on opposite sides of the globe separated, both in Europe and Northeast Asia, by power vacuums. If anything ever is inevitable in history, it was probably inevitable that the uneasy coalition Hitler had given rise to would break up,

A somewhat different version of this essay appeared in *International Security* 5, no. 4 (Spring 1981): 74–102.

once the force that had brought it together had ceased to exist. The controversies that ensued over Eastern Europe, Germany and Berlin, the Balkans, Turkey, Iran, Japan, and Korea were all part of the process of postwar adjustment among the superpowers. They grew out of the probes and counter-probes by which great states demarcate respective spheres of influence, organize blocs, establish tacit "rules of the game," and in general settle down to the perpetual condition of wary coexistence that develops when neither side can dominate the other.

The ideological competition between communism and capitalism had been present, of course, since the days of the Bolshevik Revolution, but it was not a primary cause of the Cold War. Both Russians and Americans tended to view ideology more as a justification for action than as a guide to action; both, as they showed during World War II, were capable of subordinating ideological differences to pursue common interests where those existed. Once they disappeared, though, ideology did become the chief means by which each side differentiated friend from foe. The Soviet Union moved, somewhat belatedly, to consolidate its sphere of influence in Eastern Europe by imposing communist regimes there; the United States, also somewhat belatedly, came to see in the ideological orientation of states and movements reliable evidence of where they stood in the global competition for power. Admittedly, the pattern was not always perfect. The Soviet Union did not insist on imposing communist governments everywhere within its sphere of influence—Finland was the notable exception. Nor did the United States, as the case of Yugoslavia showed, consign to the outer darkness all communist states. In general, though, and with increasing frequency as the years went on, ideology did become the mechanism by which alignments were drawn in the Cold War, even to the point that the United States refused, for many years, to cooperate with the People's Republic of China in a task in which both had a strong interest—containing the Russians.

Once it was underway, the Cold War took on yet a third dimension—that of an arms race. Here, appearances were more important than reality. We now know that throughout the first two and a half decades of the Cold War, the Soviet Union was inferior to the United States in all major categories of weapons except manpower. But until the deployment of satellite reconnaissance capabilities in the early 1960s, Washington had no reliable means of verifying that fact, nor were the Russians cooperative in providing one. As a consequence, the arms race appeared to be closer than it actually was: Until 1961 the United States perceived itself as operating from a position of strategic inferiority, or something very near to it; after 1961, when Washington convinced itself that it was in fact ahead of the Russians, it was actually in the process of losing that advantage, thanks to the Kremlin's decision to switch, in the wake of the Cuban missile crisis, from an emphasis on rhetorical weapons to real ones.

A fourth dimension the Cold War took on was that of a competition for influence in the so-called Third, or Nonaligned, World. This, again, was an aspect of the struggle that did not surface immediately: Stalin's interest in supporting national liberation movements beyond his control was notoriously tepid. With Khrushchev, though, the arena of competition did shift to Asia, Africa, and Latin America, greatly aided by the grievances inhabitants of those regions had, rightly or not, against the industrialized West.

There is yet a fifth dimension of the Cold War that is more difficult to characterize than the others, but no less important: This is the Cold War as the product of internal influences within the two major countries involved. George F. Kennan had argued as early as 1946 that the Soviet leadership required the existence of a hostile outside world in order to justify its own repressive rule; there was nothing the West could do to allay Moscow's paranoia, he seemed to be saying, because the regime needed external threats to provide internal legitimacy.[1] Similarly, revisionist critics of American foreign policy have more recently made the argument that the requirements of capitalism force the United States into an imperial posture: It is we, not the Russians, they maintain, who find it necessary regularly to disrupt the international order.[2] Whether one accepts the argument or not, it is not too difficult to suggest groups or interests within the United States who might benefit from a continuation of the Cold War: defense contractors

[1] See Kennan's telegrams from Moscow of February 22 and March 20, 1946, in U.S., Department of State, *Foreign Relations of the United States: 1946, Diplomatic Papers* vol. 6, *Eastern Europe; The Soviet Union* (Washington, D.C., 1969), pp. 696–709, 721–23.

[2] Robert W. Tucker, *The Radical Left and American Foreign Policy* (Baltimore, 1971), pp. 28–39, provides a succinct summary of the revisionist argument.

eager for arms sales, ethnic groups who for one reason or another nurse grudges against the Russians, career bureaucrats and military personnel whose budgets and promotion opportunities are tied to high levels of defense spending, and, perhaps most important, politicians attempting to win favor with the voters by the time-honored tactic of running against Moscow. Presumably parallel, though of course not precisely equivalent, impulses operate within the Soviet Union as well.

There have been, then, not one but several Cold Wars, and it is this multidimensional character that helps to explain the conflict's remarkable durability. It has had the capacity to shift from one arena of competition to another so that as settlements are reached in one area, rivalries break out elsewhere. It is as if a virus had the capacity to evolve into new and more resistant strains as each new antigen is developed against them. Although the last three dimensions of the Cold War—the arms race, the struggle for influence in the Third World, and external hostility as the product of internal interests—are the most virulent today, there is no reason to think that this process of shifting has ended, or is likely to anytime soon. It may be some time, then, before we can safely regard the Cold War, in its entirety, as history.

II

Before examining current aspects of the Cold War, though, some attempt should be made to address the tangled question of responsibility for it. Students of international affairs generally shy away from issues of responsibility: It is more important, they argue, to find out what happened; to get into arguments over "why" is to slide into the slippery realm of metaphysics.[3] That attitude may be appropriate enough for purely scholarly purposes, but when it comes to the policy implications of scholarly analysis, it will not

[3] See, for example, Daniel Yergin, *Shattered Peace: The Origins of the Cold War and the National Security State* (Boston, 1977), p. 7; also, from a methodological perspective, David Hackett Fischer, *Historians' Fallacies: Toward a Logic of Historical Thought* (New York, 1970), pp. 14–15, 182–83; and Robert Stover, "Responsibility for the Cold War—A Case Study in Historical Responsibility," *History and Theory* 11 (1972): 145–78.

do. To avoid judgments on responsibility for past events is to atrophy standards necessary for guidance in the future: We need careful thought about this question of responsibility if we are to avoid either the smug complacency of imagined moral superiority or the self-destructive effects of blaming everything that happens in this less-than-perfect world on ourselves.

In a sense, both superpowers have perceived themselves as acting primarily for defensive reasons during most of the Cold War. Whether justifiably or not, both the Soviet Union and the United States have explained their projection of influence over much of the rest of the world as necessary to protect themselves against the other. We will not get very far, then, by attempting to evaluate responsibility on the basis of where defensive motivations existed and where they did not. It is the nature of great powers that they often do offensive things for defensive reasons.

The more productive approach is to ask which great power was more capable of meeting its security requirements within the context of the existing international order and which required fundamental changes in that order to be secure. Here we come to the heart of the difference between American and Soviet behavior in the Cold War; it is from this perspective that we can best shed light on the issue of responsibility.

Americans have had the reputation, over the years, of wanting to change the international order. One thinks of Woodrow Wilson's Fourteen Points, Cordell Hull's schemes for reforming the world trade system, the Atlantic Charter, the original campaign for the United Nations. But not one of those initiatives was ever considered vital to the security of the United States: They were put forward, mostly sincerely, mostly with good intentions, but without that implacable determination—that unwillingness to compromise —that occurs when one's vital interests are at stake. Ours never really were in this somewhat utopian and certainly irregularly pursued effort to remake the world; as far as fundamental security interests were concerned, we were as content with the existing international system as the most cynical—and, in this country, most criticized—of our Old World allies.

Not so the Soviet Union. It is true that Stalin often spoke in traditional balance-of-power terms: All would be well, he implied, if the Soviet Union could only be granted its legitimate security interests. The problem was that he never made it clear how far those interests extended. The West was reluctantly prepared to grant Stalin the boundary concessions and subservient governments he wanted in Eastern Europe, nor did it balk at meeting his initial territorial demands in the Far East, despite the Soviet Union's minimal role in the war against Japan.[4] But Stalin wanted more: the northern provinces of Iran, for example, or control of the Turkish Straits, or a unified but subservient Germany, or the right to occupy Hokkaido. He also quite clearly refused to abide by promises he had made to hold free elections in the areas he occupied—notably Poland and North Korea—and he used (though somewhat cautiously) communist parties elsewhere to promote the objectives of the Soviet Union. It was not that Stalin had global ambitions or any fixed timetable for achieving them. It was just that he could not resist exploiting opportunities, and he had the patience to wait for them to arise.

There was, as a consequence, a fundamental difference in the way Soviet and American expansion proceeded in the postwar years. Soviet expansion reflected discontent with the world as it was, together with a determination to change it in such a way as to accommodate Moscow. American expansion took place, not so much out of dissatisfaction with the world as it was, as with the world as it would be if the Russians had their way. Soviet expansion took place for the most part against the wishes of the people involved; American expansion took place almost entirely at the fervent invitation of those worried about the Russians.[5]

This is not to say that both nations, once they acquired empires, did not behave in an imperial manner. Both fell into the habit of looking at the world in terms of a zero-sum game, in which gains for one invariably meant losses for the other. Both tended to lose sight, as a consequence, of the distinction between vital and peripheral interests. Both responded, at various times, by overcommitting themselves, although Americans, who tended to do their

[4] Further details can be found in John Lewis Gaddis, *The United States and the Origins of the Cold War: 1941–1947* (New York, 1972), pp. 77–79, 133–73.

[5] For a recent confirmation of this thesis, see Bruce R. Kuniholm, *The Origins of the Cold War in the Near East: Great Power Conflict and Diplomacy in Iran, Turkey, and Greece* (Princeton, 1980), pp. 345, 381–82.

own fighting, allowed this to happen more often than did the Russians, who relied more heavily on proxies.

These similarities in behavior, however, should not be allowed to obscure the very real differences in motivation that give rise to them. The fact is that the United States throughout the history of the Cold War has, on the whole, been reconciled to living with the world as it is, while the Soviet Union, more for historical and institutional than ideological reasons, has seen its security as dependent on changing it. In this sense (though not in the classic Marxist-Leninist sense), the United States has been the status quo power, the Soviet Union the revolutionary power, and that fact ought not to be lost sight of in assessing responsibility for the Cold War.

III

If we can establish, then, that the dominant pattern in the Cold War has been one of Soviet action and American reaction (for this is what is suggested by the conclusion that the Soviet Union finds it more difficult to live with the existing world order than does the United States), then the question arises: How has the United States handled this problem over the years? How, and with what results, has it responded to Moscow's successive efforts to restructure the international system to its advantage?

The answer, of course, is containment, but it is immediately necessary to differentiate between the various approaches to that strategy that have been tried over the years. All postwar administrations have seen American security as tied up with the maintenance of a global balance of power. All have seen the Soviet Union as the major threat to that balance, though they have differed over the extent to which Moscow was capable of drawing other communist nations into that enterprise. All have sought to harness American resources, along with those of allies, in a joint effort to restrict the further growth of Soviet influence in the world, in order that the diversity upon which our system depends can be maintained.[6]

Nevertheless, there have been two distinct styles of containment

[6] Seyom Brown, *The Faces of Power: Constancy and Change in United States Foreign Policy from Truman to Johnson* (New York, 1968), pp. 7–14.

in the postwar era—styles which can best be categorized as symmetrical and asymmetrical response. Symmetrical response simply means reacting to threats to the balance of power at the same location, time, and level of violence of the original provocation. It implies the idea of calibration: One tailors response to offense, doing no more but also no less than is necessary to counter the threat in question, without running the risk of escalation or suffering the humiliation of surrender. Asymmetrical response involves shifting the location or nature of one's reaction onto terrain better suited to the application of one's strengths against adversary weaknesses. One may, though, in the process run the risk of escalation or, by not countering the original provocation where it occurred, humiliation.

Both approaches have been tried at various times during the postwar period. George Kennan's original containment strategy was an example of asymmetrical response in that it sought to counter the fear brought about by the Soviet military presence in Europe and Northeast Asia after World War II, not by building up countervailing military force, but by relying on United States economic aid to rehabilitate war-shattered economies in Western Europe and Japan, thereby creating in those countries the self-confidence that would allow them to resist the Russians on their own. Containment would have been achieved, Kennan argued, if the four vital centers of industrial-military power not then in Soviet hands—the United States, the United Kingdom, the Rhine Valley, and Japan—could be prevented from becoming so.[7]

By 1950, though, out of a sense of the vulnerability the United States felt as a result of not matching perceived Soviet military capabilities (and especially after the unexpectedly early first test of a Soviet atomic bomb), Washington shifted, with NSC-68, to symmetrical response: We had to be prepared, the argument ran, to counter whatever aggression the Russians threw at us, but without resorting to nuclear weapons, where we no longer possessed a monopoly, and without capitulating, an action which, if it occurred anywhere, could lead to an erosion of credibility everywhere.[8] The

[7] George F. Kennan, *Memoirs: 1925–1905* (Boston, 1967), p. 359. See also John Lewis Gaddis, "Containment: A Reassessment," *Foreign Affairs* 55 (July 1977): 873–87.

[8] NSC–68, "United States Objectives and Programs for National Security,"

way in which we fought the Korean War was an excellent example of symmetrical response: We countered an enemy provocation at the location, time, and in the manner of its original occurrence, without surrendering, but also without setting off a wider war.

The effort proved costly, though, and the American people grew impatient with it; those frustrations contributed to the victory at the polls in 1952 of General Eisenhower and the Republicans. Their objective was to maintain American interests throughout the world against what was seen as a centrally directed monolith controlled from Moscow, but to do it at less cost than the symmetrical response strategy of NSC-68 had entailed. Accordingly, they went back to the concept of asymmetrical response, but this time with reliance on the threat to use nuclear weapons as the primary deterrent: The idea was to create uncertainty in the minds of potential adversaries as to what the United States might do if aggression took place, thereby making the risks appear to outweigh the benefits.[9] We would respond to aggression, as Dulles liked to say, with ominous vagueness, "at times and in places of our own choosing."

Unfortunately, though, the Eisenhower-Dulles strategy of asymmetrical response had two major liabilities: it seemed to run the risk of nuclear war over minor matters (Quemoy and Matsu were conspicuous examples), and it seemed incapable of preventing communist victories under the guise of national liberation movements in the Third World. It was in part by capitalizing on these deficiencies that John F. Kennedy and the Democrats gained the White House in 1961; there was nothing very original about their strategy, though, as they took the country quickly back to the symmetrical response approach of NSC-68. Like the authors of that earlier document, Kennedy and his advisors regarded American interests in the world as indivisible, but they also saw means as expandable; therefore, they argued, the United States could afford

---

April 14, 1950, *Foreign Relations of the United States: 1950*, 1: 237–92. For a recent reassessment, see Samuel F. Wells, Jr., "Sounding the Tocsin: NSC 68 and the Soviet Threat," *International Security* 4 (Fall 1979): 116–58, and subsequent commentaries on that article by Paul Nitze and the present author in 4 (Spring 1980): 164–76.

[9] The best analysis is Glenn H. Snyder, "The 'New Look' of 1953," in Warner R. Schilling, Paul Y. Hammond, and Glenn H. Snyder, *Strategy, Politics, and Defense Budgets* (New York, 1962), pp. 379–524.

to act to counter aggression wherever it occurred without either the dangers of nuclear war or the embarrassments of humiliation.

The chief result of this return to symmetry, of course, was the war in Vietnam, the most egregious American example in the postwar period of offensive actions taken for what were perceived to be defensive reasons; a war that, like Korea, was consistent with prevailing national strategy but also, by demonstrating the costs of the strategy, in the end discredited it. The debacle in Vietnam paved the way for the Nixon victory in 1968 and for a return, once again, to asymmetrical response.

The Nixon-Kissinger strategy reflected this emphasis in several respects. It called, through the Nixon Doctrine, for a cutting back of American commitments in the world: Allies, it implied, would bear a greater share of the burden of their defense, with the United States helping out, where needed, by furnishing technology but not manpower.[10] It called for countering Soviet challenges to the balance of power through a combination of pressures and inducements designed to get Moscow to accept certain "rules of the game" —to persuade the Russians that it was in their own best interests to accept the world as it was rather than to try to change it. This process was intended to work through the application of linkage— in itself an asymmetrical concept, implying the withholding of concessions in some areas until others were granted elsewhere. The goal was a multipolar world operating on balance-of-power principles—an idea not too different from what Kennan had sought some twenty-five years before.[11]

This emphasis on asymmetry continued through the end of the Ford administration, but not without coming under sharp attack from symmetrically minded critics who charged that détente had produced an erosion in American strategic and conventional capabilities relative to those of the Soviet Union.[12] Despite ample

[10] The clearest formulation of the Nixon Doctrine is in Nixon's first annual foreign policy report, February 18, 1970, *Public Papers of the Presidents: Richard M. Nixon: 1970* (Washington, D.C., 1971), pp. 905–6.

[11] See especially, in this connection, Nixon's speech at Kansas City, July 6, 1971, *Nixon Public Papers: 1971* (Washington, D.C., 1972), p. 806; and the interview with him in *Time*, January 3, 1972, p. 15.

[12] Alan Tonelson, "Nitze's World," *Foreign Policy*, no. 35 (Summer 1979),

provocation from the Russians, the Carter administration never accepted that argument, less out of respect for the strategic legacy of Henry Kissinger, one gathers, than from the fact that no one has yet demonstrated how the nation can afford a return to symmetrical response in an era of energy dependency and double-digit inflation.

What is striking, in retrospect, about this oscillation between symmetry and asymmetry, is how little most of it has had to do with what the Russians were up to at any given point. Without exception, shifts in strategies of containment since 1947 have coincided, not with new Kremlin initiatives, but with shifts in perceptions of means in Washington. Perceptions of means have played a larger role than perceptions of threats in shaping our policy toward the Soviet Union: The implications, it would seem, are not encouraging for those who seek a consistent and coherent foreign policy carefully insulated from domestic considerations.

IV

There have been several attempts at détente in postwar Soviet-American relations: the "thaw" following Stalin's death in 1953; Eisenhower's attempts, in 1959 and 1960, to establish a dialogue with Khrushchev; Kennedy's comparable efforts, partly successful after the Cuban missile crisis; Johnson's continuation of that approach, frustrated by the change of leadership in Moscow and American escalation in Vietnam. Not until 1969, though, did the same interest in a relaxation of tensions exist in roughly the same proportions on both sides: The decade that followed saw a sustained attempt on the part of both Moscow and Washington to move beyond Cold War rigidities that must now, in the light of Afghanistan and Poland, be regarded as having failed.

The reason, it would seem, is that both sides were to a greater extent prisoners of Cold War thinking than they realized at the time: Americans and Russians embraced détente with differing expectations of what it would produce—expectations colored, to a considerable degree, by legacies of the past.

---

pp. 74–90. See also the discussion of the current Committee on the Present Danger, in Wells, "Sounding the Tocsin," pp. 149–51.

Nixon and Kissinger, for example, thought of détente as an updated form of containment.[13] Their idea was to achieve nothing less than a modification of Soviet behavior by rewarding actions that showed a disposition to accept the world as it was and by discouraging, through the application of pressures and constraints, those that did not. It was a bit like trying to train a rat or a pigeon in a psychology laboratory to perform certain tricks in response to a carefully crafted and precisely measured series of rewards and punishments.[14]

The Russians, on the other hand, saw détente as a means of rendering safer the process of changing the international order. It was, they clearly said, a means of controlling competition in dangerous areas like nuclear weapons, while continuing it in others: The idea, in short, was compartmentalization.[15] True, the Soviet Union could benefit from certain concessions from the West, especially in the form of trading privileges. But it would not pay all that much to get them; in fact, Kremlin leaders probably believed they would not have to pay anything at all, given the abiding venality of Western capitalists eager to find buyers, even if communist buyers, for their products.

For a time, it seemed possible to paper over the differences. The Russians at Moscow in 1972 signed a statement of "Basic Principles" that appeared to rule out efforts to exploit Third World crises at the expense of the United States.[16] Summit meetings proceeded on more or less an annual basis during the early 1970s, with protestations of friendship covering up the fact that fewer and fewer meaningful agreements were being made. By the middle of the decade, though, cracks in the facade were becoming too noticeable to ignore.

One was Moscow's alleged failure to prevent the 1973 Egyptian attack on Israel and the 1975 North Vietnamese offensive against

---

[13] Coral Bell, *The Diplomacy of Détente: The Kissinger Era* (New York, 1977), pp. 1–3.

[14] The analogy is Stanley Hoffmann's, in *Primacy or World Order: American Foreign Policy since the Cold War* (New York, 1978), p. 46.

[15] A succinct statement of the Soviet view of détente can be found in Leonid Brezhnev, *On the Policy of the Soviet Union and the International Situation* (Garden City, N.Y., 1973), pp. 230–31.

[16] U.S., Department of State, *Bulletin* 66 (June 26, 1972), 898–99.

Containment

South Vietnam, acts of omission that seemed inconsistent with the injunctions against profiting from the discomfiture of others so solemnly invoked at the first Moscow summit. Another sign of strain came over the issue of human rights, with first Congress and then the Carter administration making changes in the Soviet treatment of Jews and dissidents a prerequisite for progress on economic and other issues. A third problem arose from the projection of Soviet power and influence into Africa, chiefly through the use of Cuban proxies, in what seemed to be a clear attempt to exploit remaining anticolonial sentiment there to the disadvantage of the West. Still another nail in the coffin of détente was the Soviet Union's continuing buildup in its strategic missile capabilities, a trend which, if it did not directly contravene the SALT I agreement, did at least seem ill-matched to the spirit of mutual restraint most Americans believed had been implied in those agreements. Afghanistan, of course, was the final blow.

It is not difficult, in retrospect, to pick out deficiencies in the American approach to détente during this period. The Nixon administration probably pushed linkage too vigorously, demanding that the Russians act to restrain countries over which they had limited leverage in the first place. It is not at all clear that the Russians could have stopped the Egyptians in 1973 or the North Vietnamese in 1975, even if they had wanted to. Then, too, linkage implied tight control—knowing just when to apply rewards and punishments, without going overboard on either. But the Nixon administration lost control of the linkage process almost at once, with the introduction in the fall of 1972 of the Jackson-Vanik amendment; in the years that followed Kissinger oscillated between yielding to and resisting congressional pressures to link détente to the Soviet performance on human rights, exerted without any clear notion on the part of the legislators of what precisely should be demanded or what should be granted in return. The Carter administration further compounded the confusion by first elevating the question of human rights to the level of universal principle but then abandoning the idea of linkage that seemed to offer the best hope of securing Soviet cooperation in that area in the first place.[17]

[17] See, on this point, Strobe Talbott, *Endgame: The Inside Story of SALT II* (New York, 1979), pp. 48–49, 146–47.

Similarly, on the issue of strategic arms, the administrations of Nixon, Ford, and Carter all tried, from an unfavorable position that saw American military power shrinking relative to that of the U.S.S.R., to negotiate arms-control treaties that would limit further Soviet gains without imposing dangerous restrictions on the United States. To a remarkable degree, they succeeded: Critics have yet to demonstrate convincingly how the SALT I agreements or their unratified SALT II counterparts left the United States inferior to the Russians in the overall calculus of strength that goes to make up deterrence.[18] But the agreements did require tolerating asymmetries, and that idea was difficult to sell to an uneasy public (and Congress) that saw quantitative indices of strategic power declining but failed to see the justification for freezing that disproportion permanently.

The United States also erred in not taking Brezhnev and his colleagues at their word when they said that détente would not preclude efforts to aid "liberation" movements in the Third World. As a result, Angola, Somalia, Ethiopia, and Yemen all became symbols of Soviet bad faith, when in fact the Russians were only honoring their own public promises, thereby meeting a standard to which Americans had often sought to hold them in the past. The most ridiculous manifestation of aggrieved American innocence came in the summer of 1979, when the Carter administration, hoping at once to defuse critics and avoid leaks, made public through Senator Frank Church the "unacceptable" presence of a Soviet combat brigade in Cuba—only to have to find it "acceptable" after all when it developed that the unit had been there for years and that Washington had no practical means of getting it out. Calling public attention to one's own impotence is, even in the best of circumstances, an unlikely way to enhance one's credibility.

Before carrying these criticisms too far, though, it is worth noting that things have not always worked out well for the Soviet Union either. The effect of the 1973 Middle East war, despite the ensuing oil embargo, was to boost the reputation of Americans, not Russians, in the Arab world. The 1975 Helsinki agreement, proposed initially by Moscow as a means of legitimizing its control over East-

---

[18] Hoffmann, *Primacy or World Order*, p. 54. See also the record of Soviet concessions on SALT II detailed in Talbott, *Endgame*, especially pp. 134–35, 181–83.

ern Europe, is now remembered more for the attention it shed on human rights violations there and in the Soviet Union than for the purposes for which the Kremlin wanted it. Soviet incursions into Africa may have won Moscow temporary control in certain countries, but they are hardly all reliable allies today. Moreover, and as a consequence, Africans are coming to see Russians rather than Americans as inheritors of the imperialist tradition there: As one observer has put it, "U.S. policy in fact lost a country [Angola] and gained a continent."[19] Moscow's clumsy handling of its relations with Japan produced similar results: For the sake of a few barren islands in the Sea of Okhotsk the Russians have managed to drive the major powers in the Far East, Japan and China, into an "antihegemonal" alignment directed, however discreetly, against them. Finally, the Soviet military buildup has now set off corresponding trends in the West, just as the Russians may have reached the stage, for economic reasons, of needing to taper off.[20]

Afghanistan is, of course, a wholly new order of provocation. For the first time since World War II, the Soviet Union has used its own troops, not proxies, in an area that has not been generally regarded as lying within its immediate sphere of influence. It is startling to realize that the Red Army has suffered more combat casualties in the past year than in the previous thirty-five. Precedents thereby established are unsettling: We can no longer rely, as we have in recent years, on the cautious nonadventurism of the Kremlin gerontocracy: the old men did bestir themselves to act, this time, in an adventurous and unpredictable way.

Taking the longer view, though, Afghanistan is likely to be regarded as a strategic error of the first order on Moscow's part, akin, in the misjudgment it reflects, to the decision to blockade Berlin in 1948, or to authorize the North Korean invasion of South Korea in 1950, or to place missiles in Cuba in 1962. It is difficult to see how whatever gains the Russians have won there outweigh their losses: (1) within the Islamic world, which, before Afghanistan, had every reason, thanks to the Palestinian impasse and events in Iran,

[19] Peter Jay, "Regionalism or Geopolitics," *Foreign Affairs* 58 ("America and the World: 1979"): 500.

[20] Andrew Marshall, "Sources of Soviet Power: The Military Potential in the 1980's," in *Prospects of Soviet Power in the 1980's*, Part II, *Adelphi Papers*, no. 152 (London, 1979), p. 11.

to be hostile to the United States; (2) in Western Europe, where NATO's sense of common danger has counterbalanced the potentially divisive effects of disproportionate energy deficiencies; (3) in American domestic politics, where the result has been to boost the fortunes of candidates the Russians would no doubt have preferred to have had defeated; (4) in the nonaligned world, where the painfully acquired leadership of a Soviet satellite, Cuba, has been abruptly discredited; and (5) in Eastern Europe and the Soviet Union itself, where the leadership has encountered as a consequence not only nuisances in the form of the American grain embargo and restrictions on technology transfers but also unaccustomed problems of public relations with regard to the Olympic boycott and, more significantly, the task of explaining what its troops are doing in Afghanistan.

One should not be too hasty, then, in deciding who gained the most from détente. All that can be said at the moment is that both sides went into it with differing expectations, that both, in varying degrees, have had their expectations disappointed, and that we are now entering a new and unpredictable stage in that long and complex phenomenon we call the Cold War.

V

Containment, therefore, will very likely remain the goal of our strategy toward the Soviet Union during the 1980s, but before suggesting what new forms it might take, we may well consider what American interests are likely to be in the decade to come and what is most likely to threaten them.

Flights of contradictory rhetoric notwithstanding, United States officials have been surprisingly consistent in defining this nation's vital interests: John F. Kennedy was only saying more explicitly what his predecessors and successors have believed when he proclaimed, two months before his death, that "the interest of the United States of America is best served by preserving and protecting a world of diversity in which no one power or combination of powers can threaten the security of the United States."[21] It has been in

[21] Kennedy speech at Salt Lake City, September 26, 1963, *Public Papers of the Presidents: John F. Kennedy: 1963* (Washington, D.C., 1964), p. 736.

the *balancing* of power, rather than in its unilateral or imperial exercise, that our security has most often been seen to rest: That there have been occasional departures from this pattern only demonstrates the untidiness of certain generalizations in history, not their overall invalidity.

What is it, then, that is most likely to threaten the existing distribution of power in the world in the 1980s? Despite Afganistan, it is not the Russians, at least not in any immediate sense: Knowing the virtues of patience, they are unlikely to undertake overt and widescale challenges to the balance of power. It is certainly not communism, not in an age when the most strident calls for Western unity and strength regularly emanate from the proletarian mandarins in Peking. It is, rather, a small and poorly understood group of states, primitive, by most standards, in their economic development, medieval in their subordination of state and even multistate interests to the dictates of religion, unsophisticated in their knowledge of the outside world and for the most part heedless of the effects of their actions upon it, and yet in a position, thanks to accidents of geology and the insatiable appetite for fossil fuels of the industrialized West, to bring it literally grinding to a halt at any moment, whether on the whim of militant students, greedy sheikhs, or fanatical ayatollahs.

The Russians, it is important to note, did not create this situation—we did that ourselves. But they are in an excellent position to exploit it, whether by gaining control of the oil-producing regions, or by interdicting lines of supply, or by simply intimidating the shaky regimes of that area to such an extent that they dole out their principal commodity, not according to the laws of economics or the needs of the West, but by a rationing plan devised in Moscow.

Coupled with this is the less immediate but no less worrisome danger posed by the Soviet Union's attainment of parity, and in certain areas, superiority, in the arms race. This achievement stems from no recent decision on the part of Kremlin leaders—the military buildup has been steady since Brezhnev and Kosygin took office in 1964, greatly aided, it should be added, by the American involvement in Vietnam, which diverted resources away from measures needed to keep up with the Russians[22] and then, by debauch-

[22] See, on this point, Harland B. Moulton, *From Superiority to Parity: The United States and the Strategic Arms Race, 1961-1971* (Westport, Conn.,

ing the currency, made it difficult if not impossible to afford to catch up. A condition of actual, as opposed to imagined, Western military inferiority is a new element in the history of the Cold War, the effects of which can be foreseen only to the point of surmising that they will not be reassuring.

What we face, then, is the task of defending our vital interests—the diversity that comes from having an international order in which no one power is dominant—from a position, not of military superiority or economic self-sufficiency, but of approaching military inferiority and already present resource dependency. It is not the most favorable position upon which to make a stand; within this general context, if not with reference to the immediate crisis in Afghanistan that gave rise to it, President Carter had some justification for making the statement that we now confront "the greatest threat to peace since the Second World War."[23]

VI

There are no quick solutions to this double problem of energy deficiency and declining military strength. Both can be dealt with, given time, but it will take years before substantial progress will be seen. What we need now are short-term measures to tide us over this crisis period, without at the same time disrupting the long-term initiatives necessary to eliminate it altogether.

Because we will be operating from a position of stringency, if not outright weakness, during this period, one thing is clear at the outset: Symmetrical response will not do. The United States and its allies cannot in the future afford to meet challenges to the balance of power on terrain and in circumstances selected by their adversaries. What this means is that we are going to have to persuade the Russians to play by our rules, rather than their own.

Moscow for years has seen détente as "compartmentalized competition"—one agrees not to compete in dangerous areas, but to do

---

1973), pp. 283–87; and, for the complaint of one who had to live with the consequences of these decisions, Henry A. Kissinger, *White House Years* (New York, 1979), p. 196.

[23] Remarks at White House briefing for members of Congress, January 8, 1980, *Weekly Compilation of Presidential Documents* 16 (January 14, 1980): 40.

so in others. But this approach gives special advantage to the power that, by its own admission, is not content with the world as it is. It allows the Russians the luxury, in setting out to change the world, of picking how and where they will do it, with the knowledge that the United States, if it follows the rules of compartmentalized competition, will not be able to shift the theater of action onto more favorable terrain. It obliges us to contest the Russians on their terms, not our own, to respond to Soviet challenges where they occur, while carrying on business as usual elsewhere.

The Russian view of détente also poses problems for the West because of its fragmented structure of political authority. Compartmentalized competition requires not only an abundance of means but also tight coordination and control; where that is lacking, as it is to a considerable extent in the United States, the NATO countries, and Japan, the way is left open for divide-and-conquer tactics. The Russians can make advantageous offers to allies, or to special interest groups within the United States—farmers, businessmen, ethnic groups, even athletes—with the expectation that self-interest can usually be counted upon to overshadow the national interest, as officially defined in Washington.

Soviet "rules of the game," not surprisingly, thus offer greater benefits to the Russians than to us. The alternative, of course, is linkage—the idea, developed by Henry Kissinger, that all elements in the Soviet-American relationship are interconnected and that concessions in one area must be compensated for by roughly equivalent concessions in others.

There are, to be sure, problems with linkage, not the least of which is that the Russians have never really accepted it. It implies leverage where none may in fact exist. It can easily be overloaded, as Congress has already demonstrated. It runs the risk of escalation —of dragging in areas, issues, or weapons previously unrelated to the question at hand for the purpose of gaining points of pressure. Given the disadvantages of compartmentalized competition, though, linkage, with all its faults, seems the preferable alternative.

How do we do it, though? What do we link? One of the lessons of the Kissinger years is that linkage ought not to be a tit-for-tat arrangement: Progress on SALT, for example, in return for restraint in Africa. The problem with such bargaining has been that it creates artificial confrontations over questions of common interest (like SALT); it assumes Moscow's willingness to attach the same value we do to the various stakes in the game; it relies on the administration's ability to insulate the linkage process from outside pressures. What we need, instead, are linkages that do not require precise calculation but will nonetheless allow the West to apply its own strengths against Soviet weaknesses, to retain the initiative while minimizing costs.

One way to do this might be to incorporate into the idea of linkage a concept not unfamiliar to the Russians—that of the "correlation of forces," the overall direction of movement in world affairs which, Kremlin ideologists believe, is progressing inexorably toward the triumph of socialism as a matter of historical imperative. It is to our advantage to do this because world trends are not in fact proceeding in that direction—if by *socialism* one means, as the Russians do, a world congenial to their own domestic institutions. The world may be moving in a confused variety of directions at once—toward triumphs of nationalism, religion, ethnicity, irrationality, even anarchy—but there is no evidence of spontaneous movement toward the kind of world Kremlin leaders would choose, if they could.

A major, if curiously unremarked, phenomenon of the 1960s and 1970s has been the declining appeal of Soviet institutions as models elsewhere.[24] Whatever gains the Russians may have made in Angola, Vietnam, Ethiopia, Yemen, or Afghanistan, they can hardly compensate for their loss of influence in China, Indonesia, Egypt, Iraq, and among the communist parties of Western Europe. The Soviet Union is bucking the trend toward diversity that characterizes the contemporary world, and that is the West's great advantage. Survival, whether one is dealing with wind, water, or world politics, is largely a matter of accommodating one's self to irresistible forces, not fighting them. And the West (using the term loosely to include Japan) is in a far better position to do that than the Soviet Union.

The objective of containment, in this context, then, should be to bring home to Soviet leaders something Americans and many of their allies found out long ago: that the "correlation of forces" in the world favors the hegemonal aspirations of no one, and that the super-power that can bring itself to accommodate diversity

[24] Helmut Sonnefeldt, "Russia, America, and Détente," *Foreign Affairs* 56 (January 1979): 285–86.

now will be the one most likely to maintain its status and position over the long haul. It is in this sense—relating irreversible trends to immediate situations—that a revised strategy of linkage can be made to work.

But what, specifically, will be necessary to accomplish this?

VII

First, the United States is going to have to achieve a much larger degree of consistency and coordination in its foreign policy than has been evident in recent years. Nebulous indecisiveness in individuals may be irritating, quaint, or even charming, but in great nations it is without exception unsettling. It is painful, but probably accurate, to acknowledge that instability in world affairs during the past half-decade has arisen as much from Washington's failure to define a strategy as from Moscow's single-minded determination to pursue one.

It is worth inquiring into the sources of Washington's present vacillations:

(1) The beginnings of the problem can be located fairly precisely in 1972, when Senator Henry Jackson prevailed upon his Capitol Hill colleagues to take a direct role in the negotiation of trade and arms-control agreements with the Soviet Union. The result, from then on, was that talks with the Russians had to be conducted with a view to what Jackson would tolerate as well as what the Kremlin would accept: that requirement significantly complicated the task of aligning pressures and inducements to produce desired effects.

(2) Domestic politics compounded the problem, as the election of 1976 vividly demonstrated. In no recent campaign has there been such a complete subordination of international priorities to internal political concerns. The sight of an incumbent President embracing a party platform that repudiated his own foreign policy was disconcerting, at best. And many of the initial blunders of the Carter administration—the letter to Sakharov, the Vance mission to Moscow on SALT, the public commitment to pull troops out of South Korea, the abandonment of linkage—reflected hasty and ill-conceived promises made during the campaign as the challenger's

means of putting distance between himself and what he perceived to be the weaknesses of the Ford-Kissinger policies.

(3) Still another source of instability was the peculiar operating style of Carter himself. As if in deliberate reaction against the centralized decision-making style of Henry Kissinger, the new chief executive encouraged openness, flexibility, and divided authority, to the point, some would say, of cultivating inconsistency as a positive good. As a consequence, his administration was slower than any of its postwar predecessors to work out and articulate a coherent set of assumptions upon which to base policy.

Now, it could conceivably be argued that inconsistency is a good thing: It keeps one receptive to new situations and ideas; it avoids the rigidities associated with more structured systems of thought; it certainly keeps enemies guessing.

But if what one is interested in is building a more stable relationship with the Soviet Union, then the kind of inconsistency the United States has manifested over the past few years is not likely to work. It undermines the linkages necessary to impress upon the Kremlin the fact that the global "correlation of forces" is not in its favor. It upsets allies: It is unsettling to make difficult and unpopular decisions in the interests of coordinating policy with Washington, and then have Washington adopt a new policy the following week. And, most important, it is the procedure least likely to establish any kind of acceptable basis for dealing with the Russians. Whether at home or abroad, there is nothing the Kremlin abhors more than unpredictability. It is, of course, odd, on the face of it, that a self-proclaimed revolutionary power should take that position; certainly it does not always exhibit predictability in its relations with others. But that is what the Soviet Union has been brought to, partly by its ideology, which does not allow for the abrupt, the idiosyncratic, the accidental, partly by its aging leadership—old men may, from time to time, inflict surprises on others, but they do not like to have them inflicted upon themselves.

The United States during recent years has startled the Russians more than once (and the rest of the world as well): It is here that action needs to be taken first if a new strategy of containment is to succeed. There can be no real improvement in Soviet-American relations—indeed, in the American position in the world generally—until the United States "gets its act together."

VIII

A second requirement for the success of any new approach to containment ought to be to take advantage of what Clausewitz a century and a half ago called "friction." The resistance an army encounters as it moves across a battlefield, he pointed out, is only in part that provided by the enemy. It arises as well from the combination of inertia, incompetence, and accident that attends any complex enterprise: Horses get tired, columns get lost, it rains, roads turn to mud, bridges wash out, ink on maps runs, boots leak, guns rust, reinforcements and supplies fail to arrive on time, and, after a while, the whole offensive can break down without encountering a single enemy soldier.[25] "Friction," in short, was Clausewitz's anticipation of Murphy's Law: What can go wrong will go wrong.

What this means, in strategy, is that an offensive movement has several strikes against it from the beginning: It must overcome powerful and at times unforeseen forces of resistance even before confronting an adversary. The effect, Clausewitz believed, was to give the advantage to the defense, all else being equal. All else has not, of course, always been equal: Asymmetries in technology, resources, or training have, from time to time, favored offense over defense, as demonstrated by Europe's colonization of much of the rest of the world in the late nineteenth century, or the Nazi blitzkrieg in the first years of World War II, or the Allied victories that ended that conflict. But these have been transitory historical phenomena; the more frequent occurrence—and surely the one most likely today, in a world whose dominant ideology is nationalism and whose technology and resources are widely diffused—is that of resistance to rather than acquiescence in efforts to achieve what the Chinese call "hegemony."

This is where the great hidden advantage of "friction" comes in. It is always more costly—and ultimately more discouraging—to try to change the world than to accommodate one's self to it. Since we, and not the Russians, seem best suited to make that accommodation, it is they, and not we, who face the uphill battle.

This raises the possibility of enlisting, in the task of contain-

[25] Carl von Clausewitz, *On War*, ed. and trans. Michael Howard and Peter Paret (Princeton, 1976), pp. 104, 119–21.

ment, Clausewitzian "friction," an accomplishment that could make the task of limiting Soviet expansion seem far less daunting —and less expensive—than it does today. But what, specifically, can be done to facilitate that process?

(1) One answer is to know when to leave well enough alone. There are situations—Afghanistan may be one—in which the natural forces of resistance are strong enough to tie down an offensive power without significant external help or with help small in comparison to the effort required to mount the offensive in the first place. Frenetic efforts on our part to organize formal alliances or overbearing aid programs might well transfer local forces of resistance in such cases from the Russians to ourselves—as happened with the ill-conceived Eisenhower Doctrine in 1957.

(2) A second thing we can do is to get away from the unfortunate habit of defining our adversaries by their ideological orientation. George Kennan used to make the argument in the 1940s that communism was a divisive, not a unifying, force in world affairs: Sooner or later, he argued, the communist world would break up, if for no other reason than from arguments over who was to say, at any given point, what the true faith was.[26] This has in fact happened; we have belatedly come to realize that the real threat to diversity in the world is not communism but the Soviet Union and that communists elsewhere can, at times, even be enlisted in defense of that goal. Still, the temptation to revert to indiscriminate anticommunism strikes deep chords in the American body politic, especially at quadrennial intervals, and it ought to be guarded against. Nothing, for example, could be better calculated to create friction for ourselves—and conversely to minimize it for the Russians—than to treat the freely elected Marxist government of Zimbabwe in the same casually myopic way that we dealt with the freely elected Marxist government of Chile a decade ago.

(3) A third thing the United States can do to avoid friction is to deny the Russians tempting opportunities. These can arise from commitments to allies that outlast their ability to command popular support, as in Nicaragua and Iran, or from such exaggerated deference to allies that it creates openings for adversaries, as in our long-standing tendency to let Israel dictate our Palestinian policy.

---

[26] See Gaddis, "Containment: A Reassessment," pp. 878–80.

The most tempting opportunity of all, though, is our energy dependency. That we have survived this far without disaster is no guarantee for the future. When a turkey obligingly places its neck on a chopping block, it is too much to expect that someone, sooner or later, will not take advantage of the opportunity and chop it off.

(4) Friction, though, will not always, by itself, defeat a determined adversary. There may well be times when the United States and its allies will have to act themselves, whether directly against the Soviet Union or (much more likely) against Moscow's proxies and accomplices. Our strategy for undertaking such operations should be to seek maximum effect at minimum cost—here we could well learn something from Mao Tse-tung and Ho Chi Minh, whose strategies achieved just this coordination of carefully selected military action with those natural forces of resistance that can cause an adversary, by his own weight, mass, and clumsiness, to defeat himself.

Friction could be a considerable asset, then, in bringing the Russians to the realization that the "correlation of forces" is not in their favor—and we would do well to make the most of it.

IX

The question of how and in what circumstances the West might need to use force to maintain the balance of power brings up the role of the military in any new strategy of containment. What strikes one immediately in looking at this question is the often remarked disparity between the amount of hardware great powers can command and their ability to project influence in the world. There seems to be no very obvious correlation between military strength and political (or economic) influence. One need only look at the capacity of small powers—at times, even factions—to manipulate larger ones, whether through the taking of hostages in Iran or the resistance a small and disorganized band of rebels have been able to maintain against the Russians in Afghanistan, to see the problem.

It might be argued that the sophistication of nations can be measured, in large part, by the extent to which they have come to recognize the multidimensional nature of power—by the extent to which they realize that influence, in international relations, does not in fact grow out of the barrel of a gun but is the product as well of political, economic, ideological, psychological, and even these days religious considerations.

The United States through painful experience has gained some appreciation of this fact in recent years, but just as it has begun, as a consequence, to broaden its means of projecting influence in the world—and certainly the Carter human rights policy, whatever its other shortcomings, had that effect—the Soviet Union has been concentrating more and more on the military instruments of power.[27] That nation, which once sought to extend influence through a broad range of ideological, social, economic, political, as well as military means, now seems to rely primarily on the latter to shape external events to its liking.

It is as if Moscow had been following Washington's lead in this respect, but from a time lag of roughly two decades. Thus, the Russians built a big missile system after we did, they built a big navy after we did, they seem now to be in the "imperial" phase we went through in the 1950s and 1960s—and they now, in Afghanistan, even have their own Vietnam. This might suggest that we should encourage their further expansion in this direction, on the grounds that if our own experience is any guide, they will sooner or later overextend, exhaust, and ultimately contain themselves.

The argument has some validity, but it ought not to be carried too far. Historical experience also suggests that power balances rarely sustain themselves automatically; even short-term disproportions of power can be destabilizing, whether by tempting the temporarily dominant side into adventurism or by wrecking self-confidence on the side that is, for the moment, behind. Since Soviet military power relative to that of the West has increased steadily in recent years,[28] we would be well advised to inquire into the state of our own defenses, lest we incur either of those risks.

United States military forces are likely to serve two main functions in the 1980s: (1) deterring the Russians from themselves

[27] Helmut Sonnenfeldt and William G. Hyland, "Soviet Perspectives on Security," *Adelphi Papers*, no. 150 (London, 1979), pp. 15, 19–20.

[28] The most complete discussion is John M. Collins, *American and Soviet Military Trends since the Cuban Missile Crisis* (Washington, D.C., 1978).

taking, or authorizing others to take, actions that could in some significant way upset the balance of power, and (2) deterring others from actions that could have the same effect, especially by exploiting the vulnerable sources and supply lines upon which the West's appetite for imported oil has now made it dependent. The first task is in some ways the simpler one, since there is only a single center of authority upon which we have to make an impression.

At the strategic level, it would appear that existing or planned forces will be adequate to do that. NATO's recent decision to deploy Pershing II and cruise missiles will counterbalance Soviet SS-20s targeted against Western Europe; the approaching vulnerability of United States land-based missiles will be remedied by the development of the MX, the Trident submarine, the air-launched cruise missile, and possibly (provided they can be reconciled with the SALT I Treaty and prove feasible) new developments in antiballistic missile technology.[29] It is likely to remain within the capacity of Western strategic forces to make deterrence work in the 1980s—not by matching the Russians missile for missile, but simply by creating sufficient uncertainty in their minds regarding the consequences of an attack as to discourage it from being attempted in the first place.

It is in the area of conventional forces that the more serious problem lies. The Russians have, of course, long had superiority in ground capabilities; they are well on the way, though, to achieving at least approximate parity at sea and in the air as well. These are areas that require careful but fairly urgent remedial action.

Particularly worrisome is the possibility of a Soviet conventional attack, say in Europe or the Middle East, that would leave the West with no means to respond other than through the use of nuclear weapons. The resulting dilemma would be a cruel one, for the informal ban on the military use of such weapons that has grown up since Hiroshima and Nagasaki has probably done more than anything else in the postwar period to limit escalation in crises. Maintenance of the nuclear-conventional weapon "firebreak" is a vital, if too often unacknowledged, interest, not to be sacrificed lightly. And yet our inferiority in ground forces together with the ap-

[29] *Aviation Week and Space Technology* 62 (June 16, 1980), 213–21, reviews the new ABM technology.

proaching stand-off at sea and in the air might require the use of nuclear weapons to preserve the balance of power—surely, if there ever was one, an example of resorting to means likely to destroy what one is trying to save.

It is an obviously difficult problem, though not a new one. What is new is the possibility of solving it, at least in part, by exploiting revolutions in guidance and reconnaissance that have taken place in conventional weaponry in recent years. Future military historians may well regard the combination of precision-guided munitions and sophisticated reconnaissance capabilities as a revolution in the fighting of wars approaching in importance the nuclear weapons revolution of 1945. At a minimum, the ability to locate and destroy targets with unprecedented precision by nonnuclear means should reinforce Clausewitz's dictum about the superiority of the defense over the offense, and ought, as a consequence, to be fully exploited by the West.

The question of precision-guided munitions brings up the second major military problem the West will face in the 1980s— that of preventing attacks on objects or areas of vital interest by smaller nations or even terrorist groups. This, in some ways, is a more difficult problem than deterring the Russians since one is frequently at a loss to know how, where, or against whom to respond. One scenario will suffice to illustrate the problem: How would the United States and its allies react if terrorists should demonstrate a capacity, using mobile but highly accurate surface to surface missiles launched from hidden shore positions, to knock out selected supertankers transiting the Straits of Hormuz or Malacca? It would not have to happen more than once for the rise in insurance rates alone to accomplish the desired effect, and yet retaliation, or the threat of it, would be no easy matter to make credible.

The long-term solution to this problem, as to so many, is to end the West's energy dependency, but that is not going to happen anytime soon. In the meantime we may have to revive some ideas little heard from since the days of mercantilism: that a nation's power is measured in large part by the degree of self-sufficiency it is able to muster; that a major function of a nation's armed forces is to protect its commerce on the high seas; that the main threat to that commerce may come, not from the rival states one has armed one's self against, but from autonomous and largely uncontrollable raiders, marauders, and pirates.

The military components of containment in the 1980s, therefore, will be neither easily developed nor implemented, although creation of a rapid deployment force—small, highly mobile elite units capable of acting anywhere on short notice—may help. Demands of both prudence and economy will dictate some compartmentalizing of our own in dealing with this problem, though: One of our main concerns will need to be to avoid confusing the two kinds of threat we face—the Russians and the *nth* powers—and in particular not to take action against one that could have the effect of bringing it into alignment with the other. Nonproliferation is an admirable objective, whether one is dealing with nuclear weapons or with adversaries who might provide occasions to use them.

X

It is worth remembering, though, that containment is and should always be regarded as a means to an end, not as an end in itself. From the beginning that strategy has been viewed as a preliminary to negotiations with the Russians, although there have been differences from administration to administration as to when those negotiations could safely take place and what was negotiable. The diplomatic component of containment complements the military and should be considered as well in any discussion of where United States policy toward the Soviet Union should go in the 1980s.

One point should be made at the outset. It is not now, and has never been, a vital interest of the United States to make progress toward reducing world tensions contingent upon changes in the internal nature of the Soviet state. Kremlin leaders resent outside interference as much as those of any sovereign nation and are likely to forego other benefits to avoid "meddling" that seems to strike at the foundations of their authority. And even if externally inspired changes in the Soviet system were feasible, there is no guarantee that they would contribute anything more to the goal of maintaining a global balance of power than does the existing one. But the main reason why we should not set out to change the internal nature of foreign governments is a deeper one: The strength of the West lies in its ability to tolerate and coexist with states of differing social systems. To try to change other systems as a matter of deliberate national policy strikes at the very advantage the West has over the Russians: Its ability to deal self-confidently with a diverse world.

This raises the question, then, of the extent to which concern over human rights should play a role in our policy toward the U.S.S.R. There is no question that the espousal of human rights is important to the United States. It is the closest thing we have to an ideology, and that is not to be taken lightly: Nations must stand for something. It is probably the case that the Carter human rights policy, on balance, won more friends for the United States than it lost.

But no nation should take its ideology so seriously that it neglects vital interests. Certainly the Soviet Union does not do this: The most consistent elements in its diplomacy over the years have been the subordination of ideological to national priorities. We have not always reciprocated: For a time during the early Carter administration our official determination to make a point about human rights was allowed, whether deliberately or not, to overshadow our interest in pursuing détente, with unfortunate results for SALT and other issues of mutual concern. A better approach might have been to take advantage of the fragmented nature of the American body politic in dealing with this issue—to have had the government remain aloof from anything other than general expressions of concern regarding the plight of dissidents inside the Soviet Union, and then rely on the very considerable capacities of private organizations to keep specific cases, as they should be kept, in the public eye.[30]

One of the illusions we have operated under during the 1970s has been that as relations with the West improved, Kremlin leaders would become more tolerant of dissent within their borders. That did not happen—indeed, the condition of the dissidents probably worsened under détente, as our concern for them fed Moscow's paranoia. Nor should we be under any illusions that the majority

[30] For a slightly different version of this idea, see William F. Buckley, Jr., "Human Rights and Foreign Policy: A Proposal," *Foreign Affairs* 58 (Spring 1980): 775–96.

of Russians sympathize with the efforts we make on behalf of the dissidents: The incentives—and genuine rewards—offered to those who work "within the system" are far too strong.[31]

We face the simple fact that concern for human rights as a matter of principle is not a universally shared aspiration, nor is the promotion of human rights a vital American interest. It is, like communism in the Soviet Union, an aspiration to be respected and, where feasible, striven for, but not one upon which the stability of the international order, or the security of the United States, crucially depends.

Apart from the issue of human rights, however, negotiations ought to play a major role in any new approach to containment, because competitors though they have been over the past thirty-five years, the United States and the Soviet Union nonetheless share a surprising number of common interests. Negotiations aimed at enhancing these can provide the inducements that complement pressures in making containment work. We ought not to allow the Russians' misadventures in Afghanistan blind us to the fact that opportunities for mutually advantageous negotiations still exist: The world is not likely soon to revert to a condition in which all gains for one side automatically mean losses for the other.

Possible areas for negotiations include:

(1) The avoidance of nuclear war, an interest so obvious that it scarcely requires mentioning, and, related to it, a less apparent but hardly less important one: that of seeing to it that the three and a half decade ban on the use of such weapons is maintained.

(2) Arms control, both at the strategic and conventional level. The costs of arms are, of course, a crushing burden for both superpowers, probably more so for the Russians than for us. It is obviously in our interests, where safe, to lower those costs, but as SALT II has shown, it is difficult to do so when technology keeps outrunning verification capabilities. Still, there are advantages simply in regularizing the procedures of verification, even if reductions in expenditures and weapons systems do not materialize. Reliable knowledge of what the other side has, and can do, consti-

---

[31] See, on this point, the analysis in Jerry F. Hough and Merle Fainsod, *How the Soviet Union Is Governed* (Cambridge, Mass., 1979), especially pp. 277–319 and 518–55.

tutes a form of arms control in itself by helping to dispel the myths upon which arms races are built.

(3) Economic relations. The Soviet Union will for some time to come be a food- and technology-importing country, items the United States and its allies are in a position to export. We cannot and should not do this in a political vacuum: Where one has leverage, one ought to use it. Nor should we fall for the demonstrably fallacious argument that economic interdependence alone will insure harmony—the experiences of Germany and Russia in 1914 or Japan and the United States in 1941, not to mention the recent history of détente, ought to be sufficient to dispel that notion. But, conducted without illusions, trade can meet complementary needs and to that extent offers opportunities for negotiations.

(4) Energy. Here there is a major potential for conflict, since the West is, and the Soviet Union is becoming, energy deficient. The most important single issue between Washington and Moscow in the 1980s may well be whether the search for foreign oil both will need to undertake is to assume competitive or cooperative forms. At the moment competition seems more likely, but since the commodity in question is volatile in more ways than one and hence capable of being lost in the rush to acquire, there may be more interest than is now apparent in an alternative approach. At any rate, the possibilities should be explored—that is what negotiations are for.

It might appear, at first glance, that *détente* and *containment* are contradictory terms: The first would seem to imply a harmonious relationship, the second an antagonistic one. But there is less incongruity here than meets the eye, if one remembers the importance of sequence: Containment is a means of bringing about the condition of mutual restraint that must precede a relaxation of tensions, if it is to last. Containment must also be coupled with opportunities for negotiation if one is to avoid reinforcing the sense of insecurity in adversaries that made the strategy necessary in the first place. In the absence of incentives for restraint, negotiations alone are unlikely to produce détente. With those provided by an updated version of containment, though, it might yet be possible to reconstitute the relatively amicable relationship of the early 1970s, but to do so this time on a basis more firmly grounded in the selfish, though not necessarily mutually exclusive, interests of both sides.

XI

To write of the future of containment is to risk dispensing bromides: There is a fine line in these matters between the profound and the platitudinous. And yet too much of our thinking in this area equates insight with complexity. There is a curious fascination with how policy is formulated at the expense of what it should contain; with process over substance. To an extent, this is unavoidable in a country where diverse centers of power contend vigorously for the privilege of saying what policy should be (and where diverse academics compete with equal vigor to chronicle the process). But the world will not indefinitely tolerate domestically derived irresolution, at however sophisticated a level, without exacting a price. The time will come when we will need to return to simple thoughts about interests, threats, and feasible responses in world affairs, and when that happens, the bromides of containment, sufficiently revised to reflect contemporary realities, are likely to provide the most appropriate mechanism.

Toward a Method to Madness: The U.S.S.R. in the 1980s

Alexander Yanov

I

THE 1980s have a quite special role in Soviet eschatology. In October 1920 Lenin promised that "the generation which is now 15 years old will see [Communist society]."[1] The elders of the present Soviet leadership are the survivors of this generation. In the 1990s they are unlikely to see anything. Their last chance to get acquainted with the final stage of human society expires in the coming decade. Do they still hope to see it, or was Lenin's prophecy a false one?

Only two decades ago it seemed that there was still promise. In October 1961, exactly forty-one years after Lenin's prediction, the Communist party through the mouth of its then leader solemnly confirmed the promise of the founding father: "We are guided by strictly scientific calculations, and these calculations show that in 20 years we will build Communist society."[2] Khrushchev described this national goal as a consumer heaven, "a cup of plenty which will always be filled to the rim."[3] Thus, for forty years the Communist Moses led his people through the biblical desert, and in the forty-first year he showed them the Promised Land. Such was Khrushchev's prediction for the U.S.S.R. in the 1980s.

I do not remember anyone laughing at this prediction. On the contrary *The Times of India*, for example, wrote that "the feasibility of the Program . . . is not subject to doubt. At least, Afro-Asian peoples are impressed by Soviet achievements, which give

---

[1] V. I. Lenin, *Poln. sobr. soch.* Complete Works, 4th Ed. (Moscow, 1969), 31:274.

[2] *XXII s"ezd Kommunisticheskoi partii Sovetskogo Soiuza: Stenograficheskii otchet*, vol. 7 (Moscow, 1962), p. 106.

[3] Ibid., p. 163.

Toward a Method to Madness 35

rise among them to the conviction that Russia will keep all her promises."[4] Even the skeptical London *Economist* agreed that "the promises of this manifesto do not seem fantastic."[5] Naturally, the Soviet press rejoiced. Here is how it pictured international reaction to the proclamation of the new national goal:

> Now in the West there is not a single periodical which does not contain something about this. Walt Rostow, in an article published in *U.S. News and World Report,* admits after all "the socialist method of planning," allowing the country to be brought in the shortest possible time from a backward to a leading one. And Gustav Johansen in the Norwegian newspaper *Neu Dag* notes that in the growth of the volume of production, the capitalist countries now have a new model. Now they attempt to achieve "the level of the Russians." "The Russians are moving full steam ahead," *Business Week* said. Arthur Goldberg, the American Secretary of Labor, reporting of the production of steel in our country, exclaimed: "An astonishing impression!"[6]

We do not hear anything of this sort upon entering the 1980s—no predictions, no exclamations, no rejoicing. The Promised Land disappeared from the Soviet media as if it never existed. Instead of a Purgatory before entering into Paradise, the 1970s turned out to be the most rotten decade in Soviet history. Here is how a remarkable Russian poet and thinker, Viktor Nekipelov, describes it: "These were ten years of deepening chaos, militarization, catastrophic disruptions in the economy, an increase in the cost of living, shortages of the basic food products, the growth of crime and drunkenness, but most of all the uncontrolled decline in the prestige of the current leadership in the eyes of the people, the moral annihilation if not of socialism in general, then at least of that which it is today."[7]

A foreign observer would perhaps find it hard to feel the awe-

[4] Ibid., p. 246.

[5] Ibid., p. 245.

[6] *Oktiabr'*, no. 5 (1961), p. 9.

[7] V. Nekipelov's article is quoted here from the journal *Kontinent*, no. 18 (1979). It was also translated and published in the *New York Times*, August 14, 1979.

some depth of this psychological metamorphosis, developing so rapidly in a great nation, before the eyes of one generation. He would, rather drily, register the facts. As a member of the Carter administration said in an interview with *Newsweek*, "We beat them in agriculture, we beat them in productivity, we beat them to the moon. No one wants to be like a Russian. . . . we don't have our ballerinas running over there to jump ship. How many more times do we have to beat them?"[8]

The Party Program, containing the promise of a consumer paradise, has been removed from circulation and is not available to ordinary Soviet citizens. The key fact, however, is that the Party *has no other program*. After twenty years it is in no condition to formulate a new alternative goal to replace the bankrupt old one. It loses the aura of majesty which causes it to be obeyed, to put it in the words of Walter Lippmann. What are the policy implications of this simple fact? Some of them are eye-openers. First, the unfulfilled promise of the "cup of plenty" nevertheless has unleashed an apparently uncontrollable growth in consumer expectations that the government is unable to meet. Secondly, this popular frustration clashes with a parallel set of expectations within the military-industrial complex, thus laying the groundwork for a collision between powerful political forces. And, finally, it has already given rise to a monstrous spiritual stagnation among the Russian intelligentsia. Here is how it is described by the well-known Russian émigré writer Viktor Nekrasov: "Something's happened to the air, there is some sort of stuffiness, something oppressive. . . . I will not compare it to Stalinist times, a bygone matter, but under Khrushchev there was still some sort of thaw, and the 20th Congress. . . . There were, it's true, Hungary and Cuba, but along with them Ivan Denisevich. And now there is no light at the end of the tunnel, rot at the root . . . depression and despair."[9] Historically, when the Russian intelligentsia has begun to feel this way, it has been a sinister omen.

Let me finish the description of the metamorphosis occurring in Russia by citing one of the most penetrating reports from Moscow in my memory. It was sent by Michael Binyon and published in the

[8] *Newsweek*, November 26, 1979, p. 47.
[9] *Kontinent*, no. 18 (1979), pp. 72–73.

Toward a Method to Madness 37

London *Times*: "There is a strange atmosphere in Moscow these days. . . . Life is perfectly normal, and yet there is a sense of malaise. . . . [A] deep unshakable apathy has settled over the country. . . . Even to the average patriotic Russian the leadership appears . . . out of touch. . . . A dangerous cynicism has crept into the people's outlook. . . . [A] sense of stagnation . . . industrial chaos . . . paralysis . . . has overtaken decision-making. . . . [An] atmosphere [of] the uncanny calm of the end of an era."[10]

II

All of this would seem to beg an awful question, one that somehow must be answered: *Which* era is likely to come to an end in Moscow in the 1980s? As a historian of Russia, I was struck by the clear sense in Binyon's report that, in describing the "strange atmosphere" of Moscow in the 1980s, the author unwittingly also had described the astonishingly similar atmosphere of Moscow in the 1680s, on the eve of Peter I: the same unshakable apathy and sense of malaise, the same sense of stagnation, and the same uncanny calm of the end of an era. This analogy may help us understand the political content of Binyon's impressionistic picture. Here is what occurred in Moscow 300 years ago: the succession of relatively "liberal" regimes, which had replaced the twenty-five-year tyrannical dictatorship of Ivan the Terrible, suddenly was broken. A powerful political crisis occurred that brought the restoration of the dictatorship.

These relatively liberal regimes that existed in the historical span between these two dictatorships could be termed the *Destalinization Era* of the time. The governments of this era tried to rule Russia by nontyrannical methods. They brought the elite of the country physical security, and its people a growth in living standards. They spared it mass terror and total militarization of the economy. They did not, however, bring it true liberalization. Its economic process was, as before, chained by serfdom. Universal obligatory military service broke the process of aristocratization and consequently the Westernization of its elite. As a result, these liberal governments appeared unable to integrate Russia into the European family of nations. The country muddled through with-

[10] London *Times*, March 31, 1980.

out hope or a national goal—until an unshakable apathy had settled over it. Economic stagnation was complicated by a spiritual stagnation. All this taken together led to a peculiar paralysis of the existing power structure, rendering it incapable of reacting adequately to the economic, social, and spiritual needs of the developing system. I call this paralysis of power, which has periodically repeated itself in Russian history, *political stagnation*, the psychological dimension of which is precisely the "uncanny calm of the end of an era" that so frightened Michael Binyon.

Since it was incapable of reforming the system internally, the government of that time attempted to replace it with an alternative means of legitimizing the regime—external political expansion (the Azov Campaign of Vasilii Golitsyn, so deplorably reminiscent of the Afghan Campaign of Leonid Brezhnev, which logically crowned the rotten 1970s). However, it was precisely the defeat of the Azov Campaign which showed that an expansionist strategy required the restoration of a strong dictatorship. All this was complicated further by a succession crisis. In the end, the dictatorship was restored in 1689, bringing Russia a new terror and new total militarization of its economy. Its elite once more were deprived of physical security, and the living standards of its people once more fell catastrophically.

The lesson of the crisis of the 1680s consisted, thus, in the following chain of events: inability to reform internally resulted in political stagnation; this in turn led to external expansion, and this to the restoration of tyranny. Speaking in modern terms, the "strange atmosphere" of Moscow in the 1680s meant that the era of medieval "de-Stalinization" had come to an end; a new era of "Stalinism" awaited a country unaware of its grim future.

III

It would, of course, be extremely naive on my part to expect that people who are now making predictions for the U.S.S.R. in the 1980s would notice this strange historical analogy. How could events occurring at the end of the Middle Ages, after all, relate to the present, or even more, to the future of the socialist empire? Therefore, it is not surprising that current predictions of Russia's future fail to reflect the psychological metamorphosis just described, even as its consequences unfold before us.

Let us look for a start at the 1978 report of CIA Director Admiral Stansfield Turner before the Joint Economic Committee of Congress. At the end of his report, the admiral says that

> the short-term shift in resources from military programs seems to us unlikely. . . . [I]n the longer term [however] if the combination of energy, manpower and capital constraints should reduce economic growth to 2 percent . . . , the Soviet leadership might be more inclined to consider cutting the growth of military spending. The pressure [in this direction] would be increased by major shortfalls in farm output.
>
> What are the options . . . that the Soviets have for coping with the 1980s? They can recognize first, that growth rates on the order of 3 percent, while conflicting with the commitment to high growth rates and satisfying consumer demands . . . , would hardly signal the economic collapse of the Soviet Union and should not be perceived as a major defeat. . . . Second, given the leadership change that we anticipate and the fact that major shifts of resources or structural changes would require a powerful political leader, we think it most likely that the Soviets will muddle through, at least into the early 1980s. Third, we think that they will, in effect, accept a slowdown in economic growth. They would seek to conserve energy and foreign exchange and use this period to concentrate domestic resources on renovating existing industrial capacity while making moderate changes in the administrative and managerial apparatus in the hope of stimulating further economic growth.[11]

In sum, for these men the 1980s will be a continuation of the 1970s; in place of Brezhnev comes another Brezhnev, and muddling through continues. In fact, the very same people who only yesterday were inspired by the triumphal promise of "a victory on a world scale, absolutely and finally," tomorrow will meekly console themselves with the fact that the Soviet economy has not yet collapsed, absolutely and finally.

The CIA's faith in the rational behavior of people—in a "rational policy paradigm," as Graham Allison calls it—may be mistaken.[12]

---

[11] U.S., Congress, *Hearings before the . . . Joint Economic Committee*, 95th Cong., 2d sess., June 26 and July 14, 1978, p. 38.

[12] Graham Allison, *Essence of Decision: Explaining the Cuban Missile Crisis* (Boston, 1971).

Should not, for example, the experience with Khomeini's government in Iran, which has proved somewhat incapable of a rational response to political challenges, convince us at least that such responses cannot be taken for granted?

If the rate of economic growth falls to 2 percent, "the Soviet leadership" could, according to the CIA, put up with a lowering of defense expenditures. But would the Russian military-industrial complex allow this assumed "Soviet leadership" to spoil the fruits of a two-decade-long struggle with the Russian consumer for access to resources—a struggle in which the military is again about to emerge totally victorious, just as in Stalin's time? Will they not prefer *another* "Soviet leadership," one that would ensure their victory regardless of the rate of economic growth? That is, even if such growth is reduced to zero, as might have been the case in 1979 (for the first time since 1921)?[13]

We can further say that the "Soviet leadership" will try to concentrate domestic resources while making moderate changes in the administrative and managerial apparatus. However, will the provincial Party prefects along with the central economic administrators whose political power depends, it seems, on the absence of any change, agree to this? Up to this point they have always been able to stop the process of change in the administrative and managerial apparatus, whether a "non-moderate" one which Khrushchev sought or a more than moderate one for which Brezhnev worked. Will they not prefer another "Soviet leadership" which would abandon administrative and managerial adventures so dangerous to their political interests?

Finally, we can say that the "Soviet leadership" will reconcile itself to the slowing of the pace of economic growth and will try to save on foreign trade. But will the consumer, already accustomed not only to drinking but also to putting on a spread and dressing up for a holiday, reconcile himself to this?

Up to a certain point all these contradictions can be tolerated, particularly as long as the growth of military expenditures (4 to 5 percent per year) more or less corresponds to the growth of the national income. But in the 1980s—and this is the kernel of the CIA

[13] Gregory Grossman, "The Economics of Virtuous Haste," Bernard Moses Memorial Lecture, May 19, 1980, unpublished manuscript.

Toward a Method to Madness

prediction—this pace of growth will fall to 3 percent, or even to 2. And now let us assume for a moment that the military-industrial complex will prove influential enough to compel the "Soviet leadership" to preserve the pace of growth of defense expenditures on the previous level. Which would be the more likely political consequences of this: the peaceful muddling through predicted by the CIA or a situation of acute conflict of interest, fraught with the possibility of a major crisis for the regime (a crisis the CIA prediction does not utter a single word about)?

In speaking of this possibility I do not by any means have in mind an "explosion" of the Soviet system or "anarchy" resulting in its collapse, as has been predicted by some practical politicians—for example, Giscard d'Estaing or Zbigniew Brzezinski.[14] I'm speaking only of the chain of events we are familiar with: the inability of the regime to reform the system internally; political stagnation; a turn toward external expansion; the restoration of tyranny. If the metamorphosis which took place in Russia in the rotten 1970s threatens anything, it is, from my point of view, not the Soviet system but

[14] In June of 1978 Arthur Comte (former director of French television) published in *Paris-Match* his impressions from conversations with the president of France on the major problems of the contemporary world. The following is said there, among other things, about the future of the U.S.S.R.: "It is not known to anyone where the crisis in the USSR will finally lead, but a crisis does exist, and on the largest scale." Accordingly, the then president is concerned primarily with such apocalyptic questions as: "Under what conditions will this shuddering volcano erupt?" And "How will the only untouched force of the regime—the army—behave?" (Quoted in the Russian translation in the journal *Posev*, no. 1 [1979], p. 49). Brzezinski's prognosis about the "degeneration of the USSR," the political expression of which was supposed to be the "alienation of [social] groups from the [Soviet] political system" and "perhaps . . . anarchy" (*Dilemmas of Change in Soviet Politics* [New York, 1969], p. 33) was first made in 1966 in conditional form ("The Soviet Political System: Transformation or Degeneration," *Problems of Communism* [Jan.-Feb. 1966]). However, in completing, three years later, the discussion which had arisen on this article, Brzezinski admits that "what in fact I intended to convey was that precisely because the necessary reforms are so major in scope, it is unlikely that they will be implemented, at least in the foreseeable future" (*Dilemmas*, p. 153). The reader thus can conclude that in 1969 the prophecy concerning the approaching anarchy in the U.S.S.R. had lost, for Brzezinski, that conditional character which it had in 1966 and had been transformed into a positive assertion and also that it was a prediction for the U.S.S.R. in the 1970s.

the regime of de-Stalinization. In trying to formulate the lessons of the 1680s, we arrive at the following: When the Russian political system does not liberalize, it Stalinizes.

IV

The CIA prediction itself muddles through the Scylla and Charybdis of diametrically opposite prophecies for the U.S.S.R. in the 1980s. At one pole, besides the prophets of "explosion" and "anarchy" mentioned above, we also find the interesting prediction of Senator Daniel Patrick Moynihan. He prophesied that, having brought Europe to its knees ("Finlandized" it) and isolated the United States, Russia would conduct a fateful assault on the oil fields of the Persian Gulf in order "to reverse the decline at home and preserve national unity." The senator develops his prophecy thus: "The short run looks good [for the U.S.S.R.], the long run bad. Therefore move. It was the calculation the Austro-Hungarian Empire made in 1914."[15] At the opposite pole we have the predictions of Professor Jerry Hough: "The preponderance of pressure is in the direction of liberalization . . . in the sense of a relaxed censorship and freer debates—more access to Western culture . . . , more tolerance of iconoclasts, and greater freedom to travel abroad—in short, movement towards a system like Hungary today."[16] Hough justifies his prognosis by the fact that the Soviet leadership in the 1970s achieved a situation in which it could play the role of "a broker facilitating agreements among competing interests,"[17] as a result of which "one might suggest that unwritten constitutional restraints of the type found in Great Britain are slowly beginning to develop in the Soviet Union."[18]

Unfortunately, it is just as difficult for me to agree with these predictions as with that of the CIA. And, once again, primarily for

---

[15] *Newsweek*, November 19, 1979, p. 147.

[16] Jerry Hough and Merle Fainsod, *How the Soviet Union Is Governed* (Cambridge, Mass., 1979), p. 570.

[17] Ibid., p. 548.

[18] Ibid., p. 555.

methodological reasons. First, each of them elevates to an absolute some single aspect of the matter, whether military-strategic, or institutional, economic—or even some single tendency, taken in isolation from the others. From such predictions we do not get the *spectrum* of alternatives. In the second place, all of them ignore the historically developed patterns in the behavior of the Russian political system in situations of major crises; in essence, they ignore history. As a result, their operational field is reduced to two generations and leaves almost no room for intellectual maneuvering. Any contemporary tendency begins to look unprecedented.

This essay attempts to expand the operational field for possible prognoses by including the historical dimension in our political discussions.

V

I understand how difficult it will be to fulfill this promise within the limits of a single essay—especially in view of the fact that Russia as a rule has disappointed the expectations of its well-wishers, just as it has those of its enemies. For example, in documents that circulated in the 1560s at the court of the Holy Roman Emperor, it was said that the Great Prince of Muscovy was the mightiest sovereign in the world after the sultan of Turkey and that "from an alliance with the Great Prince, all of Christendom would receive immeasurable profit and advantage, and he would be a fine support in the resistance to our most dangerous and tyrannical enemy, the Turk."[19] The French Protestant Hubert Langé prophesied in August 1558 in a letter to Calvin that "if any state in Europe is destined to grow, it is precisely this one."[20] History did not bear out these expectations. Instead of an "alliance with Christendom," there was the anti-European Livonian War. Instead of the "resistance to the Turk," there was a persistent attempt to make an alliance with him. Instead of growth, there was political collapse.

Had the CIA existed in the seventeenth century and had it pre-

---

[19] R. Iu. Vipper, *Ivan Groznyi* (Tashkent, 1942), p. 83.
[20] Ibid., p. 60.

dicted that the regime of medieval "de-Stalinization" would succeed in "concentrating the internal resources" and providing for "moderate changes in the administrative and managerial apparatus" in order to muddle through the 1680s, its prognosis would not have been borne out. Instead of this, as we already know, the matter ended with a repetition of the "revolution from above" of Ivan the Terrible—a rebirth of tyranny (or, speaking in habitual terms, the restoration of the ancien régime).

What followed was again quite unexpected. In fact, could Voltaire or Diderot have ever thought that after their friend Catherine the Great, with all her European charm, there would again take place in the Northern Palmyra a restoration of the medieval ancien régime? Or that the Russian throne would be occupied by a monster like Paul, who apparently intended to repeat all the horrors of the tyranny of Ivan the Terrible and Peter? Could even such first-class minds as Hegel or Shelling have expected that after the gallant Alexander I, who had just freed Europe from the tyranny of Napoleon, there would come in the course of a new restoration a somber medieval tyrant, Nicholas I, the gendarme of Europe?

For that matter, the enemies of Russia also hardly expected, after Ivan the Terrible, the "de-Stalinization" by the Tsar Vasilii Shuiskii or, after Peter, the "de-Stalinization" by Prince Dmitrii Golitsyn. In fact, did the perspicacious marquis de Custine—who described with such venomous precision in 1839 the horrors of the Nikolaian garrison state—expect the great reforms of the 1860s, which brought with them the abolition of serfdom and preliminary censorship, the introduction of local self-government, and the most modern system of justice in Europe at that time?

In the twentieth century, everything was repeated. Did such sound thinkers as Henri Barbusse or Romain Rolland, who welcomed the dawn of the socialist revolution, expect that it would end in the bloody swamp of Stalin's Gulag? But who, on the other hand, predicted de-Stalinization after Stalin?

The inertia of political thought artificially separated from history predisposes it toward unilinear prognoses—toward, let us say, expecting a new Peter after Peter, and a new Catherine after Catherine. It should be clear that I do not agree with it. And what is considerably more important, Russian history, as we have seen, does not agree with it either.

VI

I grew up at the fateful intersection of Stalinism and de-Stalinization. My personal destiny developed in such a way that I thought of the Russian political riddle precisely as a riddle ever since I can remember. And it has always seemed to me that to find a method to this madness—that is, to make Russian autocracy the object of political study—could only be done by trying to take in its entire history at a glance, by seeing it as a whole. I cannot describe here how I sought this system or to what conclusions I came as the result of my search (I describe all this in my book *The Origin of the Autocracy*.) Here I can set forth the results of my attempt only as an elementary diagram—the necessary minimum we need as a foundation for the hypothesis concerning the U.S.S.R. in the 1980s.

First of all, I would like to call attention to what lies on the surface. That is, in the course of the past fifteen generations after the famous "revolution from above" of Ivan the Terrible in the 1560s, the Russian political system (which I will here call *autocracy*) has not developed in precisely the way that its neighbors have, either in the West or in the East. In contrast to politically immobile, Oriental despotism, the autocracy proved capable of institutional modernization. It took on new forms; it became more complex; it developed. But in contrast to European absolutism it developed in a strange and, one may say, cyclical way, by means of political cataclysms that repeated themselves in a particular rhythm. Phases of rigidification (which I will call here *Stalinist*) periodically were replaced by phases of relaxation which, incapable of delivering the promise of liberalization, then passed over into political stagnation, which led in turn into a new cycle. And the new cycle always began, as we already know, with the restoration of the ancien régime (each time, of course, in a new form and on a new level of complexity).[21]

---

[21] I understand that in such a compressed exposition the hypothesis offered here may sound rather extravagant. For this reason I append to this essay an approximate chronological table of all seven Russian historical cycles as I see them. The reader can easily verify this table from the material of conventional textbooks. Certainly, the first thing which strikes the eye when one does this is the difference between the cycles. The complexity of the matter lies, however, in discovering the common parameters within this great variety.

What occurred once in English history (1660–1689) and once for a still shorter period (1815–1830) in the history of France has been repeated in Russian history regularly (and in this sense can probably be considered as a pattern of its political behavior in major crises).

However—and this probably represents the fundamental difference between autocracy and traditional despotism—none of the tyrants of Russia were able to extend the regime established by them beyond the limits of their lifetimes. Ivan the Terrible was not succeeded by another Ivan the Terrible, or Peter by Peter, or Stalin by Stalin. Just as political stagnation was fraught with the prospect of tyranny, tyranny was fraught with the *revolution of de-Stalinization*. The most diverse people could be its heralds: the Tsar Vasilii Shuiskii in the seventeenth century; or the leader of the Supreme Privy Council, Dmitrii Golitsyn in the eighteenth; Count Dmitrii Miliutin in the nineteenth; or the Party Secretary Nikita Khrushchev in the twentieth. The problem is not where these people came from, but the fact that they always came. The problem is also that they never succeeded in carrying their revolutions to their logical conclusions—that is, to the institutional and cultural-political limits beyond which restoration would have been unthinkable. The Khrushchevs of Russian history were always succeeded by its Brezhnevs.

This is the most elementary model of Russian history, if we look at it as a single unit. It looks impoverished and rigid in this short exposition. But a few conclusions nevertheless can be drawn from it. The first of these is that a political opposition has always existed in Russian political life and that powerful reformist (and, we may say, Westernizing) forces (at least in the sense of their anti-autocratic tendency) have been at work in each major crisis.[22] They

[22] The Russian political opposition (or what I understand by this term) differs just as profoundly from the opposition in contemporary democratic systems as autocracy differs from these systems. The opposition in Russia (or at least what can arbitrarily be called its Westernizing faction), which has many times been at the helm of the country, does not necessarily oppose the existing government or the regime. Its task is not to correct the current political course of the existing system, but to destroy it. This is the revolutionary meaning of de-Stalinization. Therefore, Khrushchev, from my point of view, along with the other leaders of Russian "de-Stalinizations" in other epochs (Aleksei Adashev, Dmitrii Golitsyn, or Peter Stolypin), belonged to the opposition. Stalin

proved capable of *generating* major reforms and plans for reforms (I will refer only to the most famous of these—in the 1550s, 1600s, the 1660s, the 1720s, the 1760s, the 1810s, the 1860s, the 1920s, and the 1950s) and great revolutions. This fact points to a fundamental ontological dualism in Russian political culture: The opposition to tyranny is just as organic a feature of this culture as tyranny itself.

The second conclusion is that, while capable of *generating* de-Stalinization, the Russian political opposition has never been able to stabilize it. At least this is what happened in the sixteenth and seventeenth centuries, twice in the eighteenth, twice in the nineteenth, and twice in the twentieth. Finally, the third conclusion is that as a result of the successive defeats of all the revolutions of de-Stalinization, the nature of the Russian political system has remained *medieval* up to the last quarter of the twentieth century.

VII

Only now, after this excursus into distant and archaic subject matter which at first glance has nothing to do with the case, can I explain where, in my view, the profound methodological vulnerability of all the prognoses listed above lies—whether these speak of muddling through or liberalization or "explosion." All of the prognoses look upon this political system as in principle a *modern* one even though different from the Western and, consequently, perfectly capable of rational responses to political challenges.

This is precisely why so many expectations in the past did not come through: The medieval system failed to behave in accordance with modern patterns. It played its own ancient game, governed by its own ancient rules. We have already seen some of these rules in operation: if (and as soon as) the de-Stalinizing regime abandons the effort at internal reform, the country is gripped by political stagnation. And if (and as soon as) these symptoms of political

---

apparently well understood this characteristic of the Russian opposition in declaring three members of the ruling oligarchy—Bukharin, Rykov, and Tomsky—the "right opposition." Ivan the Terrible proceeded in precisely the same way in accusing all the members of the "Government of Compromise" of treason.

stagnation appear in the behavior of Russia, this is a clear signal that a new restoration of the ancien régime is being prepared in its depths.[23]

Considering that we are living in the age of intercontinental rockets and global confrontation of authoritarianism and democracy, one more repetition of the usual Russian political cataclysm might, it seems, develop a dangerous chain of events leading to world cataclysm. This is why, in speaking of Russia in the 1980s, I am alarmed not so much about which individual—Kirilenko, Romanov, or Chernenko—will prove to be Brezhnev's immediate successor as about signals from Moscow, such as the report by Binyon or Alexander Zinov'ev's book *The Yawning Heights*, which perhaps indicate that the country is already in the grip of political stagnation.[24] This is why I am so preoccupied with Nekipelov's article "Here a Stalin, There a Stalin, Everywhere a Stalin, Stalin,"[25] or the essay by the senior specialist in Soviet affairs, Harrison Salisbury, "Stalin Makes a Comeback,"[26] or the commentary by the priest recently emigrated from Russia, Father Lev Konin, who asserts that the time has come "to speak of the Fascist danger."[27]

[23] The tyrants who came to power as the result of these restorations in Russia differed significantly from one another. They might rely either on a "new class" which they "create out of stone," as the patriarch of the Russian opposition, Prince Kurbskii, said in 1564, or on the conservative and Russophile sector of the existing establishment (like Nicholas I and Alexander III). Correspondingly, they might be really terrible or not too terrible. The terror which they established might be total or partial. It might destroy the existing elite or persecute only individual groups which seemed dangerous to the tyrant. The only thing which united all of them is the uprooting of the political opposition and the violent reproduction of the cyclical autocracy.

[24] Alexander Zinov'ev, *Ziiaiushchie vysoty* [The Yawning Heights] (Lausanne, 1979).

[25] *New York Times*, August 14, 1979.

[26] *New York Times Magazine*, December 23, 1979.

[27] "How will the new team in the Politburo be inclined," asks Father Lev, "after the natural or forced retirement of the present delapidated leadership? There are a number of signs that the right-wing, conservative bias of the leadership is beginning to show definite traditionalist and soil-worshipping features. . . . The flirtation of the elite with the leadership of the Orthodox Church serves as a confirmation of this . . . , as does also the fact that the sharp struggle against the dissidents is directed primarily toward the liberal democrats and the oppositionist Jewish intelligentsia. Along with this, the anti-Semitic ten-

In this connection, I consider it appropriate to recall that there seems to be still another rule of autocracy. The ancien régime of Ivan the Terrible led a twenty-five-year war against Livonia, Poland, Lithuania, Sweden, Denmark, the Hanseatic cities, and the German Empire that stood behind them—a sixteenth century European war. The restoration of the ancien régime under Peter led to another twenty-five-year war that ended with the conquest of the same Livonia and attempts to establish Russian hegemony in Eastern and Northern Europe. Paul, who first appeared in the role of a defender of Europe against Napoleon, later preferred the role of destroyer of the British Empire. Nicholas I was indeed for a quarter of a century the gendarme of Europe. And Stalin not only conquered the same Livonia (Baltic area) for which his two most distinguished predecessors fought but also carried out what Peter had not succeeded in doing, namely establishing Russian hegemony in Eastern Europe.

In other words, throughout the majority of the eras of the ancien régime (that is, whenever it perceived itself as strong enough), the Russian autocracy was growing toward total political irrationalism. Picture, if you will, a Khomeini with nuclear weapons handy. The policy of non-proliferation of these weapons is perfectly sound. It has, however, a terrifying flaw: What if a Stalin-Khomeini arrives at the helm of a power that already *has* nuclear weaponry?

Precisely because of this rule of interdependence between the restoration of tyranny and the increasing political irrationality of Russian autocracy, the apocalyptic prophecy of Senator Moynihan seems most plausible (although the senator himself by no means connects it with any internal-political metamorphosis in Russia).[28]

---

dencies in the country have become stronger. The specter of Stalinist chauvinism and pseudo-traditionalism has again risen up. . . . And the tendencies noted give us reason to expect a transformation [of the regime] in the direction of national-Communism." Father Lev continues: Inasmuch as "according to the fragmentary testimony of representatives of the 'shadow regime' (the KGB and the army), this nationalist-traditionalist deviation is present there also, and even much stronger . . . we may speak of a Fascist danger" (*Posev*, no. 5 [1979], pp. 23–24).

[28] I have not the least intention of analyzing here the correctness of the senator's analogy, although the probability that the rotting Austro-Hungarian Empire would unleash a world war if it did not have at its back an armored Germany appears not much different from zero. For this reason, if the analogy

VIII

It will be objected that history is not a mechanical process; that peasant Russia and the industrialized U.S.S.R.—the tsarist regime and the Communist dictatorship—are quite different things (some even say polar opposites);[29] and that, finally, it is ridiculous to expect political suicide from the establishment of a great power.

What can I answer? Hardly anyone will doubt that the historical circumstances of the 1920s that preceded the Stalinist "revolution from above" differed significantly from the circumstances of the 1550s that preceded Ivan the Terrible's "revolution from above." And certainly the Russian establishment of the sixteenth century was no more inclined toward political suicide than the Soviet establishment on the eve of collectivization. Nevertheless, it took place in both cases. Furthermore, a mere comparison of the significant parameters of both of these political catastrophes (see Appendix 1) leaves no doubt, it seems to me, that the events are analogous, although separated from each other by four centuries.

If we look from this point of view at the scenarios of "de-Stalinization" that preceded *all seven* of the Russian political cataclysms (see Appendix 2), it is hard to rid ourselves of the impression that they are connected by a certain similarity of genre—which is, moreover, quite independent of the degree of modernization or of the ideological setting. As the anti-Stalinist impulse exhausted itself and the contradictions within the victorious coalition became apparent, leaders of de-Stalinization always proved incapable of consolidating the reformist forces. Furthermore, in their attempt at

---

is accurate, then the opposite conclusion follows: Since no Germany is at the back of the rotting Soviet Empire and none is to be expected, the danger of global aggression on its part could be lightheartedly dismissed. Unfortunately, the matter is much more serious. Russian history shows, as we already know, that this country has already been *transformed* many times, if we may so express it, from a rotting Austro-Hungary into an armored Germany. In other words, the precondition for global aggression on the part of the U.S.S.R. may be only the restoration in it of the ancien régime, or using Khrushchev's expression, "a recurrence of the cult of personality" (a Soviet euphemism for the deification of tyranny).

[29] See Solzhenitsyn's article "Misconceptions about Russia Are a Threat to America," *Foreign Affairs* 58 (Spring 1980): 797–834.

reforms, they unfortunately did not rely on a competent social analysis of the society which they undertook to change and did not have experience in the creation of workable political coalitions or a clear concept of what reforms were possible—in what order or with the aid of what social forces or political blocs. They felt the nature of the system they were leading but were not able to work out a consistent, noncontradictory strategy for preventing restoration of the ancien régime. And this inevitably led to a conflict between the leaders of de-Stalinization and their own political base. As the forces opposing "liberalization"—that is, the continuation of internal reforms—were consolidated (I call these forces the *Establishment Right*), the leaders of de-Stalinization either capitulated or were removed from power. As a result, the country fell into a zone of political stagnation and everything began over again.

Thus, no one in the existing establishment had, properly speaking, an interest in the restoration of the ancien régime. The watershed between its different groups lay in the limit to which each was prepared to go in the process of "liberalization"—that is, the degree to which its political status, power, and privileges rested on retaining remnants of the ancien régime. The key to these groups' political suicide, consequently, was the fact that in all cases the artificial stopping of the internal reforms led to a destabilization of the regime, and during a major political crisis the destabilized regime proved unable to resist the restoration.[30] Thus, a generalized dia-

[30] This assertion calls perhaps for a methodological note. It might look like a challenge to the integrity of all Marxist (or Marxian) sociological postulates which assert that no major political event (and especially a revolution or a restoration) could happen unless it is backed by a certain class or stratum of the existing establishment. Indeed, the phenomenon of a "new class" repeatedly created by Russian tyrants for the purpose of carrying out their "revolutions" contradicts those postulates. But despite the absence of theoretical justification, this phenomenon seems to exist. How else can we possibly interpret Ivan the Terrible's "Oprichnina"; Peter's "Szliachta"; Lenin's "new class," combining the cadres of a revolutionary party with the "bourgeois experts" and international adventures; or Stalin's "new class" of Party appartchiki? Each of these "new classes" of Russian history was actually composed of the most variegated, disgruntled groups coming from all walks of life—from "below" as well as from "above," and even from abroad. Incidentally, it helps to explain Solzhenitsyn's insistence that the October revolution of 1917 was executed by foreigners. But after all, this same thing might be said by the contemporaries of Ivan the Terrible's or Peter's "revolutions" too. And for Mikhail Bakunin, the ruling class

gram of the historical experience of *all* of the Russian de-Stalinizations leads us to the same conclusion we arrived at from data on the
political crisis of the 1680s: If the autocracy does not liberalize, it
Stalinizes.

Whether we take as an example the story of the defeat of the so-
called Government of Compromise of Aleksei Adashev in the 1550s
(which I described in *The Origin of the Autocracy*) or the story
of the defeat of Nikolai Bukharin in the 1920s (as Stephen Cohen,
for example, described it)[31] or the collapse of the government of
Dmitrii Golitsyn in the 1720s (which I have described elsewhere)[32]
or of the government of Nikita Khrushchev in the 1960s (as described by Edward Crankshaw),[33] we see everywhere the same scenario, a scenario that testifies to the lamentable political ignorance
of the leaders of the Russian opposition and to an incompetence
that at times reaches the point of intellectual bankruptcy.

From the point of view of the hypothesis offered here, it is not
so much the *difference* between the historical settings in which the
various Russian political crises took place that really matters as
the inability to work out a strategy for preventing political stagnation, common to all of the de-Stalinizing regimes. I mean the inability to counterpose to the Establishment Right a left-centrist coalition of interests (of the kind which prevailed in Hungary in the
1970s or might prevail in Poland in the 1980s), which would have a
vital stake in preventing such a stagnation and would be capable of
defeating its opponents.

But if this was the general pattern for the behavior of the autoc-

---

of Russia under Nicholas I was the "German bureaucracy" (*Narodnoe delo: Romanov, Pugachev ili Pestel'* [M. 1917], p. 30). There was no Greek or Jew for the "new class" as long as it was directed against a traditional national elite. And it became increasingly nationalistic under Stalin when it was directed against the internationalistic elite. In any case, its purpose was the destruction of the existing establishment and its replacement by a new one. This is how the majority of Russian restorations was in fact carried out, without any class or strata of the existing establishment being interested in them.

[31] Stephen F. Cohen, *Bukharin and the Soviet Bolshevik Revolution* (New York, 1974).

[32] Alexander Yanov, "The Drama of the Time of Troubles, 1725–1730," *Canadian-American Slavic Studies* 12, no. 1, (Spring 1978): 1–53.

[33] Edward Crankshaw, *Khrushchev: A Career* (New York, 1966).

Toward a Method to Madness

racy at all the key moments in its history from 1564 to 1929, then it seems to me that we should demonstrate why the Russian political system is destined to depart significantly from this model in the 1980s. And in all fairness, the burden of proof in that case would lie with my opponents.

IX

Let us now see whether the process of de-Stalinization in the contemporary U.S.S.R. actually develops according to the scenario just described. We will need to sketch out some methodological provisions for the analysis of de-Stalinization as a historical phenomenon. Such an attempt, which requires a heavy concentration in a few pages of a multitude of unfamiliar terms (*actors of de-Stalinization*, its *tendencies, functions, formulas,* etc.), will, I'm afraid, make this section accessible only to very persistent readers. I have offered my argument in extenso in another place.[34] Here I can appeal to the reader's patience. Let us first name the main actors of de-Stalinization. Roughly speaking, there are eight of them.[35]

(1) The regional authorities, the secretaries of provincial Party committees, whom Jerry Hough calls the "Soviet prefects," whom I call the "little Stalins," and whom Harrison Salisbury describes as "the big Party guns of the Central Committee, the bosses of Sverdlovsk, of Khar'kov, of Novosibirsk, of Omsk, of the Donbas and the

[34] My book *Russia versus Russia, the Soviet 1960s* is to be published by the Institute of International Studies, Berkeley, Calif., forthcoming.

[35] The problem of "interest groups" in Soviet society and the problem of "coalitions" in the Soviet political leadership usually are considered separately from each other in the Sovietological literature. The problem of coalitions is as a rule reduced to the problem of "consensus-building"—that is, to the temporary and fragile personal or institutional blocs for the solution of this or that tactical question. In my book *Russia versus Russia* I make an attempt to connect the post-Stalinist differentiation of the Soviet establishment, which strengthened the group identification of its various elements, with the formation of a *coalition of interests*—sometimes actual and sometimes latent, sometimes conscious and sometimes intuitive, but always representing that objective background against which the "consensus-building" takes place. This political dimension of the interests of various groups is what I have in mind in speaking of the basic actors of de-Stalinization.

Kuzbas, the heavy-handed, broad-shouldered, square-headed Party mechanics."[36] By my calculations, in the previous (1971–76) makeup of the Plenum of the Party's Central Committee (which I call the Parliament of de-Stalinization), this group controlled 41 percent of the votes (in the present Plenum it controls 45 percent).

(2) The central economic administration, which in addition to its own group interests (the struggle against decentralization of management of the economy) also reflects the interests of the military-industrial complex—17.7 percent of the votes.

(3) The military—8 percent of the votes.

(4) The "high priests" of the regime, including the ideological officials on both central and local levels; tens of thousands of teachers of "Marxism-Leninism," "scientific communism," "dialectical materialism," and similar disciplines; and the quasi intellectuals of arts and sciences whose income and status totally depend on the artificial conditions of the ideocratic state.

These groups represent for me the Establishment Right in modern Russia—that is, the coalition of forces which sees danger in further internal reforms.

(5) The metropolitan establishment (the most Westernized, "aristocratizing" section of the Soviet elite)—28.8 percent of the vote in the Plenum.

(6) The middle managerial class, charged with the direct management of enterprises—2.6 percent.

(7) Workers and peasants ("consumers")—4.7 percent of the votes.[37]

[36] Harrison E. Salisbury, *The Gates of Hell* (New York, 1975), p. 84.

[37] All of the calculations are made by the author on the basis of documents kindly placed at his disposal by Radio Liberty. The complexity of the calculations consists, among other things, in a phenomenon which could be called "intersecting loyalty." How, for example, is one to determine which is greater: the loyalty of the officials of the Moscow provincial and Moscow city Party committees who, of course, live in the capital, to the metropolitan establishment or to the group of Soviet prefects? The staffs of the ministries connected with the production of consumer goods may be loyal to the central economic administration (against the managers) and may at the same time compete with the representatives of the military-industrial complex (within the central economic administration). There are disagreements between divisions in the staff of the Central Committee, and between branches of heavy industry, and even between departments of the KGB and various branches of the armed

(8) The creative intelligentsia (no votes).

I conceive of these groups as a latent left-centrist coalition with an interest in continuing the internal reforming of the country, and capable—under certain conditions—of balancing the power of the Establishment Right.

Let me now describe, equally briefly, the basic tendencies of the last Russian "revolution of de-Stalinization," and let us see at the same time how they relate to what we know of the tendencies of analogous previous "revolutions."

(1) The liquidation of the dictatorship, which presupposes the control of the security police over the Establishment.

(2) The replacement of the tyrannical power of the leader by one form or another of "collective leadership."[38]

(3) An unwritten concordat of the regime with the mass of the population (the "consumers"), obliging the regime to maintain a steady rise in the standard of living. Just as the security police were deprived of total control over the Soviet establishment, so the military-industrial complex was deprived of total control over the Soviet economy. From this point on it will compete with the consumer for the available resources.[39] I call this agreement "the first

---

forces. However, when the matter comes to fundamental questions concerning *political struggle*, such as the distribution of resources or the degree of centralization of the management of production, the various actors of de-Stalinization show themselves considerably more capable of group identification than might be expected. Nevertheless, the calculations cited certainly indicate more about general tendencies than about absolute figures.

[38] Here, of course, there were still "constitutional" questions to be decided. In the first place, in regard to the form of the leading "collective"—whether this would be a duumvirate or a triumvirate, or an oligarchy comprising the entire Politburo (Presidium). And in the second place, who will be invited to play the role of the "Soviet Parliament"? The need for such an institution flowed logically out of the fact that the "collective," as distinguished from the tyrant, conceals within itself a possibility not only of disagreements or conflicts but also of schism. To whom, in such a case, does the last word belong? In other words, the question was, which of the existing Party institutions would take on the role of arbiter: the Secretariat of the Central Committee (representing the nucleus of the Party staff), its Plenum, or the Party Congress?

[39] George Breslauer, in his *Five Images of the Soviet Future* (Berkeley, Calif., 1978), calls this agreement the "social contract" between the post-Stalinist regime and the population of the U.S.S.R.

concordat of de-Stalinization." From my point of view, this concordat constitutes its social and operational basis.

(4) An unwritten concordat of the regime with the Establishment. The "new class" which under the conditions of tyranny is destabilized to the extreme—not so much a social body as a social process, and not so much a political mass as a political energy—begins to harden under the conditions of de-Stalinization and to acquire mass and body. It claims not only physical security but also control over the strategic decisions of the regime. This agreement, which I call "the second concordat of de-Stalinization," constitutes its institutional basis.

(5) A speeding up of the development of light industry, necessary to fulfill the first concordat. It brings in its turn the necessity of economic reformation of the system—that is, the decentralization of the management of the economy, the provision of essential autonomy to the middle managerial class, and the creation of some socialist surrogate for the market (which Soviet experts timidly call "horizontal relations between enterprises").

(6) The normalization of the social process in the country, presupposing an obligation on the regime's part to assure the elementary civil rights of the population; this could be called "the third concordat of de-Stalinization." Naturally, the intelligentsia of the country have the chief interest in the realization of this concordat. The regime is interested in it to the degree to which its realization assures a normal correcting mechanism for economic and social mistakes of the bureaucracy and thus prevents the occurrence of a cold war between the regime and the intelligentsia.

(7) The political defense of all three of the concordats of de-Stalinization requiring adequate representation of the consumers, the middle managerial class, and the intelligentsia in the institutions which control the strategic decisions of the regime.

All of these tendencies of de-Stalinization are easily grouped into three historical functions:

A. Destructive (tendencies 1 and 2);
B. Stabilizing (tendencies 3 and 4);
C. Transforming (including tendencies 5, 6 and 7).

If we now, with even such an elementary method of analysis, take a brief look at all the "revolutions of de-Stalinization" in Russian history, we will see immediately that although in various historical circumstances its leaders succeeded in going various distances toward the implementation of its functions (it is sufficient to compare, let us say, the "de-Stalinization" of 1855–1881 with that of 1894–1917 or that of 1921–29), nevertheless, all these cases contained a common element: These leaders succeeded rather easily in implementing function A, sometimes succeeded in implementing function B, and never succeeded in institutionalizing function C on a firm basis. This was the nature of their inability to bring to a conclusion the process which they led. For this reason, however far it went in Russian history, this process always failed to transform the system and left an opening for the restoration of the ancien régime (by "revolution from above" or "from below").

This is how the most general historical pattern of Russian de-Stalinization looks. In complete agreement with this pattern, the leaders of the current de-Stalinization have proved incapable of implementing function C and thus of transforming the system. In other words, *the stumbling block of the present de-Stalinization appears to be its fifth tendency.* If our methodological construct is correct, the Soviet leaders should concentrate their efforts on this tendency. And it is precisely here that all of them were to suffer defeat (at least up to the moment that these lines are being written).

This assertion requires proof, and I will now try to offer it. One thing should be noted before we proceed. As we know, the mutiny in June 1957 of the Soviet Establishment against the oligarchy (the Presidium) finally confirmed the role of the Plenum as a "Parliament of de-Stalinization."[40] Thus the second concordat was insti-

---

[40] Sovietologists have taken note of a number of instances even before June 1957, in which the Plenum in fact played the role of the supreme arbiter between contending sides in the "collective"—that is, in my terms, the role of the Soviet Parliament. A. Avtorkhanov, for example, notes that when in 1954 Khrushchev first presented the idea of bringing the Virgin Lands under cultivation, "The Presidium considered this plan fantastic and rejected it. Then Khrushchev called the Plenum [which] supported the idea . . . and adopted the resolution which he proposed" (*Posev*, no. 7 [1979], p. 123). Jerry Hough notes the role of another Plenum (February 13, 1957), which was called on the day following a session of the Supreme Soviet and literally annihilated the decisions taken at it (*How the Soviet Union Is Governed*, p. 216). Seweryn Bialer (in Wolfgang Leonhard, *The Kremlin since Stalin* [New York, 1962], p. 103) asserts that still another Plenum in 1955 decided the fate of Soviet policy toward Yugoslavia. However, only at a moment of open schism in the "collec-

tutionalized. This, however, did not happen with the first one: No adequate representation for the consumer was provided in the parliament. The consumer was deprived of political protection. As a result, a curious paradox emerged which casts significant doubt upon the assertion of Hough that the Soviet leadership plays the role of "a broker facilitating agreement among competing interests." The materials at our disposal indicate the contrary: The leader of the regime himself was forced to represent the interests of the consumer. And this not only deprived him of the ability to act as arbiter or "broker" but also placed him in a position of permanent conflict with a majority of his own parliament. A fatal contradiction between two basic prerequisites of de-Stalinization—its first and second concordats—appears to have threatened the stability of the regime from its very inception. Compelled to defend the fifth tendency against a hostile parliamentary majority, the leader found himself in the end the prisoner of the Establishment Right.

If we need more proof of the fatal political incompetence of the leaders of de-Stalinization, we do have it. None of these leaders foresaw that as long as the Establishment Right remains the majority of the parliament, they would inevitably be either removed from power or forced to capitulate. None of them tried to resolve the conflict by changing the rules of the game, that is, the very means of formation of this majority. Furthermore, we have no reason to think that any of them understood the plot of the spectacle in which they were playing the chief part. In any case, Malenkov, Khrushchev,

---

tive," when the fate of the leader was being decided—and when, as one of the participants in the Plenum expressed it, "there were dangerous days for our Party" (*XXII s"ezd*, 1:394)—was it finally determined that it was the Plenum which succeeded in taking on the role of arbiter. In these "dangerous days," among other things, "instructions were given that members of the Central Committee should not be admitted into the Kremlin, and many of them" —as another participant in the Plenum later recalled—"had to resort to literally illegal methods in order to get to the place where the session of the Presidium was being held" (ibid., 2: 107). This dramatic Plenum nevertheless gathered and condemned the majority of the oligarchs to political death. From this moment its role became unquestioned to such a degree that it gives grounds for speaking of "dual power" in the Soviet system—that is, of a Soviet variant of the division of legislative and executive powers. (For details on this, see my *Détente after Brezhnev* [Berkeley, Calif., 1977].)

Toward a Method to Madness 59

Kosygin, and Brezhnev showed not the slightest sign of such awareness. Again and again they tried to assault an apparently impenetrable fortress. *They had to be defeated.*

X

Now let us illustrate this assertion by the fate of what I call "the formula of de-Stalinization," which (as *right-wing deviation* or as *capitulationism* or as *voluntarism*) each leader who came to power after Malenkov invariably anathematized and to which he invariably returned, as if drawn by a mysterious force. Let us first quote Khrushchev—not the leader of the June mutiny, flushed with success, to whom all things seemed possible, but the sobered and politically more mature Khrushchev, who, in January of 1961, understood that the coalition which had brought him to power no longer worked:

> In the first period of Soviet power [he said at that time], in the years of the first Five Year Plans, we directed all our efforts toward creating primarily heavy industry . . . , which, as we know, is the basis . . . for the reinforcement of the defense capability of the country [a Soviet euphemism to designate the military-industrial complex]. We were forced to do this when our country was subject to a hostile capitalist encirclement. . . . *The situation now is entirely different.* Our economy is in the full bloom of its powers. . . . The defense of our country is firm. The Soviet Union is not the only socialist country any more. . . . *Our opportunities to satisfy the needs of the people have now grown immeasurably.* . . . [And we cannot any more] permit lags in the development of agriculture and industry producing consumer goods. . . . I understand that some comrades have developed an appetite for giving the country more metal. . . . But the welfare of the state is determined . . . also by other indices— for example, the quantity of products received and consumed by men, the production of clothing, shoes, and in general the degree of satisfaction of all needs. . . . For this reason, one should not make oneself resemble a flounder, who is able to see only one side.[41]

[41] N. S. Khrushchev, *Stroitel'stvo kommunizma v SSSR i razvitie sel'skogo khoziaistva* (Moscow, 1963), 4: 287, 289–90 (italics mine).

To anyone who has done any reading in the speeches of Soviet leaders, it is quite clear that this is not a tactical step or, more precisely, is not *only* a tactical step. This is the formulation of a strategy. This is a philosophical historical formula that is diametrically opposed to the formula of Stalinism. Its basic feature is the division of Soviet history into two fundamentally different epochs, with two fundamentally different global strategic criteria: "The period of the First Five Year Plans," and of "capitalist encirclement" when, "in order to survive," it was necessary to "create heavy industry as the foundation of the defense capability of the country" (sacrificing the welfare of the people)—and the contemporary epoch, when "the defense of the country is firm," Russia is no longer a fortress besieged by enemies, and therefore the duty of its government is to concentrate on "fulfilling the needs of the people."

In his characteristic peasant-Marxist style of speech, Khrushchev is *repeating* the August 1953 declaration of Malenkov. What had sounded eight years earlier like a manifesto of de-Stalinization, presaging the birth of the first concordat, and which six years before was declared a great political heresy and even "a slander on our Party," is again enunciated as the general line of this same Party.

I wish to give the reader the opportunity of checking this paradoxical assertion. Here is what Georgii Malenkov said at the fifth session of the Supreme Soviet of the U.S.S.R.: "We know that the Party began the industrialization of the country with the development of heavy industry. . . . In the years of the Five Year Plans . . . there were invested . . . in heavy industry 638,000,000,000 rubles . . . and in light industry 72,000,000,000 rubles." Like Khrushchev, Malenkov piously declares that this sacrifice of the welfare of the people was justified. Also like Khrushchev, he entirely approves the fact that the "Party firmly and without deviation pursued its line in the struggle against . . . right capitulators and traitors . . . who demanded that capital be transferred from heavy industry to light." But why was this Stalinist line correct? Because "the adoption of these proposals would have meant the ruin of the revolution . . . , since we would have been disarmed before the capitalist encirclement." The contemporary epoch is a very different matter: "Now, on the basis of our successes, we have all the conditions for organizing a steep growth in the production of consumer goods. . . . Our urgent task is to raise sharply the supply of food and industrial goods available to the population."[42] This passage contains not only all the arguments within which Khrushchev will operate in 1961 but also the conclusions Khrushchev will draw from this formula. Malenkov said: "The government and the Central Committee of the Party consider it necessary to increase significantly the investment of funds in the development of light [and] food industry."[43] Was it necessary to note that this could only be done by reducing the funds invested in the military-industrial complex? Malenkov did note this. It was proposed that expenditures on defense be reduced from 23.6 to 20.8 percent of the state budget.[44] But didn't Khrushchev draw the same conclusions from the formula of de-Stalinization when he declared in London that "Soviet heavy industry is considered built. In the future, light and heavy industry will develop at the same pace,"[45] and when he continued this thought in Moscow: "Now we will reduce the expenditures on defense and devote this money to the production of mineral fertilizer"?[46] But it was not enough that the leader of the regime preferred mineral fertilizers to the glorious Soviet generals. He consistently put into practice what Malenkov had declared. In five years of de-Stalinization (until 1958), the Soviet armed forces underwent a dramatic reduction (from 5,763,000 men to 3,623.000). In 1960 there was announced another reduction by 1,200,000.

In the beginning of the 1970s we had known for a long time that Malenkov was a "capitulator" and that Khrushchev was a "voluntarist." They lost their game. They are forgotten. Logically speaking, their formula for de-Stalinization should have been buried along with them. I offer an amusing intellectual task—that of identifying the author of the passages which I will now quote. "As we know," he says, "in the first years of socialist construction, we were compelled to concentrate on the most urgent matters on which the very existence of the Soviet state depended. . . . Over the course of a long period, our opportunities were limited by virtue of certain historical causes." But what follows from this familiar jus-

---

[42] *Kommunist*, no. 12 (August 1953), pp. 14–15.
[43] Ibid.
[44] Ibid., p. 13.
[45] *New York Times*, May 21, 1961.
[46] *Stroitel'stvo kommunizma*, 8: 51.

tification of the Stalinism of the epoch of the first Five Year Plans? Something no less familiar: *"Now the situation is becoming different. . . . We can no longer dash ahead in certain areas—even if important ones, while permitting delays in others."*[47] Who is saying this? Malenkov. But he, as we know, operated with murderous and shocking figures: "Comparison of the level of production of 1953 with the pre-war level of 1940 shows that in this period the production of means of production grew by a factor of more than three, and the production of consumer goods by 72 percent. . . . We have not yet had an opportunity to develop light and food industry at the same pace as heavy industry. At the present time, we can do this, *and consequently, we must* . . . develop light industry on a crash basis by all possible means."[48] This is how the classical formula ran.

We find nothing similar in the author I just quoted. He will not, for anything in the world, say naively, "We can, and therefore we must, develop light industry on a crash basis." So this is not Malenkov. But then is it perhaps Khrushchev? After all, our author says, just like Khrushchev, "we cannot help seeing certain new features which distinguish the modern economy from that of 1930."[49] Having asked himself the question "What are we really talking about?" he answered: "Primarily, a significant increase in our opportunities." However, after this classical overture, Khrushchev, with his aggressive temperament, immediately took the bull by the horns: "We now have the opportunity to seriously increase capital expenditures in expanding [the production of] consumer goods." This simplicity, characteristic of the first post-Stalinist leaders, is completely lacking in our author. He will still go around and around for a long time, weaving a curious spiderweb of arguments explaining that "the revolution in science and technology requires the improvement of many aspects of our economic activity."[50] Or that "the increase in the welfare of the working people becomes an ever more vital necessity for our economic development itself, one of the most important economic preconditions for the swift growth

---

[47] L. I. Brezhnev, *Leninskim kursom: Rechi i stat'i* (Moscow, 1972), 3: 235, 238, 235, 236 (italics mine).

[48] *Kommunist*, no. 12 (1953), p. 15 (italics mine).

[49] *Leninskim kurhom*, 3: 235.

[50] Ibid., p. 236.

of production."[51] Therefore, this is not Khrushchev either. Then is it perhaps Kosygin? For our author, exactly like Kosygin, says: "The main task of the [Ninth] Five Year Plan consists in providing for a significant increase in the material and cultural level of living of the people."[52] But a bit later, his voice suddenly rises in a crescendo—as the muffled and colorless voice of Kosygin never did—and it reveals a power reminiscent of Khrushchev's utopian fanaticism: "In putting forward as the main task of the Ninth Five Year Plan a significant increase in the welfare of the working people, the Central Committee has in mind that this course will determine not only our activity in the next five years but also the general orientation of the economic activity of the country in the long term. In setting out such a course, the Party proceeds primarily on the assumption that the fullest satisfaction of the material and cultural needs of people is the highest goal of societal production under socialism."[53]

Therefore, this is not Kosygin. There remains a person, who along with Kosygin, not only suppressed the revolutionary impulse of de-Stalinization represented by Khrushchev but also dealt a mortal blow to the economic reform of Kosygin himself—a person who has the reputation of being a "neo-Stalinist": Leonid Brezhnev. We have no other choice. It is he, speaking before the 24th Congress of the Party on May 30, 1971, trying to breathe new life into the same fifth tendency of de-Stalinization, and following in his arguments the same formula which inspired his defeated opponents. The paths of Russian history seem to be truly inscrutable if the leader of the regime embodying its orthodox strategy practically copies it like a pupil from his politically unreliable rivals. One gets the impression that the political soul of the defeated Malenkov transmigrated into Khrushchev, who defeated him; and the political soul of the defeated Khrushchev sought refuge in Kosygin, who defeated him; and the political soul of the defeated Kosygin has been reborn in the victorious Brezhnev.

In comparing their speeches, we might conclude that we are dealing with ordinary plagiarism. But from an aesthetic point of view,

[51] Ibid., p. 238.
[52] Ibid., p. 237.
[53] Ibid., p. 238.

this is reminiscent of a paradoxical and dramatic spectacle. And this was, indeed, a drama—the drama of de-Stalinization, the eternal drama of Russia.

XI

Like his predecessors, Brezhnev did not confine himself to enunciating the formula of de-Stalinization. On the contrary, he went farther than any of them. In the plan of development of the economy for 1971–75, the forced development of light industry became the law of the state for the first time in Soviet history. At that time, in March of 1971, naive people may have supposed that even if slowly and clumsily, even if over the political deaths of Malenkov and Khrushchev, even if on the ruins of Kosygin's reform, even in spite of the violation of the third concordat and the ferocious persecution of the intelligentsia, even if eighteen years after it had been solemnly declared, the formula of de-Stalinization nevertheless was beginning to be brought to life. I was one of these naive people. My optimistic essays in the journals *Novyi mir*, *Voprosy literatury*, and *Iskusstvo-kino* for 1971 and 1972 testify to my lack of foresight.[54] But the fact that they were published and even reprinted in the U.S.S.R., that they were discussed and translated into other languages, shows that I was by no means the only one to believe in the miracle.

At that time the scenario described above had not entered my

[54] Alexander Yanov, "The Worker as a Theme: Sociological Comments on Literary Criticism," *Novyi mir*, no. 3 (1971). Also reprinted in the collection of the best articles of the year 1970 and 1971 by *Literatura i sovremennost'* (Moscow, 1972). Translated and published in the U.S.A. in *Soviet Sociology* (Winter 1971–72), and in England in *Anglo-Soviet Journal*, no. 1 (1972), and in German in *Forum*, no. 13 (1971); "The Movement of the Young Hero: Sociological Comments on Soviet Literature," *Novyi mir*, no. 7 (1972). Also translated and published in English by *International Journal of Sociology* (Summer-Fall, 1976); "The Industrial Play and the Literary Hero of the 70s," *Voprosy literatury*, no. 8 (1972), and in English by *Soviet Studies in Philosophy* (Spring, 1973); "The Movie and the Scientific-Industrial Revolution," *Iskusstvo-Kino*, no. 11 (1972). Also translated and published in German by *Kunst und Literatur*, no. 5 (1973), and in English by *International Journal of Sociology* (Summer-Fall, 1976).

mind, let alone the theoretical model of de-Stalinization. Perhaps for that reason, I did not then foresee that before two years were out Brezhnev would capitulate before the majority of his parliament, before the Establishment Right, and, just as Kosygin had two years previously, would burn what he had bowed down to and bow down to what he had burned. I did not foresee that the process of internal reform would be stopped so soon, that the country would fall into political stagnation, and that the Establishment Right would saddle it with an alternative means of legitimation of the regime such as traditionally is represented by external expansion.

For me personally, Brezhnev's capitulation was the final drop in the cup of my conflict with the regime. But was it also the final drop for Russia? Is Gregory Grossman correct in declaring in his magnificent lecture in memory of Bernard Moses that "now, perhaps, it is too late, and [Soviet] institutions are perhaps too ossified and the vested interests too strong for the system to be able to be reformed in the normal way—without cataclysm"?[55] Who can know this ahead of time? Each person has his own limits of patience and his own limits of hope. Grossman might be wrong in 1980, as I was wrong in 1974.

If he is indeed wrong—if the resources of liberalization in contemporary Russia are not ultimately exhausted and the process of de-Stalinization is destined to have a new birth in the 1980s—then perhaps we will still witness the formula of Malenkov being announced from the tribune of the Party Congress by a successor of Brezhnev. Once again, the result—and the destiny of Russia, I am convinced—will depend on whether a new leader (or leaders) is capable of counterposing to the power of the Establishment Right, which has blocked the process of internal reformation of the country, the power of what I call the left-centrist bloc. In other words, this will depend on the ability of the new leader to head up and institutionalize the political base of de-Stalinization by organizing an offensive in all seven of the directions listed above.

If he succeeds thereby in breaking up the political stagnation, Russia in the 1980s will actually depart significantly from the traditional pattern of behavior of autocracy in situations of political crisis. It will depart from this pattern because it will finally begin

[55] Grossman, "Economics," p. 8.

to tear off the rusted armor of a medieval political system. In the opposite case, I am afraid Russia could not help but submit itself to the basic law of autocracy, which I tried to formulate above: If it does not liberalize, it Stalinizes.

XII

On the basis of the foregoing, what advice could I give to American foreign-policy decision makers? What would I do if I were in their shoes? At the very least, I would ask a group of independent experts to examine whether there is indeed a method to madness, that is, a certain pattern to Russian political behavior in major crises. And if there is one, I would ask another group of experts to determine how such a pattern could be used in the best interests of American foreign policy.

In the meantime, while making all appropriate preparations for a new Russian political cataclysm in the 1980s, I would look attentively to see whether there still is an opportunity in Moscow for a new Khrushchev to appear. And if he does appear, I would help him. How effective this help will be obviously depends on how much better we understand the historical meaning of his actions than we understood that of the old Khrushchev. The aim of this essay has been to aid this understanding.

Appendix 1

Comparative Analysis of Two Russian Tyrannies

Ivan the Terrible (1564–1584)

1. The "revolution from above," halting the process of Westernization of Russia
2. Establishment of tyrannical one-man leadership
3. Destruction of the existing political establishment (boyardom)
4. Liquidation of all limitations on power
5. Terror as means of administration: liquidation of political opposition
6. Explosive modernization: the transformation of the economic and institutional structure of the state
7. Formation of a "new class"
8. Chaotic intensification of the vertical mobility of the elite ("permanent purge")
9. Enserfment of the peasantry (abolition of St. George's Day)
10. Physical extermination of the intellectual potential of the country

Joseph Stalin (1929–1953)

1. The "revolution from above," having abolished NEP (together with hope for political modernization)
2. Establishment of tyrannical one-man leadership
3. Destruction of the process of "aristocratization" of Soviet elite
4. Liquidation of all limitations on power
5. Terror as means of administration: liquidation of political opposition
6. Explosive modernization: industrialization
7. Formation of a "new class"
8. "Permanent purge"
9. Collectivization of the peasantry
10. Physical extermination of the intelligentsia

Appendix 2

Chronological Table of the Cycles of Russian History

Cycle I (1564–1689)
A Tyranny (1564–1584)
B Revolution of "de-Staliniâzation" (1584–1613)
C Attempts at reform, reâplaced by political stagnaâtion (1613–1689)

Cycle II (1689–1796)
A 1689–1725
B 1725–1730
C 1730–1796

Cycle III (1796–1825)
A 1796–1801
B 1801–1811
C 1811–1825

Cycle IV (1875–1881)
A 1825–1855
B 1855–1863
C 1863–1881

Cycle V (1881–1917)
A 1881–1894
B 1894–1908
C 1908–1917

Cycle VI (1917–1929)
A 1917–1921
B 1921–1927
C 1927–1929

Cycle VII (1929–)
A 1929–1953
B 1953–1964
C 1964–

The Future Soviet Leadership

Myron Rush

ANALYSIS of the Soviet leadership has for some years been dominated by the Brezhnev succession question. This became a live topic of discussion in 1975, when Brezhnev disappeared from public view for several months amid speculation that he was mortally ill or under political attack, or both. Similarly, the succession question dominated political analysis during the long years while Mao and Tito were aging. Mao's surrender of the post of head of state in 1958 was interpreted as a way of ordering the succession, and the initiation of the Cultural Revolution in 1966 was widely seen as due to intensified maneuvering by rivals for the succession. Actually, it was used by Mao to recover his power. In Yugoslavia, speculation about successors to Tito was rife in the mid-1960s, fifteen years before he died.

Of course, the succession issue was not a figment of observers' imagination. In fact, Tito and Mao both gave early thought to arranging their succession, and ambitious candidates maneuvered actively—some of them provocatively so—to position themselves for the succession. The point of recalling this prolonged preoccupation with succession is not to deny its central importance for an understanding of a future leadership but to underline the dangers of supposing that succession is imminent when in fact it may be years away.

Brezhnev's Current and Future Power

The Brezhnev succession has dominated speculation about future Soviet policies not only because of Brezhnev's age (he was born in

An early version of this paper was written while the author was a Scholar in Residence at the National Foreign Assessment Center of the Central Intelligence Agency. The conclusions and judgments presented are those of the author and do not necessarily represent the views of the NFAC or CIA.

1906) but even more because of his seeming frailty, repeated absences from public view, and an evident decline in his reserves of energy. He is not in robust health, but neither is he manifestly suffering from a mortal illness. Having lived man's average life span, he could be approaching an early loss of life; but he could as well continue in power for some time—to his seventy-sixth birthday; which he is due to celebrate on December 19, 1982, and beyond.

Certainly Brezhnev has acted as though he expects to remain in office indefinitely. He has been jealous of his power and clearly unwilling to make extensive arrangements for the succession, or even to countenance the efforts of others to maneuver for a favorable position in the contest to succeed him. Since 1975 three relatively young and promising leaders—A. N. Shelepin, D. S. Polyanskiy, and K. T. Mazurov—have been removed from the Politburo, and from politics, and two—K. F. Katushev and Ya. Ryabov—were removed from the powerful Secretariat. Moreover, prospective candidates who have tried to position themselves for the succession have had their pretensions publicly deflated by Brezhnev. F. D. Kulakov, the only relatively young leader in recent years to be a member of both the Politburo and Secretariat, experienced this in February 1977. (A few months later he suffered a fatal heart attack.) In early 1979 A. P. Kirilenko, who remains the second most powerful Soviet leader, was similarly undercut.

While the Brezhnev succession is a central factor in current Soviet politics, preoccupation with the issue has caused Western observers to lose sight of, or to discount, major Soviet political developments of recent years. The burgeoning cult of Brezhnev since 1975, which reached a peak at the 26th Party Congress in February 1981, has often been explained as a need to compensate for his physical decline, leaving out of account the political clout that was needed to compel Brezhnev's "colleagues" to practice the new rites of his cult. Brezhnev's repeated ouster of individual Politburo members—six have been removed since 1973—has been given the strained interpretation that he was safeguarding a weakening political position.

Preoccupation with Brezhnev's infirmities and his succession has distracted attention from the repeated and substantial increases in Brezhnev's powers. As a consequence, great turning points in Soviet internal policy have been overlooked because it was thought that a weak leadership immersed in the early phase of the Brezhnev succession was incapable of large new departures. Repeatedly it has been said that Brezhnev can make only consensual decisions, that his Politburo is dominated by bureaucracies and interest groups, that its policy decisions can bring only incremental changes. This understanding of the condition of the Soviet leadership is of course hard to reconcile with the invasion of Afghanistan in the final days of 1979. In a failed effort to effect such a reconciliation, some experienced observers found it necessary to postulate that, the Brezhnev succession being well under way, the decision to invade must have been forced on a weakened Brezhnev by hard-liners, although evidence for such a notion was hard to find.

The implication of what has just been argued is that to examine the future Soviet leadership, it is necessary in the first instance to consider the future of the Brezhnev leadership. It has the capacity to make basic decisions that may establish the direction of Soviet policy for years to come—as the decision to invade Afghanistan made abundantly clear. That the Brezhnev-dominated Politburo is capable of radical turns in policy can also be seen in the Tenth Five Year Plan, adopted in 1976. In it, the growth rate of defense was maintained at a high level and that of consumption reduced slightly, but the planned growth rate of investment was halved. This was a wrenching decision, the more remarkable because the increased scarcity of capital that resulted worsened the secular decline in the growth of national income. The choice was not of guns over butter, but of guns over growth.

The new directives for the Eleventh Five Year Plan (1981–1985) cut investment growth even more sharply, to around 2 percent a year. The absolute total increase in state investment in the five-year period is scheduled to be less than two-thirds of the increase achieved in the previous five-year plan. These decisions, which broke sharply with a half-century long Soviet practice of rapid investment growth, are not those of a leadership in the throes of succession.

Brezhnev's capacity to make such basic decisions derives from his influence over the Politburo. Lacking its own staff, the Politburo is dependent on the Secretariat and the large central apparatus attached to it. As general secretary of the Central Committee, Brezhnev has been able to dominate the Secretariat and thereby to extend his authority over the Politburo. While the Politburo remains central to the working of the system, its integrity as a deliberative body is questionable. First, it is big and unwieldy. There are fourteen full members, as against the customary ten or eleven at times when the Politburo has been most decisive, and several members are not in a position to participate effectively in its work. Three of the fourteen have posts outside Moscow (in the Ukraine, Leningrad, and Kazakhstan) and are not in a position to bring informed and independent judgment to bear on disputed issues of policy. Several others, including Yu. V. Andropov, A. A. Gromyko, A. Ia Pelshe, and D. F. Ustinov (and A. A. Grechko when he was minister of defense), have had specialized careers which limit their capacity to judge the full range of issues coming before the Politburo. Others, like the boss of the Moscow party organization, V. V. Grishin, are engaged full time in working at the jobs that helped win them membership in the Politburo. For many members and candidates, Politburo rank may confer a prestige that makes them more authoritative in their assigned posts, while leaving them without an effective voice in most Politburo decisions.

In sum, Brezhnev's capacity to manipulate the Politburo—by controlling the flow of documents, ordering the agenda, shaping and summing up deliberations, and using the requirement of voting to make Politburo members formally responsible for decisions—has not been adequately appreciated. These devices, together with a measure of indirect control over the political police and the army, help to explain Brezhnev's capacity to maintain a predominant position in the leadership despite his reduced vitality and the doubtful success of his policies. If Brezhnev remains in a position of supreme authority—after having conferred abundant resources on agriculture with poor results, having starved civilian heavy industry of needed investment, having bungled Soviet involvement in Afghanistan and then attempted to retrieve the situation by miring the army in a damaging guerrilla war—it may not be because Brezhnev's Politburo associates are really convinced he possesses the political virtues that Brezhnev's cult requires them to attribute to him. A future conjunction of political crisis and temporary physical incapacity could readily put Brezhnev's power in jeopardy. Meanwhile, the tendency to underestimate Brezhnev's political power may continue to distort perceptions of the Soviet political scene.

The Transfer of Power

A central question in the Brezhnev succession, when it finally comes, is how far will the powers be reduced that he has arrogated and that currently are attached to the office of the general secretary of the Central Committee and afford a measure of stability to the leadership? The depth of the crisis of succession will depend heavily on this issue. A severe degradation of the senior secretary's powers occurred when Khrushchev and Brezhnev succeeded to the office. The crucial question is: Has sufficient institutionalization of the office since occurred to produce a different outcome next time?[1]

Certain functions Brezhnev currently performs have not always belonged to the party's senior secretary and will not pass automatically to the new general secretary. Neither Brezhnev nor Khrushchev held the post of supreme commander in chief of the armed forces at the beginning of his tenure; nor, apparently, did either initially hold the post of chairman of the Defense Council. Brezhnev's successor as general secretary might lay strong claim to both posts on national security grounds by arguing a need in the missile-nuclear age for rapid decision-making authority. His claim would be reinforced if he were to acquire Brezhnev's additional post of chairman of the Presidium of the Supreme Soviet (virtual head of state) because, according to the 1977 Constitution (Article 121, Section 14), this body "forms the Council of Defense of the USSR and confirms its composition, appoints and dismisses the high command of the Armed Forces of the USSR." For this reason, and also because the chairman of the Presidium of the Supreme Soviet has constitutional responsibilities in the area of foreign policy, the new general secretary might argue that it was necessary to keep the top posts in the party and the state conjoined.

Although this arrangement has much to recommend it on organizational grounds, the Politburo probably would resist efforts

[1] See this author's *How Communist States Change Their Rulers* (Ithaca, N.Y., 1974).

to maintain it, and this would aggravate the first phase of the succession. Judging from historical precedent, the new general secretary would be at a disadvantage in an early test of strength with Politburo opponents. However, since his failure to obtain the post of head of state might leave the Soviet armed forces with a collective top command—with its potential disadvantages for the conduct of modern war and diplomacy—high political and military officials responsible for national security might look favorably on a new general secretary's desire to become head of state.

The new general secretary may be obliged to make an early and perhaps fateful choice between two personal strategies: (1) to bid for both the party and state offices in an attempt to resolve the crisis of succession quickly; or (2) to assure his Politburo colleagues that he is content to remain the first among real equals, in which case intense political struggle might continue over a period of years, as has generally happened in the past. As suggested above, the success of the first strategy might depend critically on support from key political leaders, particularly the heads of the armed forces (currently D. F. Ustinov, who is in poor health) and of the KGB (currently Yu. V. Andropov). If the general secretary tried to get the state post but failed, he might be allowed to stay on in circumstances that severely circumscribed his authority, or he might be replaced as general secretary by a more accommodating leader. In either case, such early maneuvering would probably result in an unstable balance that would encourage intense factional struggle among the Politburo's members, which would make it difficult for the Politburo to adopt bold, unforced decisions.[2]

On the whole, it seems doubtful that the office of the general secretary has been sufficiently institutionalized to ease the transfer of Brezhnev's full powers to his heir. The new general secretary may not even retain Brezhnev's office adjacent to the Politburo's meeting place inside the Kremlin—an important symbolic and substantive element of power that Brezhnev obtained only after several years tenure as general secretary. Whether or not the successor acquires

---

[2] A useful distinction here is that between *urgent* decisions forced by circumstances—such as whether to end the Korean War, which was decided upon after Stalin's death—and unforced decisions to initiate reforms and reorganization—such as the decision to reestablish the economic ministries, which required several months of debate following Khrushchev's removal.

this office and whether or not he acquires the post of head of state will be important indicators of the extent to which the general secretary's powers have been degraded. In the unlikely event that the new general secretary is successful in rapidly acquiring most of Brezhnev's current powers, the crisis of succession might not be deep. If so, the consequences of the Brezhnev succession for Soviet policy and institutions would depend largely on the views and the political character of the successor leadership.

Candidates for the Succession

As a result of Brezhnev's evident determination to hold on to power and to prevent the emergence of an able, ambitious, and experienced young leader as a logical heir, the circle of likely candidates within the Politburo is small and unusually unimpressive. Soviet and foreign observers have widened the circle somewhat with dubious members, while taking note of their liabilities. Andropov, for example, hardly fits the model of previous contenders: He has never been the responsible leader of a major territorial division, his health is not good, and he bears the stigma of service in the security police. His reputed liberalism is dubious.

V. V. Shcherbitskiy is another frequently listed as a leading contender. His Ukrainian ancestry, however, is a serious handicap in a contest for the succession. He as yet lacks service in Moscow, and since no one is being groomed for his key post as head of the country's second republic, an early move by him to Moscow evidently is not contemplated. G. V. Romanov and V. V. Grishin, the party bosses in Leningrad and Moscow, respectively, are plausible candidates even though they have not yet had experience in the central party apparatus. Of the candidate members of the Politburo, only M. S. Solomentsev, the head of the government of the Russian Republic, appears to be a likely candidate for the succession.

A surprise arrival in the circle of candidates is K. U. Chernenko. As head of the General Department, Chernenko has been known to the senior members of the Politburo, including A. P. Kirilenko and M. A. Suslov for fifteen years. During this time his position relative to theirs has changed from marked inferiority to equality or superiority. Chernenko doubtless has performed his sensitive and demanding task well, but his rise from nonmembership in the Central Committee in 1965 to full member of the Politburo in 1978 is a reflection of the rise in Brezhnev's power and is not a reward for brilliant accomplishment or even for assuming major new political responsibilities. Further, a sharp change in the relations of senior leaders to Chernenko is bound to have caused resentment. Thus, even before his death in 1982 Suslov's power had appreciably declined. Ustinov, Andropov, and Gromyko, as heads of the national security bureaucracies, exercise considerable authority in implementing policies, but it appears to be limited largely to the areas of their responsibility.

Chernenko has had abundant opportunity to acquire knowledge of substantive affairs in the Politburo during his sixteen-year tenure as its executive officer, although it is not known how much he has benefited. In the period ahead, if Brezhnev's health and mental faculties decline slowly, Chernenko will have further opportunity to master important affairs that are in the purview of the Politburo. If he has talents that have been obscured during the seven decades of his life, the alter ego's power may grow as the principal's power wanes. If not—and this appears more likely—his power may be dissipated.

In such a circle of candidates, Kirilenko—despite his age (75 as of September 8, 1981), his rank in the Politburo (fourth), and his limited experience (particularly in foreign and defense policy)—is a heavy favorite to succeed if Brezhnev leaves office in the near future. Kirilenko is useful to Brezhnev, who otherwise might be under pressure to prepare a younger man to replace him in the event his health suddenly failed. Kirilenko must continue to show his colleagues that he can think and act independently but must avoid provoking Brezhnev's suspicions, as seems to have happened for a time early in 1979. True, an implausible contender might come to power if the circle of possible candidates stays as small as it is; moreover, Brezhnev may still have time to decide to make new arrangements for the succession. A further weakening of Brezhnev's physical stamina, however, would increase the likelihood of his sticking with Kirilenko. On the critical question of Kirilenko's personal qualities, the evidence available to us is sparse and unclear. Even his colleagues in the Politburo may not be able to gauge him with confidence. It is useful to recall that Stalin grossly misjudged the relative capacities of G. M. Malenkov and Khrushchev, and that Khrushchev in turn thought N. V. Podgorniy could be relied on to counterbalance Brezhnev.

Should Kirilenko succeed Brezhnev, Chernenko's skill in managing the Politburo could be useful to Kirilenko's supporters in their efforts to consolidate the position of the general secretary and perhaps also, though in less degree, to Kirilenko's opponents in their effort to limit Kirilenko's power and preserve the collectivity of the leadership. Both sides might be suspicious of Chernenko's loyalties, however; unless he had somehow acquired a traditional base of power (such as control of major provincial party organizations or powerful institutions), it is questionable whether the large powers Brezhnev has conferred on Chernenko would outlast Brezhnev. If Brezhnev were forced from office, Chernenko's subsequent role in the leadership would probably depend on whether he had joined the conspiracy that ousted Brezhnev. If he had not, Chernenko probably would not be able to reach an accommodation with the new leadership as Podgorniy did in 1964.[3] Podgorniy had close personal relations with leaders of the Ukrainian party organization, as well as powerful protégés in the central party staff. Chernenko at present apparently lacks such political assets.

On balance, the elevation of Chernenko strengthened the stability of the Brezhnev leadership, but it seems doubtful that it will ease the succession. In fact, by postponing succession arrangements for bringing vigorous new leaders to the fore, Brezhnev has increased the likelihood that his succession will be troubled and disorderly.

Strategy of the New General Secretary

What strategy the new general secretary will adopt to arrogate the historical powers of his office will significantly affect the course of the succession. Another crucial early decision is whether to concentrate mainly on internal affairs in the first phase of the succession or to take on foreign affairs as well. Until now, new incumbents

[3] Chernenko's interest in such a project might be stimulated, however, by knowledge that his prospects of remaining in power after Brezhnev's departure would otherwise be poor.

to the post have left most foreign policy matters to others, directing their attention chiefly to agriculture and to winning control of the party apparatus. However, foreign policy may now be so important in Soviet politics that a new general secretary will give it serious and immediate attention. Not only do foreign affairs directly affect assessments of military and foreign aid requirements, but an activist Soviet statesman has an opportunity to associate himself in the Soviet public mind with the nation's destiny.

The new general secretary's personal strategy with respect to involvement in foreign affairs may be strongly influenced by whether he has quickly acquired the office of chairman of the Presidium of the Supreme Soviet. As head of state, Brezhnev's successor might be tempted to concentrate less on agriculture than did Khrushchev and Brezhnev and to give an appreciable share of his attention to foreign policy. His overriding political concern, however, almost certainly will be to use the post of general secretary to extend his influence over the Secretariat and in time over the party apparatus as well.

Institutional Competition

In the Stalin succession and to a lesser degree in the Khrushchev succession, there was serious competition between the government, headed by the Council of Ministers, and the party apparatus, headed by the Secretariat. Similar competition can be expected in the Brezhnev succession. The distinctiveness of the two institutions has been accentuated by the personnel policy of the Brezhnev regime. While transfers between the party and state bureaucracies are still common, cooptation of experienced economic managers to relatively high-level positions in the party apparatus has declined sharply since Khrushchev's ouster. Career-minded officials are even more aware now that they can better satisfy their ambitions in the party apparatus than in the government.

Although the hegemony of the party apparatus has lasted more than two decades and has acquired a measure of legitimacy, it may be vulnerable to attack. At present the Council of Ministers lacks the vigor and ambition necessary to compete effectively with the party or even to protect itself against encroachment by the Secretariat. Kosygin is dead and his former "first deputies," Polyanskiy and Mazurov, have been ousted, leaving N. A. Tikhonov—an aged and narrowly experienced Brezhnev protégé—as the dominant figure in the Government. Unless the economic bureaucracy acquires politically astute and ambitious young leaders in the next several years, it probably will be unable to mount a serious challenge to the party apparatus.

The Secretariat provided the basis for Brezhnev's rise and has been his chief organ of rule. But his dispersal of power within it—a device to protect his personal power—could lead to a weakening of the Secretariat after his departure. At the outset of previous successions, senior leaders broadly experienced in the work of the central Secretariat held positions in it. They were able to maintain its powers and exploit them in order to arrogate personal power, thus helping to resolve the succession. But Brezhnev has so arranged matters that experience in the Secretariat is in short supply among Politburo members. True, Kirilenko may have an opportunity during the Brezhnev succession to achieve a dominant position in the Secretariat; the absence of other vigorous and knowledgeable secretaries would even improve his chances. But if he failed (as he well might, in view of his advanced age and limited prestige), the other senior figures—being outside the Secretariat or, at best, inside it but inexperienced in its ways—might find it difficult to operate the Secretariat's powerful levers.

Since Stalin's death, the transfer of power has been facilitated by the dominant position of the Secretariat in the Communist political system in conjunction with the potential power of the general secretary within the Secretariat. This had moderated the crisis of succession not only in the U.S.S.R., but also in the several regimes modeled on it.[4] A weakening of the Secretariat in the Brezhnev succession not only would deepen the inevitable crisis of the leadership but also could lead to a crisis of Soviet institutions. Deprived of its controlling nerve center, the party apparatus would lose something of its cohesion and thus of its capacity to maintain tight control of the regime's other key institutions: the economic bureaucracy, the political police, and the army. The assertiveness of these institutions, and especially of the various interest groups that

[4] See Myron Rush, "Leadership Succession in Communist States," *Journal of International Affairs* (Fall 1978).

they harbor, should not be exaggerated. Unlike groups in democracies, they are not *pressure* groups commanding powerful resources of their own. Contrary to the expectations of many observers, interest groups in the U.S.S.R. other than the military have displayed neither a strong inclination to engage in higher Soviet politics nor great effectiveness when they have attempted to do so. Nevertheless, they have a large political potential; in a succession crisis, they could become powerful actors affecting the immediate outcome of the succession and also possibly prompting changes in the regime.

The chain of contingencies here is long: (1) Brezhnev's current mode of running the Secretariat, (2) if it continues could (3) weaken the Secretariat in the succession, thereby (4) reducing the effectiveness of the party apparatus, leading to (5) increased independence of the regime's chief agencies of rule. If in the decade ahead the character of the Soviet system experiences basic change, this may well have been brought about by such a sequence of events.

Renewal of the Leadership

Khrushchev's heirs moderated the struggle for the succession by agreeing to limit the use of political purges and patronage to win supporters. As a consequence of this policy, the leadership has now become old, and its continuation poses difficult problems. Even if Brezhnev's successors do not strive to oust their opponents and advance their partisans, natural attrition of the leadership (through death or incapacity) will compel them to replace numerous high officials. More than one-third of the members of the Central Committee are more than sixty-five years old.[5] Unless such vacancies continue to be filled by promotion on the basis of seniority, as has been typical throughout most of the Brezhnev period, new appointments are bound to bring political confrontations that will test the power of individuals and factions in the Politburo.

In addition to the effect of natural attrition on high-level politics, the obvious need to rejuvenate the leadership could lead the Politburo to adopt general rules for retiring aging Central Com-

[5] Considerable natural attrition may occur before Brezhnev's departure, and the attrition rate is likely to remain high for some years to come.

mittee members below the Politburo level. The application of such rules to particular cases and the consequent need to make additional appointments would probably increase political controversy. Since such matters are in the Politburo's domain, the balance of forces in the Politburo will be decisive. Perhaps only a stalemate in the Politburo would permit continuation of the present policy, which gives tenure to members and replaces incapacitated members with their most senior subordinates. It seems doubtful, however, that a Politburo stalemate would be prolonged, particularly since natural attrition will be high in the Politburo itself, where the average age is seventy. Only three of the fourteen Politburo members were born after 1914; seven were born before 1910. In previous successions Politburo membership has been stable in the early years. Extensive changes in the Politburo usually have followed large changes in the Central Committee. In the Brezhnev succession, however, substantial changes in the composition of the Politburo may come about by natural attrition early in the succession. A Politburo faction that gained strength from the adherence of new members would in turn be able to choose new members of the Central Committee on political grounds and perhaps even to undertake a general rejuvenation of the leadership.

Because the opportunities for patronage are so large, the stakes in the Brezhnev succession are likely to be substantially greater than in the Khrushchev succession. This will probably deepen the struggle over the succession, but it may speed up its resolution. If the general secretary were able to exploit these patronage opportunities, he would substantially improve his chances of consolidating power. The combination of a strong general secretary and a rejuvenated leadership might lead to a basic realignment of Soviet politics, perhaps even to efforts at major institutional reform. The chances of such an outcome, while considerably less than even in the short run, may be fairly good in the longer run—say, within five years of Brezhnev's departure from office.

Whatever the duration of the Brezhnev succession, in its first phase bold and controversial initiatives are not likely to be adopted, and if adopted may prove abortive. A later phase of succession, however, may bring the consolidation of a successor's personal position and his adoption and implementation of a series of bold new measures.

The New Generation of Leaders

Because the median age of the 400 member Central Committee is well above sixty, in the 1980s a new generation of leaders will enter the Central Committee and make its influence felt there. How will they differ from the men (and very few women) who have governed the U.S.S.R. in the Brezhnev period? A substantial body of analytical and speculative literature deals with this question, one that has crucial importance for the future of the Soviet Union and perhaps for the condition of mankind in the remainder of the twentieth century.[6] There is an understandable tendency to resolve our radical uncertainty about the personalities and deeper currents of higher Soviet politics by resorting to the laws of biology and to sociological and historical generalization. This is a useful exercise, although care must be taken not to build an elaborate structure of expectations on weak foundations.

Particular attention has been given to a large cohort of leaders born in the late 1920s and early 1930s whose careers have suffered from the low turnover in the Central Committee during the Brezhnev years. These men's adult lives have been spent in the more salubrious political climate created after Stalin's death. They did not know the morally corrupting pressures of Stalin's despotic rule. They are better educated and more thoroughly trained than their elders. Soviet successes have given them confidence, leaving them less insecure than the men they will replace. But does it follow that their opinions will diverge strongly from those of their elders? Will they harbor different attitudes? Will they act differently? Finally, and most important, will the new generation of leaders display a changed political character from that of the generation that now rules the U.S.S.R.?

To prevent this from happening is a basic aim of the Soviet system. The formal system of political education largely is designed to reproduce the political character of the existing rulers—to make the new leaders good *Leninists*, as this term has been understood in the past quarter century. The formal political education is

[6] See, for example, Jerry Hough, *How the Soviet Union Is Governed* (Cambridge, Mass., 1979) and Seweryn Bialer, *Stalin's Successors* (New York, 1980).

powerfully reinforced by the discipline of operating within highly stable institutions that, at least until recently, have successfully fostered the regime's objectives. Finally, informal mechanisms operating in the struggle for personal advancement have helped to socialize ambitious careerists in the prevailing political mores.

These devices may of course fail in their purpose, and the informal mechanisms that support the system may be neutralized by countervailing mechanisms. Still, the fact that the cohort born in the late 1920s has been kept in subordinate posts for a prolonged period of time, including the most impressionable years of their lives, may favor their elders' efforts to instill in them the political character that has sustained the Soviet regime in recent decades. If despite these obstacles the new generation of leaders nevertheless has acquired a different political character, they have been unable to express it actively during the long years they have been waiting to rise to the top. Their new political character, if it exists at all, is present only in latent form and lacks reinforcement by effective political action. Moreover, if this cohort (and still younger individuals who have similarly been blocked from promotion) does give expression to a new political character in a rejuvenated Central Committee leadership, its effect would be diluted by the continued presence there of still powerful remnants of older cohorts.

While it is doubtful that a new political character has been formed in the middle-aged leaders who are waiting to take control of the Politburo, this is not to argue that radical new policies will not emerge in the succession. The Brezhnev leadership will leave severe problems behind when it departs and may be badly discredited. In a confrontation with the puzzling and perhaps depressing Soviet reality of the 1980s, the failed ideas and relatively narrow ideological constraints that still limit the vision of middle-aged members of the Soviet political class may begin to dissolve. If, unlike the Brezhnev leadership, the successor leadership has faith that the system can be reformed, a combination of discredited policies and otherwise intractable problems might well persuade a new Politburo to seek out promising radical solutions. If such solutions can be found (of course, they may not even exist), the succession to Brezhnev could bring about major changes in Soviet policies and institutions.

The Impaired Brezhnev Heritage

The legacy of the Brezhnev leadership will not ease the succession, nor will it be gratefully received by the successor leadership. The severe economic problems it will inherit, in particular, are likely to exacerbate the Brezhnev succession crisis. These problems differ from the economic dislocations caused by Khrushchev's ill-conceived efforts to reform economic management, which were readily repaired by rescinding his reforms. Similarly, the depressed state of agriculture resulting from Stalin's neglect made it possible for his heirs to strengthen the economy and improve living standards simply by providing agriculture with some of the resources it desperately needed. No such "reserves" are currently available to alleviate the ills of the Soviet economy, which have worsened in the past seventeen years as the rate of economic growth has continued its decline. An acute worsening of the economic situation in a given year, perhaps brought on or exacerbated by a poor harvest, could have major repercussions in the leadership, as happened on several occasions in other Communist states (for example, Czechoslovakia in 1968 and Poland in 1970 and 1980) and in the U.S.S.R. itself in 1964. These economic problems will not be alleviated in the time remaining to Brezhnev but will probably grow substantially worse. His heirs will have to deal simultaneously with the transfer of power and the attainment of a more satisfactory rate of economic growth. The present leadership has already tried a number of remedies for the country's economic ills—organizational reform, expanded economic relations with the West, and improved incentives. The successor leadership will have to consider going beyond the modest limits previously deemed prudent in these spheres and playing one of its last cards—a cutback in the growth of military expenditures. It will also confront increasingly painful decisions in allocating a slowly growing or possibly stagnant national product among civilian consumption, civilian investment, and defense.

As noted earlier, the Brezhnev leadership has adapted itself to the reduced growth of the economy and to resource shortages by making sharp reductions in the growth of investment, rather than making substantial cuts in the growth of defense. Plans to compensate for investment cutbacks in industry by rapid increases in capital productivity have proved unrealistic. Consequently, key production targets in recent years have not been fulfilled. The economy's growth rate in the Tenth Five-Year Plan was well below that of the Ninth and will almost certainly be lower yet in the Eleventh, 1981–85—perhaps no more than 1 or 2 percent annually.

It seems most unlikely that Brezhnev will become the first top leader since Lenin whom Soviet historiography will evaluate favorably. Although all members of the Politburo and Secretariat will have attained their position of power under Brezhnev's auspices, they are not likely to feel committed to his programs, which have had but limited success. The successor leadership probably will agree to blame Brezhnev for the poor economic situation, especially the severe energy shortages they will inherit. (Soviet rulers *are* held responsible for their failures, but usually only after they have left power.)

The successor leaders may find themselves divided, however, on the issue of measures to remedy the country's economic ills. Heavy industry constitutes one powerful interest group that may try to alter Brezhnev's economic policies. This group lost its favored position as recipient of ample investment funds for expanding production and improving efficiency. It has suffered along with others from the reduced growth of investment, but it also has had to bear the diversion of investment funds to agriculture. Agriculture has not improved sufficiently to warrant eliminating large infusions of capital. The effectiveness of allotting increased funds to agriculture has been low, however; partisans of heavy industry can plausibly argue that part of the investment funds currently planned for agriculture should be diverted to heavy industry, which in recent years has been lagging in its efforts to meet even the reduced targets set for it. Agriculture is likely to suffer when Brezhnev leaves power, especially if its partisans must defend agricultural investments against powerful advocates of heavy industry. While Brezhnev's agricultural program has commanded the support of the Politburo, Brezhnev's personal advocacy probably counted for a great deal. Partisans of agriculture will probably find it expedient to blame Brezhnev for agriculture's failure to benefit more from the bounty showered on it.

It is difficult to predict the outcome of controversy over resource allocation and the relevant policy orientation of candidates for the succession. Nevertheless, Kirilenko seems a logical partisan of the claims of heavy industry. He long has been closely associated with that sector, particularly machine building, and at times he has appeared to question agriculture's claims to a growing proportion of available resources. Were Kirilenko to succeed Brezhnev as general secretary, he might depart from the pattern set by Khrushchev in 1953 and Brezhnev in 1965 of making agriculture his chief economic concern and might instead concentrate resources in heavy industry.

Defense may have to defend itself against efforts to divert funds to the heavy industrial sector. This could lead to a confrontation of two powerful sets of interests, those engaged in heavy industry and those in defense. Defense has been by far the favored sector in the Brezhnev years, even to the serious neglect of civilian investment. Partisans of heavy industry may plausibly argue that a failure to divert resources from rapidly growing military power to lagging heavy industry would lead within the next decade to a reduced economic base relative to NATO's and, consequently, to a reduced capacity to compete with NATO—and an economically strengthened China—in creating military force in the future. Here again, Kirilenko, who has not been closely associated with the military leadership, might attempt to limit the growth of defense spending, although probably not to a point that would provoke the enmity of the military chiefs.

The question of the proper level of civilian consumption may also stir contention during the succession, as it has in the Brezhnev years. Consumer advocates probably will lack strength in the Politburo, however, while advocates of a sharp reduction in the growth rate of civilian consumption will have to cope with the argument that in "a mature socialist economy" material incentives are necessary to increase productivity. In recent years, civilian consumption has grown less rapidly than previously, and in the years just ahead per capita production may not grow at all. While both Stalin's and Khrushchev's heirs were able to increase consumer goods production sharply in their efforts to enhance popular support, the heightened scarcity of resources is likely to deprive Brezhnev's successors of this option. The successor leadership may even be faced with the task of imposing new deprivations on the Soviet people: stagnant or reduced consumption levels, longer work weeks, tighter work discipline. If so, this could seriously complicate the succession.

The Brezhnev Heritage in Foreign Policy

Brezhnev is likely to be blamed not only for the poor performance of the economy but also for Soviet setbacks on the international scene. Having advocated détente with the United States by harboring exaggerated expectations of its benefits and asserting its "irreversibility," Brezhnev subsequently ventured on a course of Soviet expansion—culminating in the invasion of Afghanistan—that effectively undermined détente with the United States. By leading the retreat from détente, Brezhnev succeeded in postponing the adverse political consequences of the policy's failure, but his heirs will be faced with a need to reconcile the contradictory elements of Brezhnev's foreign policy.

The strategy adopted for dealing with economic problems may strongly condition the outcome of any foreign policy review. To the extent that the new leadership is committed to dealing seriously with the country's troubled economy, it is likely to seek improved relations with the United States. This would be desirable, at a minimum, in order to avoid provoking the United States to increase its military spending sharply, thereby initiating an accelerated arms race that would seriously hamper Soviet efforts to strengthen the economy. If, in addition, investment funds were shifted from some projected defense programs to civilian heavy industry, Soviet détente policy might enter a new phase in which a more stable international environment was a desideratum. New efforts might be made to acquire large credits from the West—less for achieving a general upgrading of Soviet technology than for intensifying exploitation of Soviet natural resources. In that event, greater restraint might be exercised in probing for gains in Third World areas. Costly aid programs, such as those adopted to support Soviet objectives in Africa and Southeast Asia, might be cut back. The leaders would continue to react strongly, of course, to any perceived threat to Soviet security.

If, on the other hand, the new leaders found Soviet economic problems intractable, they might concentrate on improving the Soviet military position, even though this would entail a further decline in the economy's growth rate. Anticipating the next phase, when the slowed economy might necessitate a reduction in the growth of defense spending, they might try to capitalize on a military-economic "window" in the mid 1980s to make foreign policy gains. Soviet military power might be placed at the service of traditional economic imperialism in order to acquire preferential access to foreign raw materials, particularly oil and natural gas. A venturesome foreign policy might be particularly attractive to a new generation of leaders. Unlike their elders, who encountered the intimidating United States preponderance of strength in the 1950s and 1960s, younger men might be less impressed by United States might. Even so, the traditional Bolshevik injunction against "adventurism" and against taking needless risks would pose a constraint.

The process of making foreign policy decisions may change in important ways as a result of the succession. Brezhnev's close foreign policy advisers—men like A. M. Aleksandrov, G. A. Arbatov, and A. I. Blatov—presumably will lose much of their current influence, but a place might be found for them in the Central Committee's growing foreign policy apparatus. The new general secretary no doubt would prefer his own foreign policy aides, although his colleagues will probably try to use the succession to reduce the size of the general secretary's personal staff. A new general secretary will lack Brezhnev's authority in foreign policy, and, at least in the short run, the collective influence of the Politburo will rise.

The Foreign Ministry will lose influence when Gromyko finally leaves, especially if the successor is a professional diplomat with initially lower party rank. Perhaps only the replacement of Gromyko by a major party figure (conceivably a Romanov or a Grishin) would preserve the Foreign Ministry's influence in the short term. In that case, ideological concerns might then be expressed more directly in the conduct of foreign affairs.[7] In either case, the authority of the Central Committee's foreign policy staff will probably grow. The assistance of academic specialists in foreign affairs will continue to be sought, although their influence might decline if party apparatchiks come to dominate the Foreign Ministry and especially the post-Brezhnev Politburo.

[7] This might also be the result if V. F. Maltsev, currently one of two first-deputy foreign ministers, succeeded Gromyko. Maltsev, who was born in Dnepropetrovsk, has had a meteoric rise in the Foreign Ministry in recent years and may be a protégé of Brezhnev or (what might favor his fortunes in the succession even more) of Kirilenko.

The Prospects

The transfer of power after Brezhnev will be complicated by a number of factors which favor extensive change in the leadership:

(1) Brezhnev's unwillingness to try to order the succession, in particular his failure to assure that there will be a powerful Secretariat to ease the transfer of power

(2) The rapid turnover of the Politburo and the Central Committee which will occur due to the advanced age of their members and which may be accelerated by politically induced turnover arising from factional struggle among candidates for the succession

(3) The severity of the problems facing the future leadership, particularly the reduced growth of annual increments to the gross national product, which will lead to intensified political struggle among claimants for resources—especially among partisans of (a) defense and agriculture, which have been favored by Brezhnev; (b) civilian consumption, which has done only moderately well; and (c) heavy industry and transportation, which by historical standards have been starved of resources

(4) The possibility of intensified ethnic rivalries, especially a more assertive nationalism of the Muslim peoples; however, the dangerous opposition of the two largest nations, Russians and Ukrainians, that Stalin encouraged has abated.

These factors pointing toward extensive change must be set against the remarkable record of the Soviet regime's stability and its demonstrated capacity for self-reform, as in purging itself of Stalin's worst practices. A key question is whether Brezhnev achieved the stability of the past seventeen years by immobilism at a cost of future instability. On balance, the Brezhnev succession promises to be considerably more far-reaching in its consequences than the Khrushchev succession, but probably less far-reaching than the Stalin succession.

Sino-Soviet Relations in the 1980s

Allen S. Whiting

GEOMETRY has little in common with international relations. The concept of a triangle with its clearly defined space and interconnecting points is far removed from the multidimensional web of interactions that enmesh governments in a world system. Moreover, geometric figures are subject to objective measurement with common agreement on their dimensions. International relations, however, are determined by subjective perceptions that define reality according to a compound of selective history, differential experience, and cultural conditioning. Last, the laws of mathematics and physics make predictable the application of geometrical principles to the real world of engineering. By contrast, the essential unpredictability of human behavior defies any comparable effort in the realm of world politics.

Yet despite these gross dissimilarities, there remains a compulsion to cast interstate behavior in terms borrowed from the realm of science, epitomized by the classic concept "balance of power." Despite a total lack of agreement as to what constitutes power, much less the obvious impossibility of maintaining a static or "stable" balance among nations whose internal properties are constantly changing, this concept has dominated the minds of policymakers and scholars over the past century and a half. In similar fashion, the notion that a triangle constitutes an enduring form within which the balance of power can operate persists in the perceptions of contemporary political leaders, pundits, and professors, whether in the Soviet Union, Japan, or the United States, irrespective of ideology or culture.

Unless we recognize the distortions that result from this approach, we can become transfixed by the simplistic model to the point of equating it with the real world. The image of a triangle, for instance, ignores the fact that under most circumstances, the dyadic, or bilateral, interaction of two states has a greater bearing on their relationship than do the ties of either with a third party. Only in the exceptional instance of an imminent conflict will the perception of hostile collusion or alliance between two countries determine the policy of a third state. Even here, however, the relationship among the three is subject to influence by other countries which lie outside the triangle but whose internal situation or external behavior may impinge on the triangular configuration.

Specifically, the interactions of Moscow-Washington, Moscow-Peking and Peking-Washington are conditioned by a host of factors not present in and largely independent of the three-way relationship. Thus, the United States-Soviet strategic balance is dominated by the super-powers' technological monopoly of global nuclear weapons systems, wherein the Chinese military capability plays a minuscule part. The Sino-Soviet dispute has a twenty-year history, persisting through a wide change in the two communist contenders' relations with the United States. And while the Sino-American détente emerged in the context of the triangle as perceived from Peking and Washington, its practical consequences have been most manifest in bilateral economic, scientific, and cultural exchanges.

The image of a tightly closed triangle is challenged further by the long list of situations in Asia, the Middle East, and Africa, where one or more of the three states finds itself challenged by or competing with one or both of the other two. It is impossible to review relations among the U.S.S.R., the United States, and the People's Republic of China over the past decade without reference to Japan, Indochina, India, Afghanistan, Ethiopia, Angola, and Zaire, to mention the more salient cases. Likewise, contention in an international forum such as the United Nations or the Nonaligned Conference involves a multiplicity of audiences for mobilizing coalitions whose votes affect prestige and status.

These observations argue for abandoning the triangular fixation that has conditioned much analysis of the past and prospective interaction among the world's three largest and potentially most powerful nations, in favor of focusing mainly on the separate bilateral relationships, in this instance that between Peking and Moscow. This does not exclude a triangular focus but rather introduces it as a secondary aspect, subsidiary to more immediate concerns that condition the two parties' interaction.

We do not know which individuals and interests will comprise the decision-making elites in the People's Republic and the Soviet

Union over the coming decade or how their respective economic situations will affect power and policy. We cannot foresee how developments external to the Sino-Soviet relationship may affect its inner workings. Yet while forecasting remains a hazardous art and not a systematic science, we nonetheless can weigh the prospects for alternative futures on the basis of recent trends and logical inference. This in turn can provide a framework for planning long-range United States foreign policy toward Northeast Asia.

Sino-Soviet Relations: The Prospects for War

Ever since the brief but bloody fighting at Damansky Island on the Ussuri River in March 1969, the outside world has speculated on the likelihood of a major war between China and the Soviet Union. During the early 1970s Chinese media warned the populace to prepare for a possible surprise attack in a war that might be conventional or nuclear. Mao's widely quoted admonition to "store grain and dig tunnels deep" resulted in a labyrinth of underground shelters and passageways beneath China's major cities. High officials subsequently downgraded the immediate Soviet threat, claiming it was a "feint to the East in order to strike at the West," but continued to stress the presence of an alleged million Soviet troops "on China's borders."

Meanwhile, Moscow sounded a war alarm in the immediate aftermath of the Damansky Island clashes but muted it shortly thereafter, perhaps because of undue apprehension on the part of the Soviet populace. The "yellow peril" image conventional in Western stereotypes is heightened for a Russian populace nurtured on the historical memory of a Mongol invasion that swept over Moscovy and Kiev, coupled with an acute awareness of a gross population asymmetry that juxtaposes 260 million against one billion. Nevertheless, recurring Soviet propaganda attacks against the alleged collusion of an expansionist China and a nascent militaristic Japan, encouraged by a hostile United States, keeps a "worst case" prospect alive.

These are not wholly paranoiac visions lacking any basis in fact on either side. Chinese awareness of a Soviet military buildup behind the 4,650-mile border was voiced by Mao in conversations with foreign visitors in 1967. Fear of a Soviet attack was openly expressed following the Soviet invasion of Czechoslovakia in 1968. By 1969 China faced a nexus of power that provided prima facie evidence of hostile intent. This included, in an arc from Central Asia to the Soviet Far East, thirty-five divisions, 500-nautical-mile-range nuclear missiles ringing the northeast provinces, and new airfields in Mongolia. In June 1969 Soviet bomber units were redeployed from East Europe to Central Asian bases whence they conducted mock air attack exercises against targets in northwest China. That summer low-level Soviet diplomats probed their foreign counterparts concerning possible reaction to a "surgical strike" against Chinese nuclear production facilities. Victor Louis, a suspected KGB journalist, publicly hinted at this prospect while *Pravda* uttered more oblique warnings. Meanwhile, further incidents, often at Soviet initiative, sparked local clashes along the Sinkiang border.

The tension ebbed somewhat in September when, in the aftermath of Ho Chi Minh's funeral in Hanoi, Kosygin and Chou En-lai met for several hours in the Peking airport and agreed to subsequent discussion of the border issue. No further fighting was reported. However, the Soviet Union continued to strengthen its military forces arrayed against China. By the end of the decade, deployment of the Backfire bomber and the SS-20 intermediate range missile had significantly strengthened the potential striking power while the ground forces had increased to approximately forty-two divisions.

As threatening as these moves may have appeared to Peking, from Moscow's vantage point they were justified by defensive need. In the early 1960s, numerous incidents occurred along the undemarcated and disputed border. Then in 1964 Mao remarked to a visiting Japanese delegation that there would have to be an "accounting" of the vast territory taken from imperial China by the Tsarist regime, including virtually all of the Soviet Far East. During the tumultuous Cultural Revolution, xenophobic demonstrations put the Soviet embassy in Peking under siege for weeks. Violence on the frontier, similar to that experienced by Vietnam and Hong Kong, may have also aroused apprehension in the Kremlin. With the vital Trans-Siberian Railroad, Moscow's only overland link with the major naval base of Vladivostok—ten miles or less from the Chinese border for much of its run along the Ussuri River, and at one point only 1.5 miles away—such apprehension is understandable.

Soviet uncertainty over the degree to which Chinese calculations rested on presumed rationality and previous caution was heightened by the action of local troops at Damansky Island. In January 1969 Moscow had warned Peking that any further physical assertion of territorial claims there would be met with force. In response, the People's Liberation Army (PLA) concealed reinforcements which that March successfully ambushed Soviet border guards resisting a fresh Chinese incursion. Although the clash was small in scale, both sides immediately inflated its significance in propaganda explicitly threatening war. In China, millions reportedly demonstrated against the "new Tsars." Moscow retaliated ten days later with a much larger force, inflicting many more casualties than it had suffered initially. Over the next five months, other clashes occurred at various points along the entire border.

Fortunately the war scare of 1969–70 eventually faded, and neither side has given evidence since that time of anticipating large-scale fighting. Ten years later a Central Intelligence Agency estimate calculated that only 12 to 15 percent of the Soviet defense budget supported the forces arrayed against China. Approximately half of the ground divisions were at one-third strength or less. Meanwhile, Chinese military missions traveled throughout West Europe in 1978–79, examining ground and air weapons systems, but failed to make any purchases. In 1979 Peking felt sufficiently confident of its northern border to invade Vietnam, despite the recent treaty between Hanoi and Moscow which included a clause on military consultation and cooperation against any third-party threat or attack.

Thus both past behavior and available evidence support the consensus of foreign observers who discount the probability of a Sino-Soviet war. Logic likewise argues against this prospect. As one high Chinese official commented privately in 1975, "The Soviet Union won't attack us until after they have defeated NATO." A prolonged war with China would expose Moscow's position in East Europe to internal and external attack. Anti-Soviet or anticommunist dissidence would be encouraged. The memory of East Germany (1953), Poland (1956), Hungary (1956), and Czechoslovakia

(1968) is a strong deterrent against inviting another such instance by engaging China's massive army in lengthy fighting. Nor could NATO be counted upon to stand passively by as it did in these past crises of Soviet control.

The chances of a "surgical strike" against China's nuclear production facilities ending hostilities quickly have decreased with each passing year as Peking's nuclear retaliatory capability improves. Moreover, Moscow must ponder Washington's experience in Vietnam and the cost of underestimating how much damage a determined enemy will suffer without surrender. China's persistent resistance against the Japanese invasion from 1937 to 1945 proved that vast nation's ability to survive despite marked military inferiority. Thus, neither nuclear nor conventional weapons superiority offers Soviet planners a sufficiently promising advantage to make a deliberate attack on China likely.

Even less reason supports a Chinese initiation of war with the U.S.S.R. Peking's gross inferiority in strategic weapons invites the wholesale devastation of urban industrial areas. Should Moscow wish to maximize the fallout from ground-burst nuclear weapons in conjunction with appropriate prevailing winds, the resulting radioactivity could lay waste to much of China's agricultural base for years to come. These are catastrophic costs, regardless of Mao's alleged observation that were half the population to be destroyed, half would still survive to leave China the largest country in the world.

Should nuclear weapons not be used, a contingency that could not be counted on in Peking, China's huge population would nonetheless be of little use in an invasion of the Soviet Union. Except in the northeast, the PLA is logistically very weak throughout the border areas adjoining Soviet territory. Once initial deployments outran their prepositioned supplies, reinforcements and resupply would be severely constrained by the absence of an adequate transportation network. Nor could a ground attack go very far without air cover, the capability for which will remain beyond Peking in the near future. The eventual modernization of the PLA air force will, in all probability, still leave it vulnerable to superior Soviet ground and air defense systems.

Thus on rational grounds a Sino-Soviet war that is planned in advance by either side seems inconceivable. An unplanned conflict that inadvertently escalates from border clashes is only slightly more plausible. These incidents have occurred at various points over more than a decade without serious consequences. Moscow and Peking appear fully capable of containing them within manageable limits. The ability to do so is enhanced by the relative isolation of border confrontations from population centers, where casualties and damage could become serious. In addition, except for the area near the Trans-Siberian Railroad, no strategic point is involved that would warrant the increasing investment of force either to capture or protect it. Finally, the remoteness of these clashes from public awareness in either country and in the world at large permits them to be handled secretly should both sides so desire, thereby reducing or eliminating considerations of prestige and national honor. These conditions offer considerable assurance against a Sino-Soviet war arising from the dynamics of uncontrollable escalation initiated by border incidents.

As a third case to be considered of somewhat greater likelihood, renewed Sino-Vietnamese warfare might prompt Moscow to pressure Peking, consonant with its 1978 treaty commitment to Hanoi. The three sides have already survived one such test without an expansion of hostilities. But because three sides are involved instead of two, the possibility of unanticipated or uncontrolled escalation is much greater than with the Sino-Soviet border. Moreover, border incidents can be kept secret if both parties want to avoid an open confrontation. This is not possible for serious and prolonged Sino-Vietnamese hostilities. Once the news becomes known, prestige abroad and politics at home can narrow the options available to the leadership in Hanoi, Peking, and Moscow.

One potential flashpoint in Sino-Vietnamese relations is the South China Sea, where both sides dispute ownership of many islands and reefs. In January 1974 the PLA defeated Saigon's annual military excursion to the Paracel Islands in a brief skirmish that firmly secured China's control. Similar action might aim at taking the Spratly Islands from Hanoi. Alternatively, offshore oil activities might be contested by either side. Both contingencies raise the likelihood of Soviet involvement. Not only does the 1978 pact obligate Moscow to make a response at some point, but there is also the possible incentive of a permanent Soviet naval base in Camranh Bay, as opposed to the present use of facilities there for brief visits.

A still more complicated scenario posits serious fighting between Vietnam and Thailand that could prompt Peking to help Bangkok by a diversionary attack on Laos or Vietnam. This in turn might force Hanoi to call on Moscow for compensatory action against China. Much would depend on the command and control of the respective armies as well as the nature of the fighting. This sequence of events might be confined to peripheral areas with carefully limited levels of combat, but it conceivably could get out of hand and result in a major Sino-Soviet war.

The consequences of such a war are truly incalculable but it is difficult to see how they could benefit other nations, particularly those contiguous to both countries. If nuclear weapons were used, as seems probable, the potential radioactive fallout could imperil the entire West Pacific region, and perhaps the world. At a minimum, the tacit prohibition against such warfare, which has lasted nearly four decades, would have ended. A prolonged conventional war could leave a burden of refugees and reconstruction that would spill over national boundaries.

Under the circumstances, United States policy should not encourage or seek to perpetuate situations that increase the likelihood of a Sino-Soviet war. It may appear tactically advantageous to have two or three communist countries fighting one another, as with Vietnam, China, and the U.S.S.R., but the potential risks far outweigh the probable gains. While these relationships have their own dynamics and are not readily susceptible to manipulation by outside powers, the United States can nevertheless have some influence as, for instance, through the provision or denial of military equipment to China. At a later point we will address the question of arms sales to the People's Republic more fully, but it is worth noting here as relevant to the issues in Sino-Soviet relations that can lead to war.

Sino-Soviet Relations: The Prospects for Peace

War and peace are commonly juxtaposed as dichotomous, each defined as the absence of the other with no middle or mixed ground between the two conditions. The term *Cold War* emerged to characterize the Soviet-American relationship which, at the time, consisted of total ideological, political, economic, and military confrontation without actual fighting. This "no peace, no war" state of mind best describes Sino-Soviet relations from 1960 to 1980, border clashes to the contrary notwithstanding.

The prospects for a genuine easing of this confrontation are highly uncertain. Against such a development stand two decades of patterned behavior, during which time a host of reinforcing experiences have established syndromes of hostile interaction, whether in United Nations debates, public media exchanges, or local crises that invite outside intervention. Each side has treated the other as a virtual enemy where the stakes are zero-sum. Each has defined the other as the worst threat to other countries and to world peace. Each has denied the feasibility of improving relations until the other undergoes a basic change of view and probably of leadership.

The indirect benefits from this confrontation have varied in time but generally serve Moscow and Peking well in their relations with third countries. In the communist world the Soviet position in Mongolia and Indochina has been enhanced as a direct result of the dispute with China, as has the Chinese position in Rumania, Albania for many years, and more recently, Yugoslavia. In the capitalist world, Moscow won economic benefits from détente with Washington during the 1960s, in part because it appeared to be more moderate than Peking. The situation was reversed in the 1970s when China won recognition and economic assistance from the United States and Japan partly because of its dispute with the expansionistic U.S.S.R. Among Third World countries, the gains have been less clear, less constant, and less clearly a consequence of the dispute itself. However, Peking's position in Egypt and Moscow's influence in India stem in large part from Sino-Soviet competition and confrontation.

In addition to patterned behavior and indirect benefits, domestic politics and bureaucratic inertia tend to perpetuate the dispute. Both societies are authoritarian. Debate and dissent are discouraged, particularly on such sensitive issues as foreign affairs. This inhibits innovative analysis and policy prescription which challenges established positions. For the individual, advancement is more secure in accepting the status quo without argument. Similarly, bureaucratic interests, military and civilian, become locked into existing policy and tend to resist any change which threatens those interests.

History, however, reminds us that there are no permanent enemies in world politics, least of all for Peking. The People's Republic of China allied with the Soviet Union against the United States during the 1950s, opposed both superpowers in the 1960s, and sided with the United States against the Soviet Union in the latter 1970s. Another change by the 1990s cannot be entirely ruled out. It need not be so extreme a swing as in the past; indeed, a total reversal is unlikely. Neither Moscow nor Peking will again entrust its military security to alliance with the other, given the past record. But a moderation of the dispute that might include a settlement of the border dispute and a partial drawdown of military forces in confrontation is conceivable.

One step in this direction since the death of Mao in 1976 was Peking's virtual abandonment of the charge that Moscow is a "revisionist" regime. The accusation of ideological heresy had lasted nearly two decades, first appearing through surrogate attacks against "Yugoslav revisionism" in the late 1950s. Its international manifestation emerged during the 1960s when the Chinese Communist Party (CCP) identified radical splinter groups in Europe as "true Marxist-Leninists" and rejected all association with the established communist parties of France, Italy, and elsewhere. By the thirteenth anniversary of the PRC in 1979, however, China's most senior Long March veteran, Yeh Chien-ying declared that "revisionism" had been "incorrectly defined" at the start of the Cultural Revolution. In 1980, the CCP hosted the Italian Communist Party leadership. Thus the ideological controversy, like the celebrated Cheshire cat, simply faded away, although no improvement in party relations followed.

Instead of indictments against revisionism, Peking concentrated its fire on "social imperialism" and "hegemonism" to vilify Moscow. But while this ostensibly proved that the Soviet Union was not socialist, the question was nonetheless debated in academic circles and occasionally aired in the press. Moreover, the singular emphasis on Soviet foreign policy transformed the dispute into a traditional "Great Power" struggle of national interests without an ideological basis. This lacked the incompatible dichotomy of moral good versus heretical evil which brooked no compromise. On the contrary, by defining the differences in terms of world politics, China removed one obstacle to a negotiated settlement which now ostensibly depended only on external Soviet behavior and not on the nature of domestic Soviet rule.

Two indicators of possible improvement in state relations came in 1977. That November, considerable foreign speculation accompanied the visit of Foreign Minister Huang Hua to the Soviet embassy on the anniversary of the Bolshevik Revolution, the highest such official presence there in eleven years. This seemed particularly significant because earlier in September the two sides had quietly arrived at a compromise settlement of their long-standing differences concerning navigation at the juncture of the Amur and Ussuri rivers opposite Khabarovsk. This agreement was explicitly disavowed by Peking as abandoning its claim to the large island overlooking the key industrial city, and Moscow continued to insist that the boundary between the two countries lay west of the island rather than east. Nevertheless the settlement betokened the possibility of improved relations. Revival of Sino-Soviet friendship associations in both countries provided added symbolism. Unfortunately, the Chinese hosts received their Soviet counterparts for the first time on February 17, 1979, the day Peking staged its "defensive counterattack" against Vietnam. The Soviet delegation returned to Moscow the next day.

China's invasion of Vietnam seemed to close the door to any further progress in ameliorating the dispute. In April, Peking announced it would not renew the Sino-Soviet Treaty of Friendship and Mutual Assistance at its formal point of termination one year later. However, the PRC also said it was prepared to discuss Sino-Soviet relations without preconditions, contrary to the stance it had adopted over previous years. In September talks began at the deputy foreign minister level in Moscow. No agreement was reached and the meetings were adjourned, supposedly to resume in Peking at an unspecified date. Then the Soviet invasion of Afghanistan prompted Peking to declare the exchanges indefinitely suspended, presumably until Moscow withdrew its forces. Meanwhile, Chinese propaganda attacks against "Soviet expansionism and hegemony" reached new levels of intensity as the leadership proclaimed to one and all that Afghanistan proved Moscow's global strategy to be aimed at strangling the West and Japan by control over vital Middle East oil supplies.

As a final factor, economic relations remained stagnant and at a low level, at a time when China's program of "four modernizations" greatly increased trade with Japan, West Europe, and the United States. The total exchange of roughly $500 million each year in 1978–79 amounted to less than 2 percent of each side's aggregate foreign trade. Annual negotiations will probably show marginal increases, but in contrast with other major economies China's trade with the Soviet Union is confined to virtual barter terms, no credits or loans being involved.

All things considered, the prospects for resolution of Sino-Soviet differences appear dim for at least the next several years. While the disappearance of ideology as a point of controversy should presumably facilitate compromise, the emergence of powerful national security concerns as an overriding issue, manifest in developments in Indochina and Afghanistan, makes such compromise exceedingly difficult. Moreover, the asymmetry of power inhibits Moscow as the dominant party from any felt need to make concessions and constrains Peking as the weaker side from backtracking on its demands. Domestic politics may also limit flexibility with changes in leadership, imminent in Moscow and recent in Peking, narrowing the range of debate in each capital on so sensitive and volatile a question. In this regard it is difficult to exaggerate the degree to which each has raised the stakes of prestige and status in defending its position against the other. By comparison, the factors that might induce some compromise which would improve relations are few and of lesser importance. The risk of border incidents escalating into larger conflict is slight in view of the record since 1969 and the apparent routinization of responses on both sides. The economic cost of confrontation is marginal for the U.S.S.R. although this could become more important as China's acquisition of modern weapons raises the investment for both parties. Labor shortages in the U.S.S.R. might also prompt a search for ways to reduce the large standing army. In themselves, however, these considerations seem outweighed by the impediments to a compromise settlement.

Peking initiated the dispute and has pressed it to the present, whereas Moscow has persisted in intermittent attempts to patch up the quarrel, without success. This suggests that if any real breakthrough is to occur, it will come on the Chinese side. Unlikely as this seems, one development which might bring this about could be a loss of confidence in the utility of siding with the United States against the U.S.S.R. This introduces triangular considerations at an appropriate point in our analysis. Other things being equal, the calculation of cost and benefit in leaning to one side could be determining for Chinese policy.

Such a calculation could be affected by several factors. The relative power of the Soviet Union compared with the United States and their respective records of expansion and contraction of influence might tilt so decisively to Moscow's advantage as to persuade Peking that accommodation is wiser than confrontation, Moscow's terms permitting. Alternatively, developments on Taiwan could take an alarming turn from Peking's perspective, moving toward independence when Chiang Ching-kuo leaves the scene. Regaining Taiwan, by force if necessary, could take priority over placating Washington. Under these circumstances, the leadership might want to reduce the need to safeguard its long Soviet frontier against attack and seek a settlement with Moscow toward that end.

None of these contingencies appear imminent, but they cannot be ruled out for the more distant future. Détente between Peking and Moscow is not impossible, any more than was détente between Peking and Washington. In the latter case, China had suffered 300,000 casualties fighting the United States in Korea. It had faced a total American embargo on trade for twenty years with spillover effects on many other countries. Washington's defense of Taiwan had frustrated certain communist victory in the prolonged Chinese civil war in addition to separating the island province from mainland rule. Moscow's record of hostile interaction pales by comparison.

Moreover, whereas Soviet proposals for collective security arrangements in Asia have found few takers in ten years of effort, largely because of the implicit anti-Chinese flavor, United States military bases and allies confronted China with a semicircle of hostile power extending from Korea and Japan to Thailand during the 1950s and 1960s. Nor was this power alignment passively confined to "containment." Clandestine operations for espionage and sabotage mounted from Taiwan and the offshore islands combined with U-2 reconnaissance overflights as constant reminders of the "U.S. imperialist–Chiang Kai-shek clique" effort to undermine Chinese Communist rule. In the case of Tibet, this effort succeeded in making a bad situation worse. By comparison, only in Sinkiang did Soviet subversion arouse the explicit charge of attempting to "separate" the region from Chinese control. Otherwise, Moscow's maneuvers failed to elicit accusations similar to those directed against Washington.

This brief recapitulation of Sino-American relations does not predict a precise parallel of détente in the evolution of Sino-Soviet relations. It does, however, serve as a cautionary reminder against a simple extrapolation of the future from the recent past. Just as the Nazi-Soviet pact in 1939 demonstrated the power of realpolitik in overcoming deep-seated patterns of behavior, seemingly reinforced by strong ideological commitment, so too did the Nixon handshake with Mao symbolize the ability of strong-willed leaderships abruptly to reverse course when circumstances demand it. The fact of that handshake occurring while American forces were fighting in Vietnam and shortly before a Nixon-Brezhnev summit meeting was scheduled in Moscow underscored the observation cited earlier; namely, there are no permanent enemies in international relations.

We have suggested that the absence of war may not be a sufficient condition to bring peace. There also may be relationships wherein two sides are neither enemies nor friends. Even should détente occur in the Sino-Soviet case, it is difficult to conceive of the competition for influence in third countries being amicably resolved. During the heyday of "monolithic unity" and the flourishing of the alliance, manifest in wholesale military and economic assistance to China, the two regimes already vied for position in the Third World, then known as the Afro-Asian world. This competition ranged across the political spectrum, whether in local communist insurgencies or among monarchical, feudal regimes. Eventually, this tacit rivalry burst into open polemics when the Sino-Soviet split became formalized, but its more subtle beginning in the mid-1950s foreshadowed subsequent developments.

This rivalry seems certain to continue, regardless of bilateral relations. In addition to the imperatives of world politics which compel aspirants to Great Power status to play the competitive game, third parties often seek to exploit competition between potential patrons so as to extract more largesse. Such calculation is likely to draw Peking and Moscow into contention in the Middle East, Africa, and ultimately Latin America over the coming years. In some cases, a close balance may shift their roles back and forth, as in North Korea. In other instances, such as Tanzania or South Yemen, one side may hold the advantage for a considerable time. But the dynamics of international politics will keep each attempting to outmaneuver the other throughout the Third World. In this sense, if they are no longer enemies, they will not become friends.

Beyond Détente

Détente, strictly defined, refers only to the reduction of tension. We have examined the prospects for this minimal moderation in Sino-Soviet relations and found them to be dubious and distant but not inconceivable. We have also suggested that the contingencies which might bring it about involve setbacks, implied or expressed, for United States interests, at least in the short run. But this does not necessarily mean that the consequences of a Sino-Soviet détente are to the long-run detriment of American interests or those of its allies and friends in Asia.

Our analysis has shown that there is no likelihood of Moscow and Peking once again forming a hostile coalition against their neighbors in Asia. Beyond this negative assurance, a reduction of tension between the two communist powers is both positive and necessary if they are to have cooperative multilateral relations with other countries in the region. For example, the ocean resources in the West Pacific and adjacent waters can become a focal point for contention over fishing rights and offshore oil exploration, or they can be jointly exploited through mutually beneficial arrangements. The problems of sea and air pollution can be addressed collectively by contiguous states or they can remain unsolved through unilateral action. In these and other issue areas, Chinese and Soviet negotiators must be able to assume that joint benefit for their common interests will result from negotiations sincerely entered into. Otherwise, any comprehensive regional effort will be defeated by communist polemics, provided that the two sides even agree to take part at all.

In the past, Sino-Russian relations have provided some precedent for collaborative effort. During the 1950s a joint Sino-Soviet commission surveyed the Amur River and its tributaries to assess the prospects for a multipurpose project which would provide flood control, irrigation, navigation, and hydroelectric power. One account, published in Russian, bore the now ironic title, "Amur— River of Friendship." Nothing came of the study because of the subsequent dispute, but it suggests one basis for future cooperation.

In addition, trade between the Soviet Far East and northeast China, or Manchuria, as it was then known, traditionally evidenced a symbiotic economic relationship that may still be relevant. The Soviet side is seriously deficient in foodstuffs; the Chinese side enjoyed a surplus before and may again. China is desperately short of timber and wood products; Siberia has virtually limitless reserves. A major obstacle to exploiting those reserves is a severe Soviet labor shortage; this can be readily remedied with surplus Chinese labor. Already in 1954 Khrushchev proposed that Chinese workers fell Siberian timber. Mao agreed, and 200,000 served an initial two-year term, although the project was not renewed when relations worsened. More recently, North Koreans have helped to meet this need, but now that the People's Republic is exporting labor elsewhere, an agreement with the U.S.S.R. would be of mutual benefit.

Chinese participation in Siberian development would be welcomed by Japan as removing a possible point of sensitivity which could limit future Japanese participation. In 1974–75 Peking protested to Tokyo over Moscow's proposal for a joint pipeline and railroad project to transport oil from West Siberia eastward because of its strategic implications. No such problem has arisen since but Chinese sensitivities remain a consideration in Japanese planning.

In the context of a Sino-Soviet détente, East Siberia's basic resources could be exploited for the benefit of all three countries. One of the largest copper reserves in the U.S.S.R. is in this region but it requires foreign capital and foreign buyers for its development. While China's copper reserves have not yet been fully determined, estimates to date suggest a possible deficiency as the economy modernizes. The Siberian mine would also provide a major source close to Japan to meet future need in a highly volatile commodity market.

The transformation of this traditional triangle of tension into one of cooperation should be a policy goal for all who are involved with the stability of northeast Asia. An important step in this direction has already moved the U.S.S.R. and Japan from their historic struggle over the island of Sakhalin to joint exploration of its offshore oil reserves. This has occurred despite the fact that oil is a strategic commodity which is in short supply for the Soviet Far East. Moreover, a peace treaty between the two countries remains obstructed by the Soviet occupation of former Japanese islands north of Hokkaido not ceded by the World War II agreements.

A parallel development finds Japan and China, bitter enemies throughout much of the twentieth century, joining to exploit oil deposits in the Bohai Gulf. This has taken place despite Peking's refusal to renounce its claim to the Senkaku (Diaoyutai) Islands, administered by Tokyo, which lie on the edge of the continental shelf between Tokyo and the Ryukyus. In both cases, the economic advantage of shelving political differences for the sake of mutual interest suggests a new pattern of relations emerging in northeast Asia. These interactions are as yet too tenuous and nascent to be characterized as a web of interdependency. However, if allowed to run its course, such a development could make a major contribution to the interests of peace and stability as one consequence of Sino-Soviet détente.

Implications for United States Policy

Our analysis has widened from a focus on Sino-Soviet relations to triangular aspects involving the United States on the one hand and Japan on the other. We have suggested that while bilateral relations are primary, third-party policy can influence the behavior of one or both sides. In this regard, the relevance of United States military sales to China has been mentioned. Other aspects, such as American participation in Siberian development and technology transfer to the U.S.S.R., also deserve attention.

Fundamental to these and other questions is the determination of

Soviet policy goals and their implementation. If these are anticipated to include world domination through exploitation of any weakness or vulnerability among noncommunist nations, a different set of United States policy responses is necessary as compared with a projection of Kremlin goals that combine defensive and developmental objectives with offensive, strategic designs. In the first instance, deterrent strength and combat supremacy are the sine qua non of prudent planning. In the second case, a mixed approach combines political-military confrontation with economic cooperation to maintain a relationship stable enough to minimize the likelihood of general war. The following observations will be premised on the second alternative.

On the negative side, the United States should sharply restrict the sale of military equipment to China. It is difficult to determine the political volatility of the China factor in Soviet calculations. Objectively, Moscow's overwhelming preponderance of military power at all levels and in all categories of weapons should provide ample reassurance that no serious threat from China need be contemplated for at least a decade. Subjectively, however, twenty years of bitter relations combine with a gross population disparity to produce an acute sensitivity to indicators of an anti-Soviet coalition that might include China.

We know too little about the actual process and content of Soviet policy formation to make any hard-and-fast conclusion on the balance between objective reality and subjective perception. But whatever may be the actual level of Soviet concern over China's military modernization (as differentiated from political posturing for domestic and foreign audiences), the basis for such concern cannot be dismissed out of hand as irrational nor its existence held to be irrelevant for United States policy. Both logic and analogy with other modern bureaucratic systems suggest that the greater the perceived Chinese threat, the more likely is the Kremlin to strengthen its armed forces, and the more hostile will it perceive American policy to be. The consequence will be to encourage, if not intensify, tension in Sino-Soviet and Soviet-American relations.

This is a dangerous risk compared with the potential gain of tying down Soviet divisions opposite China that otherwise might be used in the Middle East or Europe. In quantitative terms, this argument has considerably less merit than is often assumed from the simple calculation of Soviet deployments in Central Asia and Siberia. The Sino-Soviet border has never been a demilitarized frontier like that between Canada and the United States, nor would it be in the event of a border settlement. When the alliance was presumably alive and well, twelve or fifteen divisions were positioned in the Soviet republics adjacent to China.

Moreover, the increase of this deployment to thirty-five divisions by 1969 and a total of 600,000 troops by 1978 occurred without any outside strengthening of China's military capability. Conceivably, such a strengthening might prompt Moscow to assign still more units that otherwise might confront NATO or move to trouble spots in the Middle East and Africa. But this is not certain. As for the alleged deterrent aspect of Chinese hostility, this did not constrain the Soviet invasion of Afghanistan. In West Europe, the American troop presence and treaty commitment is almost certainly the operative deterrent, while the build-up of Soviet conventional and nuclear strength in East Europe has not been visibly slowed by demands on the China front. In sum, the advantages in global terms of strengthening China's military forces are highly conjectual and marginal at best while the disadvantages, admittedly also conjectural, are more central to the prospects for peace and stability in Asia.

We must be sensitive to the role of symbols as well as of substance. Perceptions and expectations are shaped by speeches, visits, and media messages triggered by calculated briefings and backgrounders. Short-run tactical moves can cause long-run strategic problems if they are not carefully designed as part of an overall policy calculation of potential gains and risks. Sino-American relations, whether addressed unilaterally or through interaction between Peking and Washington, must not be construed by either side or by third parties as based on any such concept as "mutual security." Many points of divergence exist between China's definition of its security and that held by the United States, its allies, and its friends in Asia. The more common term, *parallel strategic interests*, reminds us that parallel lines may be proximately or widely separated but they never meet. But this ignores the agreement between China and the United States on such questions as the United States-Japan security treaty and the Soviet presence in Southeast Asia.

Given these complications, it would be better to abandon the effort for catchwords and phrases that become clichés at best and policy traps at worst, the most notorious example being the so-called China card. Rhetoric can not only obscure reality; it can create a reality of its own. The Sino-American relationship is now entering a stage where hard facts and plain speaking should determine the image as well as the content of United States policy, especially where military aspects are concerned.

On the positive side, differential embargo lists for dual purpose technology should be applied to the U.S.S.R. and China. The potential use of such technology in a highly advanced economy such as the United States, or by a military superpower such as the Soviet Union, is not possible for China at its present stage of development. The strategic implications, therefore, are much less serious when such equipment is sold to Peking as compared with Moscow. Furthermore, technology is more easily copied or acquired through a competitive world market than are advanced weapons. United States allies, particularly Japan, are less likely to agree to constraints in this area than they are in arms sales to China.

In this regard, however, it is important that the United States support its major Asian ally, Japan, in whatever course it adopts concerning the development of Siberia. Japan's interests in this regard are primary; ours are secondary. The potential effect on Soviet power and policy combine with access to valuable resources to compel a careful weighing in Tokyo of risks and gains. Participation in Siberian development is seen there as an essential corollary to support for China's economic modernization. This makes "omnidirectional diplomacy" a credible assurance to Moscow that Tokyo will not join an anti-Soviet coalition. Moreover, Japan's assessment of the implications of Siberian development is based on long experience in dealing with Russia as well as a decade of involvement in Siberian projects. On all these counts we should respect and respond positively to Japanese judgment in this matter.

Our posture is particularly relevant for the future of Siberian energy resources. The restrictions on Export-Import Bank credits for the U.S.S.R. in general, and for energy research development in particular, virtually eliminate the prospects for opening up the Yakutia natural gas fields, for example. The economic costs are too great for Japan to accept unilaterally and the physical hazards call for a sharing of the risk. American firms have shown interest in the three-way investment proposed by Moscow with the commensurate sharing of production, but their level of involvement is severely restricted by the Jackson-Vanik and Stevenson Amendments to the 1974 Trade Act. A presidential request for a waiver to these enactments because of Japan's need to diversify its energy dependency makes good sense.

This recommendation is reinforced by the administration's intelligence forecasts, on the one hand, of an impending shortage of domestic Soviet oil in the mid-1980s and its professed concern, on the other hand, over a future Soviet move into the Middle East. Under these circumstances, denying the U.S.S.R. access to its own energy resources by an embargo against high technology transfer seems short-sighted in the extreme. The granting in June 1980 of a license for the sale of a $5 million offshore drilling rig through an American subsidiary to be used near Sakhalin was a wise exception to the general posture adopted by the Carter Administration in the aftermath of the Afghanistan invasion.

True, the Sakhalin project has more symbolic than substantive significance. Progress has been slow and discoveries limited in scale. Tokyo, however, sees it as an important signal of "balanced diplomacy" in its relations with Moscow and Peking. As one official remarked, "We want to show that we are willing to help both sides in their economic development to prove we are not hostile to either nor can we be pressured by either." Thus, when China finally decided to seek government credits, the Japanese Export-Import Bank opened the window for $2 billion, slightly more than the amount already available for Siberian development of the previous years.

Japanese policy clearly differentiates Soviet military and civilian interests, reacting to them accordingly. Tokyo responds negatively to intrusions on its air and sea space while protesting deployments to contested islands above Hokkaido. It also negotiates patiently but positively on proposals for timber, coal, port, and natural gas projects, provided that these are economically sound. Officials admit there is no certainty that this dual approach will affect perceptions and policy in Moscow. But they see little risk, some economic benefit, and at least the possibility that Soviet-Japanese relations will ultimately improve. They see no such possibility in adopting American assumptions of linkage and leverage to be applied through negative economic policies such as credit restrictions and technology embargoes.

China's tacit acquiescence in this policy is evident in the granting of the Bohai Gulf concession to the same Japanese firm already engaged in exploring for Sakhalin oil. Another Japanese company providing engineering equipment for construction of the Baikal-Amur Mainland (BAM), a second trans-Siberian railroad, negotiated successfully for a major contract in China. If Peking does not welcome Tokyo's participation in Siberian development, at least it has not made any objections in recent years.

The economic evolution of bilateral relations along two legs of the northeast Asian triangle, Soviet-Japanese and Sino-Japanese, should be welcomed and supported by United States policy. If the third leg, Sino-Soviet, eventually follows suit, the prospect of regional interdependency might mitigate political tensions. This would augment, not replace, the security arrangements manifest in the United States-Japan treaty and joint military dispositions in the area. However, it might reduce the likelihood of local conflict while helping to meet local economic needs, to this extent enhancing Japan's security, and thereby advance United States interests.

A former Japanese cabinet official responsible for national security planning noted, "Security has two aspects, negative and positive. Negative security requires a strong defense against attack. Positive security lies in economic cooperation which reduces the perception of hostility. We should not have one without the other." This formula is not universally shared in Tokyo, nor is it certain of success. Yet it offers an important expansion to a key concept in American policy normally defined in strictly military terms. It lies at the heart of Japan's "omnidirectional diplomacy" as demonstrated in its relations with the Soviet Union. It deserves the fullest American consideration and evaluation as relations between the two superpowers make their way through the 1980s.

American Policy in the Strategic Triangle
Thomas W. Robinson

I

SINCE the early 1970s, United States foreign policy has been based on the three-sided relationship among itself, the Soviet Union, and China. As its relative power vis-à-vis Moscow has declined, Washington has come to depend on increasingly close relations with Peking and on the adoption of a series of "parallel" policies toward the Soviets. The actions and statements of the United States and China are little different from what is normally termed alliance behavior. And in their perceived weakness, America and China now depend on each other for protection against predatory Russian actions.

Other important elements inform policy in Washington and Peking to be sure. The United States is vitally concerned with continuing Middle Eastern oil supplies at reasonable prices, the North-South problem, global issues, and the problems of American society and its economy. China is consumed with domestic problems ranging from the politics of the Maoist succession to problems of economic development; China also has to pay close attention to the configuration of power in Southeast Asia. But at the center of American and Chinese foreign policies and of Sino-American relations is the issue of how to deal with the rapidly growing power of the Soviet Union and the Kremlin's ensuing policy activism. In the Chinese case, every other aspect of policy has been subordinated to dealing with the perceived danger from the North. In the American case, Soviet-American détente has been set back, a Cold War–like atmosphere has rapidly reappeared, and most American policy is made and judged on the basis of its effect on American rivalry with the Soviet Union.

The result of Soviet gains in relative power, the resultant aggressiveness of Soviet policy, and American and Chinese weakness and policy defensiveness is a severe distortion of the strategic triangle.

While the Chinese kept their distance as much as possible from both Washington and Moscow between 1960 and the early 1970s, their subsequent move toward Washington out of fear and prudence was itself enough to destroy the relative equality in the triangle. But American actions since the mid-1970s, moving away from Moscow and toward Peking, accentuated that trend. The net result is that the triangle has assumed a shape nearly the mirror image of that of the early and mid-1950s: two of the three states on one side, each opposed to the third.

As for the Soviets, they naturally feel on the one hand a combination of injury and betrayal that their former closest ally and their détente partner now combine against them; and resentment and pugnacity on the other hand that America and China do not willingly acknowledge the rightfully gained Soviet place of primacy. The Soviets thus set about doing what the Americans did in the early 1950s, when Washington felt itself in a similar predicament. First, they redouble their efforts—strengthening their military even more, tightening up socially at home, and enforcing greater discipline over their dependencies abroad. And, second, they attempt to forestall a reversal of the balance of power within the strategic triangle by increasing the number of their allies and welding them together into a single Moscow-centered system. These Russian actions accentuate even further the skewed nature of the triangle; together with the American and Chinese measures just mentioned, they seem to guarantee perpetuation of the present freeze in Soviet-American and Sino-Soviet relations and continued warmth in Sino-American ties.

Just as in the early 1950s, then, the prospect is for a Cold War, with all the attendant crises: politicization of otherwise extrapolitical activities, estrangement of personal ties, low levels of trade and technological transfer, tightening of geographic and other boundaries among independent systems, and high military budgets. If the new configuration of power continues, there would seem to be only three outcomes. One would be war. The Soviet Union, perceiving that the American-Chinese-European-Japanese coalition prevents it from attaining its goals and that the balance of power between the Soviet-led system of states and the coalition threatens to turn decisively against it, attempts to sunder the opposition by attacking one or more of the partners—say, China or West Germany.[1] The rest come to the aid of the injured party and the world is thus plunged into war. In essence, this is a repetition of the formula for disaster so graphically demonstrated by World War I.

A second outcome is more benign. After an extended period of crises, "small" wars, and threatening maneuvers lasting for perhaps the remainder of the twentieth century, Moscow decides to forego its most pretentious ambitions and settles back, through a series of compromises, to enjoy the status of a satisfied power and to concentrate on the perfection of Soviet society at home. The rest of the international system, and particularly the Sino-American–led coalition, make adjustments in turn, accepting the Russians for what they have become: a superpower in every sense, with a voice in every international matter of consequence anywhere in the globe. The coalition, losing its purpose, withers away, and a new stage in world politics begins—either a new form of the balance of power as the relationship among the five major centers of power changes (say, through the growth of Chinese power) or a common quest for that transnational, internationally organized world order that was

[1] It may be objected that the term *coalition* is too strong, or at least premature. And it is true that there is no formal document among the five states (or organizations, in the case of NATO) pledging mutual cooperation against the Soviet Union in peacetime or assistance in case of conflict. But history indicates that such formality does not always guarantee the existence of a coalition. Actual behavior is the more important criterion. If all five entities take the Soviet Union as their common opponent, if there is some coordination and similarity of policy—ranging from the "parallel policies" of the United States and China and Japan and China to highly organized behavior of NATO—and if there is some modicum of consultation and cooperation vis-à-vis Moscow, a coalition exists. The anti-Soviet set of arrangements among the five entities, such as they are, meets these criteria.

Perhaps the term *proto-coalition*, or *entente*, is a more accurate description of the present, admittedly very loose, situation. It is surely not an alliance in the full meaning of the term. And yet the degree of consultation, coordination, and cooperation is relatively advanced—nearly as much, for instance, as that between Britain and France a few years before World War I. It took the outbreak of war, in that case, to solidify the arrangement formally, but all but the final step had been taken previously. Indeed, if a broader and more formal arrangement among Germany's several opponents had been worked out sufficiently in advance, World War I might not have occurred.

The situation is similar in the 1980s. While there is no alliance at present, there are nonetheless allies and alliancelike behavior. Thus, the term *coalition* is not inappropriate.

the noble but stillborn dream of the early Carter Administration.

A third possible outcome is transformation of the triangle from inside or the outside. This would occur if one or more of the trends in the international system becomes so important that it overshadows the present dominance of the strategic triangle. Oil diplomacy not only might concentrate politics on the Middle East but also could focus the attention of all three members of the triangle on making their separate deals with the Arab oil states. Revolution might occur in the Soviet Union, say; China might evolve into a Soviet-like system and make its peace with Moscow; or racial disturbances or depression might cripple the United States. The Third world might find the unity that has so long eluded it, led perhaps by the Arab oil states or Brazil or India. Or, finally, each of the three strategic triangle members might find their dominance increasingly challenged by regions hitherto thought to be within their sphere of influence: the United States by Central and South America, the Soviet Union by East Europe, and China by Southeast Asia. In this last instance, however, the matter would be better described as China's having to pay inordinate attention to regional politics rather than restore its rule over the area, which it does not yet have.

I do not think the United States can avoid in the near term (i.e., 5 years) a new Cold War with the Soviet Union. Nor can it avoid becoming still more dependent on Chinese anti-Sovietism in resisting further Soviet moves to change the triangular and international system balance in its favor. Part of the rest of this essay considers the consequences of these highly likely developments. The other part inspects the three longer-range alternatives to the new Cold War and discusses how to minimize the probability of war, maximize the chance for peaceful settlement, and prepare for systematic transformation in ways advantageous to the United States.

II

There is a mechanism that, once in place, tends to set up a Cold War cycle. In the case of the strategic triangle, the cycle has already proceeded through the first stages. Stage one, beginning in the mid-1970s, saw the Soviet Union making rapid strides in gross national power, especially military, whereas America and China tended to lag behind in terms of yearly percentage gains and overall amounts. Moscow took advantage of this disparity by achieving gains in areas that presented comparatively little risk: Ethiopia, Angola, Yemen, Vietnam, and Afghanistan, and in the realm of strategic weapons. The Kremlin also invested in weaponry and troop dispositions on its Western and Eastern fronts, facing NATO and China. All these developments caused the other two members of the triangle to take fright. Realizing that there was little each could do by itself in the short run due to domestic insufficiencies, they drew together—initiating foreign minister talks, exchanging defense ministers, beginning staff talks, stepping up trade and overall exchanges, and in general cooperating against the Russians (taking "parallel actions," as each has come to term it). They also took the offensive with regard to the other relevant centers of power—West Europe, Japan, and the Arab oil states—drawing at least the first two into a tighter bond against the Soviets and compromising with the latter (in the American case, aiding their defense against Soviet incursion).

The second stage, which began in early 1980, finds the United States, China, and probably West Europe and Japan responding separately or together to the Soviet challenge by increasing their arms budgets, pledging further cooperation in the face of Soviet threats, and preparing to counter Soviet activism by dynamism of their own. The trouble is that they are not able to move ahead fast enough to counter the Soviet buildup and the Russians' geographic and issue-related initiative. The balance, therefore, will continue to swing in favor of Moscow for some time. Indeed, with regard to the military balance, at least the first five years of the 1980s will see no major improvement. Only in the latter half of the decade will the balance begin to right itself, and then only slowly, since the Soviet Union will probably accelerate its efforts. This could be the time of maximum danger for the United States: Moscow may feel it should, and must, take advantage of the chance to make major, even permanent, changes favorable to itself in the regime-character of many states. A series of crises may ensue, any one of which could escalate to central war.

As a distinguishable part of this stage, the Soviet Union feels the need to take measures to protect its lead in the military sphere and to insulate itself from the effects of allied countermeasures in the diplomatic, economic, technological, and cultural realm. The first and most obvious Soviet response is to step up the rate of arms procurement—a task they can perform relatively easily, given excess capacity in the Russian economy's military sector. This could precipitate a new arms race. Because the United States and its coalition partners probably also will be rapidly increasing their arms budgets, such a race generally would be ruinous to the economies of all, would bring no greater net security to any, and would require major increases in military expenditures. The second Soviet response is to tighten their grip at home and over East Europe. This is a natural response of any ruling elite to perceived threats from abroad; in the case of the Soviet Communist Party it is even more likely, given that it places a premium on ideological control and that it possesses the organizational means by which to tighten the socioeconomic screws. Moreover, the Kremlin wants to assure itself that Soviet participation in crises abroad will not be linked to disturbances at home or in East Europe. It cannot afford to fight in both at the same time.

The third Soviet response would be to accelerate efforts to fashion its own global alliance system. Moscow has already proceeded in this direction by signing "friendship" treaties with a number of Third World states. More states will be encouraged to sign such bilateral accords, and existing arrangements will be renewed, strengthened, and where possible upgraded into full-fledged alliances. It is probable that Moscow will seek to draw these together into a single "collective security" system—perhaps as an extension of the Warsaw Pact or as regional arrangements like Brezhnev's proposal years ago for a Soviet-led Asian "collective security" system. The final Soviet response would be to weaken the ties between the states which they see as opposing Moscow's interests and to help start brushfire wars or exacerbate existing disturbances in areas associated with one or another of the presumed coalition partners. These Soviet activities need not be purely military or insurrectionary in character. Moscow does have economic instruments of policy —oil purchase power, economic assistance, and trading ability—that are already strong and will increase substantially in the 1980s. The Soviets also have a demonstrated long-range intervention capability and military-supply potential that will grow even further. As with the economic-policy instrument, this military capability will be used as a means of demonstrating Soviet resolve and showing that Moscow is a superpower by rights and not by assertion. Policy instruments tend to be put into service once they are in place.

The 1980s will probably see a series of confrontations between Moscow and the Sino-American led coalition in disparte regions of the world, continued stringent contention for local regime alignment and loyalty, Soviet use of the subversive instrument, and economic competition. For reasons outlined below, I believe that confrontations will not involve China directly, nor will they take place in the NATO-Warsaw Pact arena, although surely Moscow will continue to maintain strong forces along the Sino-Soviet border and in East Europe. Rather, Soviet-Western confrontation will tend to diffuse around the globe—concentrating, say, in the Persian Gulf, then transferring to Central America, and then reappearing in Southern Africa. Economic, diplomatic, subversive, and ideological competition also will tend to be global.

This state of tension between the Soviet Union and America, China, Japan, and Europe, together with a series of indirect and perhaps direct military confrontations, defines the third state of renewed Cold War. These states, together and separately (the latter characterizing most Chinese actions), will respond to the Soviet challenge in nearly identical manner: Force will meet force, subversion will counter subversion, foreign aid, military assistance, and arms sales will balance Soviet efforts in those fields, and a campaign will be conducted to induce Third World states to eschew close ties with Moscow, if not actually sign alliance or alignment agreements with the West. Such confrontation *cum* competition will encourage the Soviet Union to broaden its own efforts, thus bringing matters back to the equivalent of stage one and thereby establishing a vicious cycle.

Such vicious cycles are, unfortunately, a "normal" component of international politics. Until the nuclear era, quite often they eventuated in war. That may well happen this time, since both sides feel that the other has—or may have—a fatal dominance and may at any time after initiation of the cycle feel inclined to exploit fleeting advantages. Moreover, when most of the essential political actors are engaged on one of the two sides, otherwise small matters magnify in importance, and competition intensifies for the allegiance of third states or political parties. Further, all participants in the system find that, because they are caught in the operations of the cycle, they cannot defend or advance the whole range of their interests. Rather, they must let them slide for the duration or compromise an increasing percentage of them in face of the greater danger emanating from the constant threat of war. Frustration thus increases, accompanied by the probability of irrational or impetuous behavior. Finally, the uncertain nature of the nuclear balance itself with its changing deterrence and employment doctrines, its systems rapidly becoming obsolete due to the accelerating technological pace, and the very great cost of replacing existing systems—heightens the probability that nuclear war might occur.

What can be done in this critical decade to avoid war, manage crises, achieve national goals despite external threats, and pave the way for systematic transformation? The first and most important issue is whether a grand coalition (or some modified form thereof) is the best means of staving off the Russian challenge to the postwar balance of power. It seems to be that some sort of cooperative arrangement that brings together the United States, China, West Europe, and Japan is surely a necessary component of any strategy for containing the expansion of Soviet power. In an era of weakness in one or another vital aspect of national power of each of the four states or regions vis-à-vis the Soviet Union, no other short-term measure will give the Russians pause in their impulse to use their newly developed potency. The United States must confront many domestic social problems simultaneously—urban, racial, environmental, and industrial—during the 1980s and still find enough money, national will, and raw energy to face the Soviets in the various strategic and regional realms (this to say nothing of playing a principal role in the North-South question and dealing with challenges to its authority in the Western Hemisphere). China cannot even defend its own borders against serious Soviet attack, much less attain its other foreign policy goals of national reunification, becoming Asia's (particularly Southeast Asia's) power center, and beginning anew the task of spreading the gospel of the Chinese road to socialism. Japan discovers that it must wean itself from dependence on America for defense—at the very time when it is most vulnerable to the Russians militarily, when the United States is least able to devote the necessary sea and air forces to protect the Japanese islands, when the rest of the industrialized world seems ready to turn on Tokyo in retribution for being so successful economically, and when critical energy supplies and the sea lines of supply become increasingly tenuous. Western Europe's defense problems are a composite of those of China and Japan: It has not been able to secure itself against the Soviet threat without external assistance but now it is being asked to augment its military budget greatly to provide for that defense. Moreover, Western Europe is still in transition to some form of supranational government and common economic institutions, a process that requires careful attention and a minimum of interference from the outside. Yet the external realm does pose major threats, not merely in the form of Warsaw Pact forces but also from Europe's high degree of dependence on Middle Eastern oil.

Some sort of common arrangement is necessary also when one inspects the Soviet situation. It is true that Moscow is also beset with internal problems. There are the questions of non–Great Russian nationalities, consumer goods and the balance among various sectors of industry, productivity in agriculture, and religious and political dissidents. But each of these by itself is unlikely to impede a Leninist party from continuing to rule, however inefficiently, and from moving toward its domestic goals, however ponderously. And the Soviet Communist Party can always summon additional resources through partial re-Stalinization of the economy and the society. Indeed, among the five principal powers or regions, the Soviet Union has its domestic situation under better control than all the others, with the possible exception of Japan.

It is the external side of the equation, of course, that gives Moscow so much trouble. Like every other emergent power before it (Britain, France, Germany, Japan, and America), the Soviet Union's growth by itself disturbs the international equilibrium. And like the others, Moscow feels that its added capability carries with it the right to insist that its interests be taken into account throughout the globe. Soviet interests, national *and* ideological, expand commensurately with Soviet power, making systematic adjustment more difficult. Finally, the failure of most nonmilitary subversive instruments of Soviet policy means, and will continue to mean, that the struggle over the shape of the new international equilibrium will tend to be military or at least will employ means that threaten the use of force or that could lead rapidly to conflict.

American Policy in the Strategic Triangle

Historically, the international system has employed a number of equilibrating instruments in situations of major disturbance by an emerging power. They include: alliances and alignments, arms races and other means of internally generating contervailing power, establishing buffer states, demonstration of force, economic assistance and advice of various forms to weak but potentially important states, cultural appeal, propaganda, ideological persuasion, subversion, threats of force, trade, and finally war in its various manifestations. The Soviet Union also could use these same instruments. But the Soviet Union has no cultural diplomacy, eschews organizational and legal methods of dispute settlement except for tactical gain, finds its economic assistance program has little appeal or effect, has not been able to enlist major support through its propaganda and ideological programs, and has not been sufficiently successful in converting trade to political influence. It must therefore concentrate its efforts in areas where it finds natural advantage: arms production, threat of force, military assistance as a means of influence, subversion, and war. Moscow does use to its advantage two of the diplomatic instruments of policy: alliance and buffer states. But it is not now interested in establishing, or participating in, a reasonably stable balance of power. Its goal is to modify to its advantage the existing balance and to forestall or fracture potential balances that would hem it in geographically or prevent it from expanding its range of substantive interests.

The Soviet issue is therefore fourfold: the inability of the international system to accommodate swiftly enough to the growth in Soviet power, the tendency for Moscow to be too quick in matching its newly discovered interests with its expanded power, the Kremlin's relative poverty of foreign policy instruments, and the relative shortcomings of those states that, by their strength, must be charged with committing their resources and organizing the international system's response to the Soviet challenge. Under these circumstances, it appears that the only appropriate means short of war is for the major powers to band together in an anti-Soviet united front for whatever duration is necessary (my estimate is two decades) or—amounting to the same thing—to pursue separate but parallel policies of resistance. (A third option is often discussed: a combination of firmness *and compromise* by each of the four major states or regions, acting more or less independently. But given the dynamism of Soviet expansionism, the weakness of Moscow's opponents when facing the Kremlin alone, and the ever-present threat of systematic breakdown into nuclear war, that option seems to me to be unlikely to succeed. Accordingly, I consider it an evil to be avoided and not a positive good to be embraced.) In either option, united front or parallel policies, all of the available means of policy noted above must be not only used but also coordinated, firmly or loosely.

If a united front or parallel policies are necessary if unfortunate responses to the challenge of Soviet power, the question remains: Are they sufficient to the task? Two considerations need to be made clear. One is that the Cold War ahead will be even more vicious in nature than that of the 1950s. Costs, domestically and internationally, will be high, and the threat of war involving one or both of the superpowers and perhaps the other three regional powers may be equally high. The most important question is whether an arrangement designed to prevent permanent and fatal altering of the balance of power will lead to a decision by the Soviet Union or the coalition to employ large-scale force against the other. Thus, the dilemma is simultaneously to arrange a balance of power that forces the Soviet Union to give up its expansionist ambitions, accommodates (if gradually) Moscow's legitimate aspiration to be accepted as a central part of the system, and trains the Russians into behaving acceptably by threatening force against them but never using too much (e.g., nuclear).

The second consideration is that the linchpin of any such containment system must be the character of the arrangement between the United States and China. Of America's three coalition partners, only China can and may change its Soviet policy overnight. Neither West Europe nor Japan will suddenly, or even gradually, modify its present Soviet policy to the point of dropping out of the new cooperative arrangement in either of its manifestations; turn neutral between the Russians and the others; or actually join Moscow against its former partners. China can do any of those things, and any would be disastrous to the United States. Washington therefore must do all it can to maintain and strengthen the anti-Soviet inclination of Chinese policy. But that very policy involves the United States in a serious dilemma. Those measures that most appeal to the Chinese to remain anti-Soviet over the two decades' duration of the Soviet challenge are the same ones that eventually will lead the Chinese to modify their current policy set in Moscow's favor.

China seeks to restore its policy freedom vis-à-vis Moscow. Its goal is to strengthen the country sufficiently to approach the Kremlin with proposals for compromising their major but not irreconcilable differences. One means to that end is the policy of economic modernization *über alles* at home. Another is the establishment of large flows of technological, military, and economic assistance from the West, especially the United States. Washington is, of course, motivated to encourage such Chinese desires, for three reasons. First, they are the currency of Sino-American relations (a currency, it must be remembered, that did not exist for most of the post-1949 period). Second, Chinese dependence on the United States minimizes the danger of Sino-Soviet détente. And third, Chinese modernization so far has meant domestic liberalization and some movement toward democracy. But as China grows in power, thanks partly to Western assistance, the tendency will be for Peking to wean itself from dependence and to approach Moscow from the resultant position of strength to solve most, if not all, outstanding differences.

Although any Moscow-Peking agreement on more than minor matters would be disastrous for the United States, the risk must be run, given the precarious state of American-Soviet relations. Certain implications follow. One is that Washington is racing against time. The United States must improve its position vis-à-vis Moscow before the Chinese return to a position of balance between the superpowers. And the United States must provide the Chinese with enough reasons—diplomatic, economic, technological, and personal—for not moving any more than minimally in the Soviet's direction when the time comes. A second implication: To keep the Chinese sufficiently anti-Soviet, the United States must constantly increase the level and broaden the kind of its ties with Peking. Of course, China will understand this American fear and may increase the level of its requirements as insurance against playing a Soviet card. A subtle form of blackmail may thus become a part of Sino-American relations. The third implication is that, after a time, the ante could be raised too high and Washington and Peking could come to a parting of the ways. Sino-American separation may also come for other reasons: a swing once again of the internal

Chinese political pendulum; Chinese criticism of the diverse and ponderous nature of American society and politics; China's decreasing need for the technology and likely disagreement over Taiwan.

It appears reasonable to conclude that a grand anti-Soviet coalition is not a sufficient condition for deterring Soviet expansionism or avoiding wars and crises. It tends to produce crises, if not necessarily wars, and its base in Sino-American relations is weak. Other means must therefore be found to supplement the force of the coalition and make it more effective. Perhaps the most important is the internal strengthening of the United States. A major reversal of the continued decline of American power is in order, including reindustrialization, resuscitation of the public school system, overcoming urban blight and the racial problem, national service, some version of national health insurance, energy independence, monetary stability, and a greatly lowered rate of unemployment. All are needed for their own sake but will also translate into power applicable abroad in one form or another.

A second means is a change in how the United States treats the Soviet Union. A finely honed carrot-and-stick policy is called for. Simply put, the Soviet Union should be rewarded for good behavior and punished for being bad. Rewards should be highly desirable and punishments increasingly hurtful. For instance, if the United States seeks to punish Moscow for its Afghan transgression, it should support the indigenous rebels with the kinds and levels of equipment and training that will make that adventure increasingly dysfunctional for Moscow. Correspondingly, the United States should engage in a crash program to provide itself with a sufficiently large and readily transportable rapid deployment force; if the Soviets think to respond to American support of the Afghan rebels with further acts of force in South and Southwest Asia, they will have to contend with a major American force in place ahead of them. More positively, Washington should pledge to reinstate the kinds of relations the Russians want from us—high levels of trade, transfer of significant types of technology, meaningful exchanges of personnel, and resumption of progress on arms control—only when and if Soviet behavior improves.

In American-Soviet relations the Russians should be made aware of two operational principles of American policy. First, all issues, instruments of policy, and relationships should be considered mutually interchangeable. If the Soviets wish to be Machiavellian, the United States will be forced to play that game—with a vengeance. Indeed, the United States might find it desirable, in view of its interests, to adopt a standard of absolute invariability toward the Soviet Union, in contrast with how it treats other states. A regime of strict reward and punishments *with no exceptions* may be best for the Soviet Union. Then they will know where they stand and can choose and act accordingly.

The United States also should act toward the Soviet Union *and* all others according to another operational principle of policy. American acts and promises should never outrun the material resources pledged or readily available to serve them. At present, America is vastly overextended, and everyone knows it. It must choose between severely cutting back the level of its commitments and the kinds of interests it pretends to have, or expanding its resources to protect its interests and the commitments made in their name. It is easier in the short run to do the former, but in the long run it would be much more costly. Sometimes a policy of bluff—which is the inevitable consequence of such imbalance—can see a country through a period of weakness or manage a crisis. But it will not do as a habitual policy. This is another reason, therefore, for putting major effort into strengthening America.

A third means concerns the way in which the United States treats its relations with China. Should Washington deliberately vary its closeness to or distance from Peking, depending on the character of its relations with Moscow? The question is not easily answered. Some have claimed that both countries already are using each other for anti-Soviet purposes and that the common threat from Moscow is the principal reason for the present Sino-American closeness. If that threat were removed, Sino-American relations would be very different; surely they would not be nearly so friendly. There is no escaping the utilitarian nature of that relationship, a feature that will likely continue into the foreseeable future. Moreover, hinging the quality of Sino-American relations on the kind of attitudes exhibited by the Soviet Union signals to Moscow undeniable seriousness and meaning. It will remain part of the carrot-and-stick policy that the United States must apply to its relations with the Soviet Union.

Nevertheless, American-Chinese ties should develop for their own sake, at their own pace, and for their own reasons. And American policy should infuse still more of this attitude into its relations with Peking (and Peking with Washington) as time proceeds. Trust will never grow on either side if each knows that the other's policies are entirely manipulative and fickle. The very character of triangular relations inevitably pulls both countries in that direction. Whenever possible it should be America's policy to talk and act to the Chinese as though the Russians really did not matter so much and that what is more important for the United States is constructing a firm foundation for long-term American-Chinese relations. Indeed, that is the only basis on which other than hostile relations will ensue. Fortunately, policymakers in Washington and Peking seem aware of that need and have spoken and acted accordingly. That needs to be persisted in, especially when the going gets rough—as it surely will—in American-Chinese relations.

A final means is to make the coalition internally more effective. The major issue is whether the present loose collection of states united only by opposition to Soviet expansionism should or can be drawn together more tightly. One option to that end would be to make more formal the connections between China and the other three entities and to effectuate some sort of defense ties between Japan and NATO. Such arrangements seem down the road a bit. Moreover, they might not serve a useful purpose. For example, China would probably become interested in forming a close working defense relation with Europe and Japan only in response to Soviet aggression, not as a means of preventing it. Japan is still in the preliminary stages of rearmament, and its contribution to the common deterrence or defense would not be very great. Indeed, a Japanese-European defense tie could be counterproductive, if it invited a highly disproportionate Soviet response.

A Japanese-Chinese defense tie is sometimes discussed. But for the five-year future it is unlikely to be of interest to Japan, given the vast disparity in arms in China's favor. Tokyo would probably consider any defense arrangement as asking for Chinese arms protection, diluting the American security treaty unnecessarily, and unduly alarming the Russians. If the United States were brought in on (or, rather engineered) a tripartite Northeast Asian tie, matters would be somewhat different. Intracoalition equality would be preserved, and the resulting arrangement could provide a meaningful defense against Soviet adventurism in that part of Asia. But nothing could happen unless the Korean question were addressed and, by agreement of all parties, shelved as with Taiwan or "solved" as in the case of the two Germanys. Just to mention this necessity is to indicate how unlikely it is.

Formalizing and tightening the coalition fails also from the viewpoint of American interests. First, the situation does not now require it. Second, it would be counterproductive by causing the Soviet Union to confirm, even more than at present, its fears that the others were ganging up. Moscow might thus take those very actions which tightening the coalition would be designed to prevent. Finally, Chinese and Japanese ties with Europe and between themselves would tend to dilute American authority and centrality. As it is, all alliance ties and working arrangements go through Washington. The United States thus enjoys a unique position, while the others are at the periphery. American dominance will undoubtedly have to be diluted at some point, but there is no sense hastening the process without good cause.

Even a major tightening of the coalition—a formal treaty binding North America, Western Europe, China, and Japan together in event of Soviet attack—would be necessary only in response to a sudden major shift in the balance of power in the Soviets' favor. That is highly unlikely under present and foreseeable circumstances. The only instance of that sort would be Soviet attack on one or more of the coalition members, in which case a formal treaty would be both unnecessary and post hoc (since the purpose of a formal treaty is to prevent war).

Formalizing the present arrangement does not seem to be a desirable means of preventing conflict or even of hemming in Soviet expansionism. Closer parallelism of policy is a more attractive option. In this case, alliancelike behavior might be enhanced without the need for a formal, written multilateral document. Some mechanism would be needed to coordinate policies toward the Soviet Union beyond the occasional bilateral consultation process presently in effect. Perhaps a regularized conference of foreign ministers or a sort of working level contingency planning committee would be in order. In the case of a foreign minister conference, a periodic meeting announced ahead of time would avoid the shortcomings of formal ties noted above. Both the conference and the contingency committees would be relatively nonthreatening to Moscow. If set into place ahead of the next instance of Soviet expansionism they could help prevent war or mitigate crises.

III

The measures described above seem to me those necessary, unfortunately, to balance the enormous increase in Soviet power and activism that the next two decades will witness. Without them, or even with halfhearted adoption of some of them, the probabilities for war or a fatal overthrow of the balance are great. Yet even if all of them (or other devices found to be useful) were extant and working at peak efficiency, the world—and the United States—would not necessarily be a safer or more pleasant place to live. The present global holding operation must be transformed into more positive, system-transforming trends. War preparations, domestic reforms, coalition arrangement, carrot-and-stick policies, and the balancing of power with power do not address the question: What should be the nature of international relations once the Soviet Union has turned status quo internationally and sociopolitically progressive domestically?

One way to prepare for the post–twentieth century world is to put major effort into peaceful settlement of two kinds of disputes. One is disputes between states that are members of the anti-Soviet coalition or between them and minor national entities within the great area compromising the principal geographic regions of the coalition. Thus, in Northeast Asia, the Korean and Taiwan problems should not be put off as long as possible but rather should be addressed jointly by America and China; the Sino-Indian border controversy should be worked out; the Kashmir dispute between India and Pakistan should be brought up again for mediation; the Greek-Turkish conflict over Cyprus must be solved within the confines of NATO; Japanese-American trade issues should be attacked in a cooperative spirit; and the emerging American-Mexican dispute over a number of issues should be addressed in both capitals. Listing is not solving, of course, but these urgent problems require serious attention at the same time as decision makers in the major capitals grapple with the Soviet problem. Solving these issues not only will provide fewer targets of opportunity for Moscow but also will enhance the probability of a peaceful transition to the next configuration of the international system.

The second kind of dispute is that between members of the coalition and states and other entities geographically external to their areas of primary interest, and issues that transcend geographic boundaries—the so-called global issues. These include all the transfer-of-wealth issues grouped under the North-South question, the Arab-Israeli conflict, the racial problem in South Africa, the energy question in all its manifestations, and the various international monetary and trade issues that arise from rapid expansion of trade, interdependence, multinational corporations, and the inadequacies of the international monetary system. There is no better way in the long run to deal with the Soviet challenge and to set the stage for eventual improvement than to redouble efforts to overcome these shortcomings. Moreover, in no other arena does the United States have a greater comparative advantage in leadership and experience. Unless the United States shows the way, these issues may not merely become the occasions for Soviet-American confrontation but may combine to plunge the globe into economic, racial, religious, and ecological crises.

There is a third type of dispute that must be addressed on its merits and separated, as best as possible, from the problem of Soviet power: the military-revolutionary activism of regional communist states. Cuba and Vietnam are today's examples; there may be others tomorrow in Africa, the Middle East, and South America. One such state per region is enough to alter radically the politics and economics of the entire area. When these radical regimes attach themselves to the Soviet Union for security, the politics of their regions become enmeshed with the Soviet issue and threaten confrontation and war between the two rival global systems.

It would be better if the connection were broken, not merely because the Soviet Union would be deprived of local allies and of a way to insert itself into regional matters but also because the question of the role of these states in their respective regions cannot otherwise be addressed on its merits. The more local communist states, the greater will be the difficulty of eventual settlement with the Soviet Union, and it is tempting to argue that the United States should do what it can to prevent their numbers from increasing. The situation may be too late in Africa, given the present status of Ethiopia, and perhaps in the Middle East, where South Yemen may occupy the same role. But perhaps the United States should resist the next Soviet attempt to extend the "Brezhnev doctrine" to establish protectorates over these states. At the least, the coalition may have to work out a common policy toward these states, lest Moscow treat each issue as between itself and only one of its members (e.g., with China vis-à-vis Vietnam and with the United States regarding Cuba); in this way Moscow isolates the problem and deals with it from a position of strength.

More positive measures must be found to induce regional communist states to separate themselves from the Soviet Union and to concentrate their energies on domestic development. When the openings occur, these stages must be recognized diplomatically, offered trade and technological transfer opportunities, and shown both how they can make their peace with their putative regional opponents and why the export of revolution will not benefit them. The United States has a comparative advantage in the economic and technological realms and there is no reason why direct competition with Moscow for their favor cannot be won in the long run. One of the most effective devices is to make showcase societies of at least one of the regional rivals of these communist regimes. Not only does that render them less susceptible to domestic upheaval and external penetration but it demonstrates that there are less stringent yet more effective paths to modernization and social-political unity than Stalinist communism. In this regard, the United States would be making a wise investment, in every sense, if it were to reverse its historic attitude of inattention to Central America and the Caribbean; work out a long-range and practical economic development relationship with the Association of Southeast Asian Nations; take steps to implement massive improvement of the economies of the Horn of Africa; and buttress Egypt, Tunisia, and Morocco in both defense and development.

A second way to prepare for the post–twentieth century world is to address the status the Soviet Union is likely to have (and should have) within the strategic triangle and in the international system, and what the overall configuration of postconfrontational power is likely to be. Moscow must be made to feel that it is a legitimate and vital component of the international system and that it is not America's desire to organize all other relevant stages against it on general principles. The United States must make it plain that Soviet rights of participation as a global power in every region and issue will be respected, indeed welcomed, so long as the Soviet Union plays a constructive role. Once again it seems advisable to establish a clearly stated and executed policy rewarding the Kremlin when its actions are helpful and punishing it when they are not. Constructing a *cordon sanitaire* around the Soviet Union in the long run will only force Moscow to overcome it by exhibiting more of the kinds of behavior the Sino-American coalition is designed to oppose in the short run.

At some point, then, the coalition must cease acting purely in a reactive manner and make room for the Russians as vital players of world politics, as essential contributors to international regional development, and as important actors in effectuating cooperative solutions to global issues. There are no easy formulae for transforming zero-sum opposition and military confrontation to cooperative participation in common efforts. But even as the military balance occupies the center of world attention during the next half decade, the door can be kept open to cooperation. If the Soviets are invited to participate in solving common problems (rather than feeling that they are being deliberately kept out or that they have to push their way into acceptability), perhaps they will come to act in good faith, with a stake in stability instead of disorder.

What will be the role of the two potential major powers, India and Brazil? Should they be induced to join the Sino-American–led coalition, thus completing the array against Moscow? Should they be hindered in their growth to major power status? Or should their development be fostered and the international system modified deliberately in their favor? It may not be possible or desirable to try to gain their affiliation with the anti-Soviet group. Newly emerging powers always guard their independence carefully. More importantly, a bipolar Cold War system desperately needs balancers; these two states could play a constructive role by contributing to systemic stability—that is, by staying out of the coalition and Moscow's embrace. Of course, it is not totally in the American interest to amplify the status of Brazil, since Washington would then have to contend with a serious Western Hemispheric rival for the first time in its history. But Brazil will achieve that status eventually, regardless of America's wishes. Perhaps it is better to arrange the way rather than hinder it.

Further, the long-term position of China needs to be addressed. How should the United States conduct itself when Peking moves, progressively, to negotiate its differences with Moscow? The "rules" of behavior should be, I believe, to show no panic at the possibility of closer Sino-Soviet ties; to encourage the Chinese to stretch out over a long period their movement toward Moscow; to maintain the full range of established ties with the United States; and to modulate Washington's relations with Moscow for the better (if at all possible) at the same rate and along the same lines as improvement in Sino-Soviet relations. In that manner, a sea change in intra-triangular relations will neither occur nor unduly threaten the United States. The United States also should look to the peaceful integration of China into the international system—just as, from about 1990 forward, it will be the task of the United States to lead the way to peaceful systemic integration of the Soviet Union. It would be disastrous for the last four decades of American difficulties with the Russians to be repeated with the Chinese. It need not be, if Washington plans now for that eventuality by deciding which of its interests it wishes to maximize and which it may have to modify or even forego. In the twenty-first century, a China of superpower status could well threaten the global balance of power, just as the Soviet Union does now. Surely China will demand political-military primacy, if not economic supremacy, in Asia. The Asian international landscape could suffer considerable modification, principally by the exclusion of a dominant or even a major role of America and Russia. That would indicate an Asian balance of power centered around China, Japan, and India, and a commanding role for China in Southeast Asia.

But China need not necessarily come to threaten all of Asia. It will always have enormous internal problems. The United States and the Soviet Union will always be Asian actors of consequence. India and Japan can always ally themselves with either of the two other superpowers, thus balancing China. And Southeast Asia need not become a sphere of exclusive Chinese influence: It is large, variegated, and capable of rapid development, strong defense and Kautilya-like relations with extraregional powers. Of equal importance for the United States, Washington can lead the way to gain general acceptance of necessary regional changes in China's favor while at the same time working with Peking to modify its more extreme demands. In essence, the same "rules" in relations with the Soviet Union noted above will have to be applied, when the time comes, to China.

America has a unique position and the requisite ability to lead the other major powers to construct a more secure, highly developed, and interdependent system which avoids most of the errors of the twentieth century. The United States can be instrumental in building a new type of system based not so much on the power and destructive potential of very large national states as on a tripartite division among states, supranational and transnational institutions, and subnational, more or less autonomous cultural entities. For the next twenty years Washington must center its policies on the cut-throat politics of the strategic triangle and must operate within the international system that it largely produced. But at the same time it can prepare for a new stage in world politics which, because of the greater power and number of new actors, can be relatively safer than the present. And even now it can invest policy attention and resources in moving beyond the state-based, power-politics system altogether. The task is thus threefold: security now, based on a frank return to Cold War and containment through coalition building and management; transition by the end of the century to a new configuration of power that sees the Soviet Union a decreasing threat and China a responsible and accepted global power; and transformation after that—perhaps by the middle of the twenty-first century—to a very different kind of system and politics.

Human Rights and Soviet-American Relations

Kenneth W. Thompson

THE Carter administration placed human rights at the center of its foreign policy partly because of the convictions of the new president, partly because of the political thought of some of his advisers, partly as a result of political accident, and partly because of the unfolding campaign for the presidency in 1976. Few would claim that he defined human rights as "the soul" of his policy after cautiously weighing competing goals and establishing a hierarchy of objectives with human rights at the pinnacle.

Human rights was a happening in the campaign, not a well-formulated aim of Carter's campaign. He was slow to invoke the principle. Not until late 1975 at a Democratic issues forum at Louisville did the candidate pose the question. The following March he returned to human rights in a speech in Chicago and again in October at the home of one of his moral mentors, Father Theodore Hesburgh, at Notre Dame. Only in the second Carter-Ford debate did Carter make a determined political statement attacking President Ford and Secretary Kissinger for not protesting Soviet violations of Basket Three of the Helsinki agreement. (The first basket dealt with security and postwar European boundaries; the second with trade and scientific and technological exchanges; and the third with freedom of travel, marriage between citizens of different states, and reunification of families.) The human rights appeal in the campaign was what pollster Patrick Caddell called a strong issue across the board. It found the candidate reaching out to conservatives and liberals alike, to the followers of Sen. Henry Jackson and to Jewish labor leaders concerned with Soviet treatment of the Jews and to those who took note of the statement in his Notre Dame speech about five million Russian Baptists. At another point on the political spectrum, his words stirred liberals who were dissatisfied with American policies in Korea and Chile.

In retrospect, the Carter crusade for human rights had an air of inevitability about it. As certain observers have noted, it fit the candidate like a glove. The determinants were his religious beliefs, his fundamentalist origins, an irrepressible moralistic streak, and a genuine commitment to the movement of the New South toward an expansion of civil rights. With all his well-publicized devotion to America's foremost theologian, Reinhold Niebuhr, Carter in practice took exception to Niebuhr's stress on complexity and ambiguity in two important respects. His populism was hardly Niebuhrian, and his political instincts were more attuned to the early reformist Niebuhr than to the later Niebuhr who found in political prudence deriving from Burke the surest guide for political action. In any event, Niebuhr had passed from the scene and more immediate counselors called for action, not ambiguity. A surer guide to action than prudence was activism grounded in moral indignation over Watergate and Vietnam and a fervor for doing worldwide what Carter's generation had succeeded in doing for civil rights domestically. It was no accident that the new president found the cadre for his human rights campaign not in experienced foreign policy experts or foreign area specialists but in resolute civil rights workers.

Whatever the differences between those who advised him on foreign policy and on human rights, the two groups made common cause because of the foreign policy advisers' quest for every means of demonstrating differences with the realpolitik of Henry Kissinger. The lifelong rivalry between two Harvard men, Kissinger and Zbigniew Brzezinski, all too familiar to academics, was to play itself out with far-reaching effects on American foreign policy. The former had submerged human rights in the quest for peace and world order. The latter, who would not accept a position in which he remained overshadowed by a longtime rival, reinforced the President's natural moral instincts and those of his civil rights workers.

One other factor should not be overlooked in 1981: the moral and intellectual climate of the mid-1970s. America's image had been tarnished and its position as world leader undermined by Watergate and Vietnam. Again and again those who were closest to Carter proclaimed that the United States had exercised leadership in the counsels of state in the past because it stood for something in the world. There was an urgent need to restore confidence in American integrity at home and abroad and to reinstate the higher-law principles on which democracy was based. Only the unrepentant cynic would claim that Carter and his advisers were motivated exclusively by politics, not morality, in what soon became a political crusade. In politics, however, the affirming of positive goals moves imperceptibly into political denunciations of the enemy at home and abroad.

Carter's first impulse had been to shy away from foreign policy issues in the campaign. He departed from this strategy for at least two reasons. First, he soon recognized that he faced a political problem. His critics had begun to charge that he was too passive on the threat of Eurocommunism and too inclined to leftist leanings on foreign policy. Second, he discovered in the second debate an issue that reversed his position and enabled him to argue that President Ford was slow to answer the evils of communism. Overnight, he turned the tables on the president and rallied forces on the left and right to his side. Liberal Democrats discovered that their candidate was offering human rights as a moral base for arresting support for repressive right-wing regimes which they found morally offensive. Conservatives in labor and business joined Carter in blaming the amorality of American negotiators for the concessions which had been made to the Soviet Union. The challenger found some of his most effective political targets in the foreign policy arena, including not only Soviet-American relations but the CIA scandal and the Chilean coup d'etat. As the campaign unfolded, Carter was able to combine a new and more positive call for human rights with negative attacks on those who had neglected human rights while in office.

It is beside the point to suggest that Carter should have shown greater restraint and wisdom in formulating a human rights policy. The recent human rights campaign, no matter how deep and abiding the President's convictions are, must be seen as an aspect of the political process. As one Carter adviser explained: "I know there was no specific planning for a particular human rights campaign or program, such as it is.... Fate intervened—happenchance things, letters—that blew the issue up unexpectedly.... [Response] drew such enormous attention and acclaim—especially from the right... [and] gave the President maneuvering room."[1] It is probably asking too much of any political candidate in the heat of battle to sharpen

[1] Quoted by Elizabeth Drew, "Human Rights," *New Yorker*, July 18, 1977, p. 41.

or refine moral judgments when an election is at stake. The most that political observers can expect is that those engaged in political combat not become burdened with commitments that make discriminate political judgments impossible.

The problem facing every political leader is to steer a course between cynicism and moralism. In this regard, the architects of a human rights policy share a common dilemma with those who champion any other worthy cause, whether participation in the League of Nations or the United Nations, the promotion of international law, collective security, or peace in our time. The cynic errs by supposing that people or nations are incapable of embracing any moral purpose. Inevitably, nations—and particularly democratic nations, and most particularly the United States—tend to view political actions as taking place within a moral framework. Such nations look to national goals and traditions as explaining and justifying the course they follow. Only in certain exceptional periods, made possible in part by extraordinary leaders, has foreign policy been successfully articulated solely in the language of national power or narrow self-interest. Historically, claims are made that actions rest on moral purposes beyond the state. Foreign policy characteristically is expressed in moral terms even by authoritarian regimes, whether social democracy, economic planning, anticolonialism, national liberation, or revolution. Cynicism falters because it asks too little of people and nations.

Moralism fails as the grounding of foreign policy for the opposite reason. It claims too much for a single moral purpose. Moralism is the tendency to single out one worthy objective—to make it supreme and to apply it indiscriminately without regard to time and place. Moralism deals in absolutes viewed not as objects of ultimate concern but as immediate and practical possibilities. Whatever their moral worth, lesser concerns become, in theological language, icons or objects of idolatry. Historians such as Toynbee have maintained that the most common form of idolatry in the present era is the nation-state. A more subtle form of idolatry may be the worship of a particular expression of nationalism or of a certain national attainment in one society that is universalized as immediately attainable in every national community.

Woodrow Wilson found such an attainment in national self-determination which had brought a tolerable measure of harmony to certain developed nation-states. However, writers beginning with John Maynard Keynes warned that national self-determination applied indiscriminately would sever the economic unities that had bound together the states of eastern and central Europe. Nor should it be forgotten that Hitler invoked the concept of national self-determination to justify overrunning the Sudetenland.

Moralism imperils the international community not only through predatory abuse at the hand of demoniac leaders but also as employed by relatively good and virtuous leaders. Moralism is capable of poisoning relations among states which turn against those who claim too much for their virtue. It was Niebuhr who warned fellow Americans that the more they indulged in an uncritical reverence for the American way of life, the more odious they would become in the eyes of the world, and the more they would destroy their moral authority, without which both military and economic power become impotent. American leaders will not be forgiven their moralism by claiming ignorance of the harsh circumstances which prevent the transformation of the world. "The irony of our situation lies in the fact that we could not be virtuous (in the sense of practicing the virtues which are implicit in meeting our vast world responsibilities) if we were really as innocent as we pretend to be."[2] Moralism and innocence may go together.

Fortunately, those Americans who look for a framework of moral choice are not condemned to choosing between cynicism or moralism. Another tradition presents itself which has an ancient and respected history. Morality, as distinguished from moralism, is the endless quest for what is right amidst the complexity of competing and sometimes conflicting moral ends. It is the tradition of moral reasoning, the essence of which is weighing not only good and evil but also competing goods.

Paradoxically, men and women are accustomed to employing moral reasoning and taking its requirements in stride in the more intimate communities of their common life, within the family, the locality, the nation, and the domestic legal system. They learn to live within communities that enshrine multiple, not single moral principles. They struggle to do what is right balancing obligations that if they stood alone would make for a far simpler life. Yet every-

[2] Reinhold Niebuhr, *The Irony of American History* (New York, 1952), p. 23.

one knows that most of their lives will be lived at the juncture of contradictions. In their workaday communities, men and women come to expect that moral choice will be fraught with tragic and agonizing decisions. Within the family and in daily work, people must choose between devotion to the family and professional advancement; few people of conscience rest easy with such a choice. Tocqueville found Americans unique in their commitment to voluntarism and public service, but who has served community without cost to family? Democracy draws its strength from the grass roots, yet states' rights from the Founding have been in tension with national requirements; when the conflict went unresolved, a tragic civil war resulted. If the nation is to prosper, freedom of speech and assembly must be balanced with order and security; correspondingly, the Supreme Court proclaimed that the right of free speech cannot mean the right to cry "Fire" in a crowded theater. Within the law, the right to a fair trial has been said to conflict with freedom of the press and the right to know, and magistrates must weigh and balance the two in given cases.

Every political and constitutional principle coexists and must be interpreted in relation to other constitutional principles, prompting Justice Oliver Wendell Holmes to observe: "People are always extolling the man of principle; but I think the superior man is one who knows that he must find his way in a maze of principles." Freedom coexists with order, leading Reinhold Niebuhr to write: "Our best hope . . . rests upon our ability to observe the limits of human freedom even while we responsibly exploit its creative possibilities."[3] Within the nation, freedom and order, justice and security, and equality and economic progress are at best a partial expression of morality. For democracies the triumph of common sense prevents anyone's exclusive commitment from being carried through to its logical conclusion, whether the prosperous person's devotion to freedom or the poor person's demand for justice. Democratic theorists have staunchly held that there is an element of truth in each of the historic claims made for particular rights, but they become falsehoods when carried forward too consistently and too exclusively.

For politicians on the hustings, especially in times of disorder

---

[3] Niebuhr, *The Structure of Nations and Empires* (New York, 1959), p. 299.

where national unity is in jeopardy, the truths of democratic theory are difficult to sustain. It is tempting to take hold of a single principle and erect it into a political absolute. The public rallies to those who simplify; it turns on those who call for discriminating judgments. The leader then is confronted with the most fateful choice between oversimplifications that almost certainly lead to disillusionment or measured responses that seek to inform and educate but carry political risks. In no realm is the choice more fraught with consequences than with issues that engage national pride and prevailing national moods. When international tensions abate, leaders prefer to speak more of détente than of continuing rivalry; when conflicts multiply, they call for arming against aggression, not negotiating peace. Extraordinary and rare are those like Churchill, who declared "we arm to parlay," or an American secretary of state who spoke of "negotiating from strength."

The beginning of a human rights policy is the search for an approach more enduring than cynicism or moralism, a perspective that balances moral and political objectives. One case study for such a framework is to seek to relate human rights and Soviet-American relations.

A Cynical Framework

Two forms of cynicism are apparent in the quest for a framework for human rights and Soviet-American relations. One involves resigning oneself to the fact that human rights as we understand them are virtually unknown in totalitarian regimes. The Western conception of individual rights goes back to the Magna Carta, if not to Graeco-Roman thought. According to the Western political tradition, rights inhere in the individual and are preserved in documents such as the Bill of Rights. For totalitarian governments, rights reside in the state and the individual is subordinate to the state. The individual enjoys only such rights as are assumed by the state when it obligates itself to provide economic and social rights such as housing and health. The cynic maintains, therefore, that human rights as Westerners conceive them have no place in totalitarian states.

A second form of cynicism is expressed by those who assume that in the relating of human rights and Soviet-American affairs, policies must be judged exclusively from the standpoint of the Cold War and in terms of the military balance of power. The criteria of policy, we are told, must be hard, not soft; military estimates must prevail. Human rights have validity not in and of themselves but as weapons in a protracted conflict in which America or the Soviet Union ultimately will triumph. Viewed from this perspective, human rights are the main instrument of ideological warfare for the West—subordinate to missiles, submarines, and aircraft because of the Soviet design of world conquest, but a contributing element of national power nonetheless. In other words, rights are part of America's armory of weapons for waging war in the irrepressible conflict.

One way of classifying the two forms of cynicism is to consider the first as a cynicism of the liberal left and the second as of the conservative right. Within liberalism, one strain of reformist thought has looked to institutions as the preconditions of all progress. In the absence of liberal institutions, societies are doomed to chaos and retrogression. On the world stage, social and political advancement presupposes the construction of world institutions. Federal Union Now and World Federalism as political movements rest on intellectual foundations of the liberal left. Common to their prescriptions for the North Atlantic Community and the world is the belief that only new international institutions can save mankind. Contrary to their predictions, international cooperation has been gradualist and incremental, inching ahead on the basis of such improbable forms of collaboration as the European Coal and Steel Community and wider functional groups within and outside the United Nations.

The critics of the cynics of the left maintain that for human rights, as for every form of international advancement, the best is oftentimes the enemy of the good. Ideally, for purist liberals the world would be composed of freedom-loving states bound together in a federal union. Actually, the task of those who would promote freedom is to seek out men and women who cherish freedom and who can be found in every civilized nation. Persons of this stripe *were* present in Nazi Germany. They might have been embraced and prompted to come forward if Hitler's imperialism had been contained and if time and circumstances had been allowed to work their civilizing leaven. For those who would condemn a whole people, overarching cynicism about Germans appears to have been refuted by the democratic attainments of the Federal German Republic. The dissidents in the Soviet Union, particularly if they are viewed as the tip of the iceberg rather than as an insignificant antigovernment group, may in the long view of history offer a similar refutation of blatant cynicism.

In any event, one authority on the Soviet Union, Dean Edward L. Kennan can write: "I feel that a stable life, a stable society, and a modern figuration of social relations exist now, or are coming into existence, in the Soviet Union. It is only the selfish behavior of those who were the first to seize its fruits and levers that is holding back an evolution toward more modern attitudes about man and his individual rights."[4] Or Shao-Chuan Leng of the University of Virginia, writing of China, can say: "Human rights are not just a Western contribution but have a universal validity, with contributions from all major civilizations."[5]

If cynicism on the left falters as a world perspective on human rights, cynicism advanced by spokesmen of the conservative right is no less defective. By comparison with recent American conservatism, the virtue of Western conservatism has been its stress on political evolution and organic growth. Conservatives such as Edmund Burke took the long view, emphasizing that the historical process of government "moves on through the varied tenor of perpetual decay, full renovation and progression."[6] As with nature, so with the state, Burke argued: "In what we improve we are never wholly new, in what we retain we are never wholly obsolete."[7] For conservatives, the state must deal with the greatest variety of ends and the entire circle of human desires; whatever its makeup, it must ultimately contend with individual feeling and individual

[4] Edward L. Kennan, "Human Rights in Soviet Political Culture," in *The Moral Imperatives of Human Rights*, ed. Kenneth W. Thompson (Washington, D.C., 1980), pp. 79–80.

[5] Shao-Chuan Leng, "Human Rights in Chinese Political Culture," in *Moral Imperatives*, p. 81.

[6] Edmund Burke, "Regicide Peace," *Works of the Right Honourable Edmund Burke*, rev. ed., 12 vols. (Boston, 1865–67), 5: 374.

[7] Ibid.

interest. Conservatism finds its treasures in tradition and custom. In Karl Mannheim's words: "The Conservative type of knowledge originally is the sort of knowledge giving practical control. It consists of habitual orientations towards those factors which are immanent in the present situation."[8] A man of the far left, Harold Laski, in recognition of the intrinsic qualities of conservatism, observed: "Burke has endured as the permanent manual of political wisdom without which statesmen are as sailors on an uncharted sea." Conservatives historically have opposed too rapid social change. Burke distinguished profound and natural alterations from the radical infatuation of the day, preferring a gradual course in order to prevent "unfixing old interests at once: a thing which is apt to breed a black and sullen discontent in those who are at once dispossessed of all their influence and consideration [and at the same time] . . . prevent men, long under depression, from being intoxicated with a large draught of new power."[9]

American conservatism, however, is not the traditional conservatism of Western political history. In foreign policy, it has fluctuated between isolationism and imperialism; between underestimating the nation's responsibilities and overestimating its power, between withdrawing from the world and embarking on moral crusades. It has derided mere politics and the role of expediency and ignored the moral predicament about which conservative historians like Herbert Butterfield wrote: "While there is battle and hatred . . . the enemy is [seen as] the cause of all the troubles; but long, long afterwards, when all passion has been spent, the historian often sees that it was a conflict between one half-right that was perhaps too wilful, and another half-right that was too proud." Nor have American conservatives understood the distinction between force and power. They accept the former, but "that power should become an objective in itself, a goal for individual, social or state action, is considered both undesirable and wicked." The late Clinton Rossiter concluded that American conservatives "were the . . . only Right in Western history to push individualism

[8] Quoted in Richard Crossman et al., *The New Fabian Essays* (New York, 1952), p. 162.

[9] Quoted in Clinton Rossiter, *Conservatism in America* (New York, 1955), p. 41.

so far as to assert that a man could never be helped, only harmed, by the assistance of the community."[10] And he added: "The extra measure of moral indignation that George Kennan finds in our foreign policy; the worst excesses of tariff legislation, the moral blindness of those who insist on the identity of Socialism and Soviet Communism . . . all these are the major counts in the indictment of political conservatism."[11]

American conservatism, which stands as the arch defender of nineteenth century liberalism, has proved itself strangely inept in the one sphere where conservatism historically has enjoyed an unquestioned superiority: foreign policy. It has seen the world through the narrow squint of upper-middle-class American life. Only conservatives like President Eisenhower, with a devotion to America's international responsibilities and a sense of the limits of American power in the vast expanses of Asia, have transcended the peculiarities and parochialism of American conservatism.

If cynics of the liberal left have underestimated the prospects for human rights, those of the conservative right have overestimated the chances that human rights can be installed on Soviet soil in the wake of a more aggressive American foreign policy. Viewed from the right, stronger and more sustained military pressure and economic penalties and rewards, accompanied by intervention in Soviet affairs on behalf of human rights, are capable of bringing about social change. While the liberal left and its intellectual proponents hold out little hope of the broadening of rights within another sovereign state, the conservative right, while not relaxing its defense of American sovereignty, is sanguine that the sovereignty of the Soviet state can be abridged through American strength.

Thus, two forms of cynicism lead to opposite conclusions about human rights within the Soviet Union and presumably within other totalitarian states. In their practical effects, one form becomes a cynicism of limitations and the other of imposition of human rights. One is reminiscent of moral isolationism before World War II and the other of John Foster Dulles's liberation foreign policy, which cynically offered what America could not provide. Neither confronts the issue of the slow and gradual growth of rights within

[10] Ibid., pp. 162–63.
[11] Ibid., p. 239.

widely differing cultures. If the one asks too little of American foreign policy, the other expects too much.

A Moralistic Framework

The moralistic framework for human rights matches the pessimism and doubts of cynicism with an overriding optimism. In a world shrouded in fear and burdened with despair, sounding a note of hope should never be disparaged. In the early days of the Carter administration, observers pointed to a resurgence of America's belief in itself, leaving behind the grim days of Watergate. Yet a regime which began so auspiciously had faltered before it reached mid-course. Its failures may be explained in part by its persistent moralism.

To reiterate, moralism is the tendency to single out one worthy objective in foreign policy, to make it supreme, and seek to apply it indiscriminately. Morality, by contrast, is finding one's way in a maze of principles. In June 1977 some fifteen government officials and scholars in international relations met in Charlottesville, Virginia, to discuss human rights. Their differences arose less from opposing attitudes toward human rights than from divergent assumptions about morality. Almost without exception, administration spokesmen, then in their first six months in office, saw no contradiction or even any tension between a strong human rights campaign and the pursuit of other objectives in foreign policy. It was argued that strategies to advance SALT II and nuclear nonproliferation would not be influenced by the crusade for human rights. Opposing this viewpoint, the scholars who participated warned against supposing that the Soviet Union would negotiate on SALT without regard to the human rights campaign being waged against them. One was inseparably connected with the other. Later in his administration, the president was to express surprise that the Soviets had linked the two issues. That surprise has been attributed by some to his innocence in foreign policy—an indictment that, if true, must be shared by some of his more prominent advisers. If the policymakers were wrong and the scholars generally right in prophesying the path and pitfalls that human rights would encounter, one important reason was the fact that the former espoused moralism and the latter morality. Even a rather idealistic international lawyer warned participants at Charlottesville against moralistic finger-shaking. It was an obstacle, he warned, to progress toward noble goals.

Yet moralism has offered an attractive framework for human rights for reasons apart from the personalities of President Carter and his national security adviser. In the aftermath of Watergate, moralism appealed to those who sought a sharp break with the past. It suited the personal and party politics of the principal actors, driven to prove how different they were from their predecessors. A moral crusade for human rights abroad appeared consistent with a populist crusade to rally the people against the bureaucracy in Washington. Above all, moralism as a political strategy throws off the weight of cynicism that surrounded the Nixon-Kissinger foreign policy. For a new administration coming to power in an era of righteous indignation against the malefactors of the past, it was a natural response for Carter but one nonetheless that carried seeds of future problems.

Moralism as a framework for human rights unfettered by other issues was the unchallenged framework of the Carter administration through the spring of 1977. The president received a letter from Andrei Sakharov on January 28, 1977, and made public his reply on February 17. The State Department leveled its charge against Czechoslovakia for arresting and harassing the signers of "Charter 77" (a petition outlined in the Helsinki agreement). In messages to Brezhnev and Ambassador Dobrynin and in various public statements, the president made clear his intention to speak out when human rights were threatened. In March he declared before the General Assembly: "No member of the United Nations can claim that mistreatment of its citizens is solely its own business." An independent unit was established within the State Department to deal with human rights as both the executive branch and the Congress sought to introduce human rights considerations into foreign policy across the board. It was understood that human rights would be applied in specific new areas, such as the issue of military assistance to certain Latin American, African, and Asian countries.

Not until April 30, 1977, did the administration undertake to place its human rights program in broader perspective. In a speech at the University of Georgia Law School, Secretary of State Cyrus

Vance warned against "stridency" in public statements and appeared to hold open the possibility of quiet diplomacy and private initiatives. Further, he offered instead of an undifferentiated mass of universally valid principles new concepts of human rights that distinguished among governmental violation of the integrity of the person (torture, arbitrary arrest, denial of a fair public trial); fulfillment of vital human needs, such as food, shelter, health care, and education; and the right to civil and political liberties, such as freedom of speech, press, religion, and assembly. Moralism began to break down and political discrimination take its place with Vance's speech; it continued with development loan assistance efforts of multinational assistance organizations such as the World Bank, through which the United States channels one-third of its aid, proceeding independently of the Carter human rights crusade.

The deteriorating climate for negotiating a SALT agreement, mounting tension in crisis areas such as South Korea and certain key Latin American countries which Carter had condemned, the difficulties in balancing urgent human needs in developing countries with improved practices of human rights, and mounting differences within the State Department led to a more tentative, pragmatic approach. Although leading officials such as the assistant secretary of human rights, Patt Derian, had opposed the selection of carefully targeted areas for the promotion of human rights when the issue was raised in Charlottesville in mid-1977, the administration grew sympathetic to concentrating on more favorable opportunities. The public heard less about any early transformation of countries that had been slow to support human rights (an internal report contained in the PRM review under the chairmanship of Undersecretary Warren Christopher had referred to eighteen months as the period required for dramatic changes).

The price of moralism in human rights has been to introduce an additional element of uncertainty into foreign policy. To engage the president as the primary spokesman in public declaration is to exhaust prematurely a court of last resort. When presidential initiatives dropped off in 1979 and 1980, other voices were unprepared to speak out as they had done in the past in supporting the creation of the United Nations. In other Western countries, parliaments, political parties, and civic and religious bodies had shared part of the responsibility. Because human rights was initially presented by the administration as a clear-cut moral issue and a matter of absolute right and wrong, it has been difficult to preserve a strong human rights policy as complexity and disillusionment have made moralism an unconvincing approach. As moralism declined, the human rights question, having been equated with moralism, has been pushed into the background. Rightly or not, the fate of the one became the fate of the other, and the decline of moralism has meant the decline of human rights.

A Third Framework

It can be argued that human rights might have enjoyed a longer life if the architects of the Carter foreign policy had provided a framework other than moralism. Human rights politics are not the only aspect of foreign policy dominated by moralism. *A New York Times* editorial concluded: "The Pentagon too often puts strategic arguments in absolute terms."[12] The same can be said of those who defend foreign economic assistance as a universal in American foreign policy.

An alternate framework to moralism would stress the broad-gauged character of foreign policy and the necessity for balancing painful choices. Those who talked only of human rights in the early days of the Carter administration saw the world in one dimension. Pursuing the national interest requires equal if not greater attention to political and strategic concerns. The issues of foreign policy must be arrayed in hierarchical, not random, terms. No other concern is more vital than the avoidance of a nuclear holocaust, and every departing secretary of state has cited its abeyance as the major accomplishment of his office. To approach human rights in Russia and the SALT negotiations as though they were equally vital to human survival suggests a foreign policy not grounded in realism. Surely it would be difficult to chart advances in human rights if a nuclear war left only a handful of survivors.

A third framework would approach human rights from the standpoint of moral reasoning. It would seek to weigh alternatives and assess priorities. It would strive to relate power and morality while not forgetting that their essential disjunction in international poli-

[12] *New York Times*, editorial, February 27, 1977.

tics is never wholly resolved. It may be useful to consider the framework put forward by the renowned British military historian Michael Howard, who wrote:

> Political activity takes place in a two-dimension field—a field which can be defined by the two coordinates of ethics and power. The ethical coordinate (which we may appropriately conceive as vertical) indicates the purposes which should govern political action: the achievement of a harmonious society of mankind in which conflicts can be peacefully resolved and a community of cultures peacefully coexist within which every individual can find fulfillment. The horizontal coordinate measures the capacity of each actor to impose his will on his environment, whether by economic, military or psychological pressure.[13]

Obsession with ethical values, with no concern for their implementation, is itself unethical. The more far-reaching the ethical goals, the greater the capacity and power required to achieve them. For the pursuit of human rights, the first task is to be ready to relate them to other goals, weighing and judging their importance to the national interest. The second task is to recognize that the proclamation of human rights is the beginning and not the end of forging a policy. Ethics and power must be harnessed together and purpose balanced by capacity.

I have written elsewhere:

> Michael Howard's framework for relating morality and power has its application to human rights not in offering politics for concrete and individual sectors of rights but in suggesting directions and a course to follow. The statesman in pursuing his diagonal course guided by the two coordinates must be like a pilot reading a compass bearing from which he cannot diverge too far in either direction. Too fanatical a concern with moral absolutes may destroy capacity for effective action; too little concern for ethical values may produce short-run military or political advantages but destroy a nation's moral standing and prestige. Again Niebuhr's phrase best articulates the principle underlying this approach: "Politics will, to the end of history, be an area where conscience and power meet, where the ethical and coercive factors of human life will interpenetrate and work out

[13] Michael Howard, "Ethics and Power in International Politics," The Third Martin Wight Memorial Lecture, January 12, 1977, p. 373.

their tentative and uneasy compromises." One can only hope that President Carter will find this phrase a helpful guide as he continues to reflect and act on human rights.[14]

To that I would merely add, one would also hope that whoever occupies the presidency will turn to this or a similar guide in pursuing the worthy goal of human rights.

[14] Kenneth W. Thompson, "New Reflections on Ethics and Foreign Policy: The Problem of Human Rights," *The Journal of Politics* 40, no. 4 (November 1978): 1010.

Human Rights and Soviet-American Relations: The Role of NGOs

Laurie S. Wiseberg
and
Harry M. Scoble

THIS essay explores the impact of political interest groups that profess to be committed to the defense of human rights on United States policy toward the Soviet Union. The human rights nongovernmental organizations (NGOs) under consideration are largely, although not exclusively, American-based organizations. While the impact of some international or European-based NGOs will, of necessity, form part of the analysis and while it is equally important to consider the interaction of the Soviet human rights movement with the American one, the focus is on organizations that have sought to affect directly the policies of the United States government.

A number of methodological problems are apparent. First, American-Soviet relations are affected by a multiplicity of United States-based private groups, only a portion of which direct their attention to official United States policy and only a tiny subset of which concern themselves with United States human rights policy. Many interest groups exist and take actions that impinge positively or negatively upon American-Soviet relations: the Yale Russian Chorus, in its annual good-neighbor tours to Russia; Armand Hammer, chairman of the Board of Occidental Petroleum, both in cutting a deal for a multibillion dollar, multiyear petrochemical/technology transfer contract with the U.S.S.R. and in funding a series of "Pugwash-type" conferences (on "Human Rights = Peace; Peace = Human Rights") which have now been institutionalized;[1]

[1] Armand Hammer thus far has funded three conferences on this theme: in Oslo (1978), Campobello (1979), and Warsaw (1980). After the meeting in

McGeorge Bundy, in closing out an illustrious career as chief executive officer of the Ford Foundation by presenting $400,000 to endow a United States Helsinki Watch Committee, preparatory to the Madrid November 1980 review conference;[2] the American Political Science Association, in participating in the International Political Science Association Congress in Moscow in the summer of 1979;[3] Bella Abzug's law firm, in representing American claimants in Russian courts; and Puerto Rican athletes who decided to participate in the 1980 Moscow Olympics, Afghanistan and President Carter notwithstanding.

In addition to these private groups, whose behavior may indirectly affect United States policy and thereby shape American-Soviet relations, a wide variety of political interest groups more directly seek to affect United States policy. Examples include: a large number of sophisticated pro-détente business corporations with their academic and foundations allies (e.g., the Committee on Economic Development, the Council on Foreign Relations, the Trilateral Commission, the Committee on East-West Trade); organizations speaking for all or part of the military-industrial complex in the United States (e.g., the American Security Council); nativist, patriotic, and Protestant fundamentalist organizations (e.g., the Moral Majority, Daughters of the American Revolution, Veterans of Foreign Wars); the peace and disarmament lobbies (e.g., the Quakers, SANE, Federation of American Scientists, and the Americans for SALT); American-based labor unions, especially the AFL-CIO under President George Meany; the quality media (e.g., *New York*

Poland, the decision was made to institutionalize the Armand Hammer Conference.

[2] In addition to this U.S. Helsinki Watch Committee, based in New York and concentrating most of its attention on the violation of human rights in Eastern Europe and the U.S.S.R., a second Helsinki monitoring group is based in Washington, D.C. The latter group, which is a coalition of U.S. domestic civil rights organizations, has never been able to attract any substantial foundation funding, although it is more in keeping with the Helsinki monitoring ideas of holding one's own government accountable for living up to the Helsinki Accords.

[3] The authors participated in that meeting and wrote a report following the IPSA Moscow Congress. Portions of it are excerpted in "The Moscow Congress of the International Political Science Association," *A Chronicle of Human Rights in the USSR*, no. 35 (July-September 1979), pp. 35-47.

Times, Washington Post, Los Angeles Times, and *Christian Science Monitor*); and ethnic-religious groups (e.g., Jewish organizations, the Polish American Congress, and the many organizations of Americans of East European descent, and organizations of Russian exiles or émigrés). (The last category of ethnic-religious groups does, of course, include many organizations genuinely committed to human rights advocacy.)

Given the exceedingly large universe of United States-based groups that directly or indirectly influence American-Soviet relations or influence United States policy with regard to the U.S.S.R., two things should be evident. First, we can focus only on the very small subset of private associations that seek to influence the human rights component of official United States policy toward Russia; secondly, it will be impossible to determine, with social scientific precision, any causal relations.

The problem of determining influence is compounded further by the fact that groups with no particular interest in United States-Soviet relations, in a direct sense, nonetheless may help shape those relations. To illustrate, a country-specific campaign, such as that directed toward Pinochet's Chile and the denial of labor union rights there, produced an official United States condemnation that made it exceedingly difficult to maintain official silence with regard to similar violations in the U.S.S.R. Indeed, most of the United States human rights legislation of the 1973–76 period evolved without any direct reference to or real concern for violations of human rights in the Soviet Union; the Jackson-Vanik Amendment of 1974 is the significant exception.

A second methodological problem is how to define the key concept of lobbying. We do not accept a strict-constructionist interpretation of this central political communication act.[4] Broadly speaking, by lobbying we mean the informed communication from private individuals and groups to public decision makers (not merely elected or appointed executive officials or legislators but also the judiciary), as well as the less well researched lobbying of interest groups in the public at large. Such communications need not con-

---

[4] That is, we think the federal court decisions since the 1946 so-called Federal Regulation of Lobbying Act (Title III of the 1946 Legislative Reorganization Act) and the 1976 legislation are so narrowly legalistic as to be useless from a social science point of view.

vey specific policy recommendations, but the information conveyed is always conceived as being policy-relevant. To illustrate, Amnesty International does no formal lobbying, narrowly construed; yet when Amnesty International testifies about psychiatric abuse in the Soviet Union, when it launches a public campaign for the ratification of international human rights covenants, or when it delivers its Annual Report to legislators and the Department of State, it is indeed lobbying. The intent of the information conveyed is to shape American policy in a pro-human rights direction. Additionally, it is important to recognize that the policy process is not described by a simplistic model of interest groups acting in a unidirectional fashion upon public decision makers. Frequently the initiatives originate within the governmental elite: the pressuring by the White House of both executive and legislative institutions, the logrolling by one legislator of his colleagues, and also the initiation of contacts by governmental institutions and officers themselves to stimulate "a public ground swell" in support of (or in opposition to) some pending policy decision.

The third methodological problem concerns how we are to define political interest groups committed to the promotion and protection of human rights. A major difficulty here is that ever since Carter raised high the banner of human rights and Brzezinski declared human rights to be "the historical inevitability of our times," the term has been co-opted by groups across a wide political spectrum and pursuing diverse special interests.[5] As Sandy Vogelgesang has noted, the term *human rights* "serves as many purposes as there are protagonists: from furthering actual respect for human rights to massaging the American ego, from advancing group causes and individual careers to rallying support for larger national objectives. It represents a selfless enterprise in behalf of victims of repression, as well as an unholy alliance of self-serving interests."[6] Rather than attempt the impossible task of setting objective criteria for defining a human rights NGO, we will discuss this below in the context of describing the universe of relevant actors.

[5] Brzezinski has used this phrase several times, most recently in his briefing to human rights NGOs concerning the forthcoming Madrid Conference, at the White House, July 29, 1980.

[6] Sandy Vogelgesang, *American Dream—Global Nightmare: The Dilemma of U.S. Human Rights Policy* (New York, 1980), p. 110.

The Universe of Political Interest Groups Concerned with Human Rights

In 1980 in the United States the universe of political interest groups professed to be concerned with the promotion and protection of human rights is large and still expanding. The Human Rights Internet identified and described over four hundred such organizations in its *1980 North American Human Rights Directory*,[7] and at least another twenty-five or thirty have emerged since the manuscript went to press. Perhaps as many as 80 percent of these organizations either did not exist before 1970 or—as with most professional associations, churches, and labor unions—did not consider themselves to be engaged in human rights work until the post-Vietnam era. That is, the development of public interest human rights constituencies is a relatively recent phenomenon in the United States. The notable exceptions to this will be discussed below, particularly the preexistence of universalistic human rights NGOs such as the International League for Human Rights and the development ten years earlier of Soviet Jewry groups.

During the past ten years there has been a virtual explosion in the human rights NGO community in the United States in West and East Europe, and also in the Third World.[8] The explosion has been coincidental with and in part stimulated by the Carter human rights policy. Yet historical perspective is needed. Some human rights NGOs date back to the turn of the century or even earlier. These include the London-based Anti-Slavery Society, whose origin lies in the movement to abolish slavery and the slave trade;[9] the

[7] Laurie S. Wiseberg and Harry M. Scoble, *1980 North American Human Rights Directory* (Garrett Park, Md., 1980).

[8] For an elaboration of this point, see Wiseberg and Scoble, "Recent Trends in the Expanding Universe of Non-governmental Organizations Dedicated to the Protection of Human Rights," *Denver Journal of International Law and Policy* 8 (Special Issue 1979): 627–58.

[9] Peter Archer, "Action by Unofficial Organizations on Human Rights," in Evan Luard, ed., *The International Protection of Human Rights* (New York, 1967), pp. 160–82. On pp. 162–64, Archer cites C. W. W. Greenidge, *Slavery* (London, 1958), "for a full history of the Society and its activities." Reports of the recent work of the Anti-Slavery Society are found in diverse issues of the *Human Rights Internet Newsletter*, hereinafter cited as *HRI*

International Federation for Human Rights, whose affiliate (and parent organization), the French League for Human Rights, was created in 1902 in response to the Dreyfus Affair;[10] and the International Committee of the Red Cross in Geneva, created in 1863 by Henry Dunant after the Battle of Solferino.[11] Other organizations were established during World War II. The New York-based International League for Human Rights emerged in 1942 as a result of the French Federation taking haven in the United States when the Nazis overran Europe.[12] Freedom House, also New York-based, was founded in 1941 "to defend America by aiding the Allies" and "to fight for freedom."[13] And in the immediate postwar period United Nations associations sprang up in many countries which, while concerned more broadly with providing support for the incipient world organization, often took seriously the human rights provisions of the charter.

A variety of other organizations also emerged in the 1950s and 1960s. The Geneva-based International Commission of Jurists, today one of the most widely respected of the universal human rights organizations dedicated to the promotion of the rule of law in all countries, was established in 1952, largely to follow up inquiries into abuses of justice in the Warsaw Pact countries in the context of the Cold War.[14] Amnesty International, recipient of the 1977

Newsletter, published since 1976 by the Human Rights Internet, Washington, D.C.

[10] Reports of the current activities of the International Federation for Human Rights are carried in the *HRI Newsletter*.

[11] One of the most comprehensive studies of the ICRC is David P. Forsythe, *Humanitarian Politics: The International Committee of the Red Cross* (Baltimore, 1977).

[12] Scoble and Wiseberg, "The International League for Human Rights: The Strategy and Tactics of a Human Rights NGO," *Georgia Journal of International and Comparative Law* 7 (1977): 289–313.

[13] Freedom House publishes an annual comparative survey of the status of civil and political rights around the world in its periodical *Freedom at Issue*. For an analysis of that survey, see Scoble and Wiseberg, "Problems of Comparative Research on Human Rights," a chapter in a forthcoming book edited by Professors Ved Nanda, J. Scarritt, and George Shepherd, Jr., Westview Press, 1980.

[14] See Scoble and Wiseberg, "Human Rights NGO's: Notes toward Com-

Nobel Peace Prize and today a worldwide movement on behalf of "prisoners-of-conscience" and against torture and the death penalty, was created in 1961, simply as a year-long campaign to secure amnesty for students in Salazar's Portugal who had been arrested for peacefully protesting.[15]

In addition to these universalistic NGOs, a wide variety of groups emerged with more specialized concerns. Until the mid-1970s they did not consider themselves part of the human rights movement or community, yet they now so identify themselves. We refer, for example, to the antiapartheid movement which was largely responsible for forcing the United Nations Human Rights Commission finally to assume some responsibility for investigating gross violations of human rights by establishing the ECOSOC 1503 procedure.[16] In the United States, the American Committee on Africa and the African American Institute, which launched the antiapartheid movement in this country, were created in 1953.[17] Most Latin American groups are of more recent origin, however; the Inter-American Association for Democracy and Freedom (IAADF) was created in 1966 in response to the United States invasion of the Dominican Republic. These, too, did not consider themselves human rights actors at the time of their creation: IAADF saw itself as providing support to Western-style democracies in the hemisphere under the threat of Communist advances, while the North American Congress on Latin America saw its role as opposition to United

---

parative Analysis," *Human Rights Journal* 9, no. 4 (1976): 611–44; Philip L. Ray, Jr., and J. Sherrod Taylor, "The Role of Non-governmental Organizations in Implementing Human Rights in Latin America," *Georgia Journal of International and Comparative Law*, 7 (1977): 477–506; and reports of the recent activities of the ICJ in issues of the *HRI Newsletter*.

[15] Scoble and Wiseberg, "Human Rights and Amnesty International," *Annals* of the American Academy of Political Science, vol. 413 (May 1974), pp. 11–26; and Egon Larsen, *A Flame in Barbed Wire: The Story of Amnesty International* (New York, 1979).

[16] On the antiapartheid movement, see George W. Shepherd, Jr., *Anti-apartheid: Transnational Conflict and Western Policy in the Liberation of South Africa* (Westport, Conn., 1977); on the U.N.'s adoption of 1503 procedures, see Warren Weinstein, "Africa's Approach to Human Rights at the United Nations," *Issue* 6, no. 4 (Winter 1976): 14–21.

[17] Shepherd, *Anti-apartheid*, and descriptions of these organizations in the *1980 North American Human Rights Directory*.

States imperialism. Today both are listed as groups concerned with human rights in the Internet's human rights directory.

Groups concerned with human rights violations in Eastern Europe are, in one sense, of fairly recent vintage and in another sense of some longevity. Following World War II and the Communist conquest of Eastern Europe, a large number of East European émigré organizations were created. In the United States these often took the form of ethnic-American organizations: the Polish American Congress, the Council of Free Czechoslovakia, the ELTA Information Service of the Supreme Committee for the Liberation of Lithuania or the Joint Baltic American National Committee. Similar groups (or branches of the same organizations) existed in Western Europe. While these organizations expressed concern for the violations of human rights in Eastern Europe and the U.S.S.R., they were concerned more with the overthrow of Communism than its humanization—in part because they did not believe in the possibility of its humanization. These organizations were, therefore, Cold Warriors par excellence. Thus, an irony developed: Those organizations which in the 1950s and 1960s were most articulate in denouncing the excesses of Communist totalitarianism were also prepared to embrace uncritically any and all dictatorial allies in the Third World, as long as they would espouse the anti-Communist creed; at the same time, they were insensitive to violations perpetrated against blacks or Indians in the United States itself. That their views on this coincided with those of white Anglo-Saxon Protestants is hardly an explanatory factor.

This situation began to change only in the late 1960s, in the context of the emergence of a human rights movement in the Soviet Union. The movement of dissent within the U.S.S.R. is normally taken to have begun on December 5 (Soviet Constitution Day), 1965, when some fifty people gathered in Pushkin Square, at the poets' monument, calling for freedom for Andrei Sinyavsky and Yuri Daniel—two writers accused of publishing their books abroad —and calling on the Soviet authorities to "Respect the Constitution, the Basic Document of the USSR."[18] These demonstrations were

[18] See, e.g., Pavel Litvinov, "The Human Rights Movement in the Soviet Union," in David Sidorsky, ed., *Essays in Human Rights: Contemporary Issues and Jewish Perspectives* (Philadelphia, 1979), pp. 114–25.

broken up, and Sinyavsky and Daniel received seven and five years, respectively, in labor camp. But their trial produced the "White Book" compiled by Yuri Galanskov and Aleksandr Ginzburg, who were subsequently arrested and tried in January 1968 for protesting the persecution of their colleagues. The sentencing of Ginzburg and Galanskov, followed in August 1968 by the Soviet invasion of Czechoslovakia, crystallized the movement of dissent.[19] On April 30, 1968, *A Chronicle of Current Events* was launched, marking the transformation of *samizdat* from its literary to its political form. While it was comprised of diverse factions—Alexander Solzhenitsyn arguing that Communism was an unremitting evil;[20] Roy Medvedev, a Marxist, believing that repression is the vestige of Stalinism and not the inherent characteristic of Soviet Communism;[21] and Andrei Sakharov in the middle, arguing that Western pressure and support for Soviet dissidents could return the U.S.S.R. to the path of socialist legality and humanity[22]—the movement for human rights (which experienced its greatest growth in the Soviet Union

[19] Ginzburg received 5 years, Galanskov received 7; but the latter died in prison in November 1972. See "The Death of Yury Galanskov," *A Chronicle of Human Rights in the USSR*, no. 1 (November 1972–March 1973), pp. 5–7.

[20] Aleksandr Solzhenitsyn, "Misconceptions about Russia Are a Threat to America," *Foreign Affairs* 58, no. 4 (Spring 1980): 797–834. The Cold War rhetoric of this article matches, if it doesn't surpass, anything written in the U.S. in the 1950s. Thus, in his third paragraph, Solzhenitsyn comments on the two mistakes of the West: "One is failure to understand the radical hostility of communism to mankind as a whole—the failure to realize that communism is irredeemable, that there exist no 'better' variants of communism; that it is incapable of growing 'kinder,' that it cannot survive as an ideology without using terror, and that, consequently, to coexist with communism on the same planet is impossible. Either it will spread, cancer-like, to destroy mankind, or else mankind will have to rid itself of communism (and even then face lengthy treatment for secondary tumors)." The second mistake "is to assume an indissoluble link between the universal disease of communism and the country where it first seized control—Russia" (p. 797).

[21] See, e.g., Roy A. Medvedev, *On Socialist Democracy* (New York, 1975).

[22] See, e.g., Andrei D. Sakharov, *Alarm and Hope* (New York, 1978) and *Sakharov Speaks*, ed. Harrison E. Salisbury (New York, 1974). Also, for a comparison of the three positions, see Harvey Fireside, "The Conceptualization of Dissent: Soviet Behavior in Comparative Perspective," *Universal Human Rights* 2, no. 1 (January-March 1980): 31–45.

in 1968) primarily took the form of "solidly based letters and documents, restrained in language and always public."[23] Thus, it differed markedly from the vitriolic rhetoric of the Cold War and tended to focus narrowly on the objective documents of cases of violations of human rights embodied both in the Soviet Constitution and in international standards. This pattern became even more pronounced after the signing of the Helsinki Final Act; Helsinki Monitoring groups emerged throughout Eastern Europe, invoking international instruments as well as socialist legality.[24]

By and large, these cues were picked up by the West, helping to dampen the ideology surrounding the question of human rights violations in Eastern Europe. While it was clearly not possible, in the context of continued East-West confrontation (even in the "spirit of détente"), to make human rights violations in Eastern Europe or the U.S.S.R. simply a humanitarian issue, the Cold War aspects were de-emphasized when groups with no ideological ax to grind became active in this arena. To illustrate, although the Soviet Union might consider Amnesty International as a tool of the CIA and Western imperialism,[25] more objective observers saw no Cold War motives behind the decision of Amnesty International's International Executive Committee to recognize the formation of an AI group in Moscow in September 1974. And even earlier (in June 1971) the Board of the International League for Human Rights took the unprecedented step of accepting the Moscow Human Rights Committee (formed in November 1970 by Andrei Sakharov, A. N. Tverdokhelebov, and V. N. Chalidze) as a League affiliate.[26] In like manner, to the extent that West European and North American support groups for East European Helsinki Monitors have tried to confine themselves to violations of the Helsinki accords or

[23] Litvinov, "Human Rights Movement," p. 119.

[24] The exception to this is clearly the Solzhenitsyn-style argument; but this contrasts markedly with much of the samizdat which has appeared in the West during the past years, much better typified by A Chronicle of Current Events, published by Amnesty International in London.

[25] The Soviet Union has frequently launched vicious attacks on Amnesty International and has so harassed the Moscow Amnesty group that it was largely inoperative by 1979.

[26] See Scoble and Wiseberg, "International League for Human Rights," pp. 307-8.

the United Nations Covenant on Human Rights (e.g., Khronika Press in the United States or Index on Censorship in the United Kingdom), the tone of the debate over violations of human rights in communist Europe has been very different from the 1950s. Yet strains of the 1950s have persisted and have often been strident.

One final group of NGOs requires discussion: those NGOs in the United States and elsewhere that have focused solely on one issue— the plight of Soviet Jewry. This NGO cluster also predates Carter, and in the United States its emergence dates back to 1963. American Jewish establishment organizations—such as, B'nai Brith, the American Jewish Committee, the Conference of Presidents of Major American Jewish Organizations, the National Jewish Community Relations Advisory Council—had, of course, an even longer-standing concern for Soviet Jewry, but they also had a much broader range of concerns (including support for Israel and opposition to anti-Semitism worldwide). In 1963 Soviet Jewry (single-issue) grass-roots organizations arose both as competitors and spurs to the Jewish establishment. According to Orbach, developments within the Soviet Union provided the stimulus, notably the Soviet reinstatement of capital punishment for economic offenses (over two hundred people were sentenced to death for such crimes in the U.S.S.R. between 1961 and 1964, a disproportionate number of whom were Jewish); the Soviet ban on the baking of matzoth for Passover; the decision of the Kiev Town Council to build a park and stadium on the site of Babi Yar; and the publication by the Ukranian Academy of Science in 1963 of *Judaism without Embellishment*, the blatantly anti-Semitic tract of Korneyevick Kichko.[27] Against this background, the Cleveland Committee on Soviet Anti-Semitism was founded in October 1963 and the first Conference on the Status of Soviet Jews was held. The Conference issued an "Appeal of Conscience for Jews in the Soviet Union," enumerating seven specific protests against the U.S.S.R. These grass-roots initiatives led, the following year, to the convening of the American Jewish Conference on Soviet Jewry—an establishment initiative, concerned that its prerogatives were being usurped. It took seven years until the National Conference on Soviet Jewry was established (in 1971) as a permanent organization; however, a substantial grass-roots move-

[27] The discussion which follows draws heavily on William W. Orbach, *The American Movement to Aid Soviet Jews* (Amherst, Mass., 1979).

ment on behalf of Soviet Jewry developed during the 1960s. The movement spawned a plethora of organizations, such as the Student Struggle for Soviet Jewry (1964) and the Bay Area Council on Soviet Jewry (1967); it gave rise to the Union of Councils on Soviet Jewry (1970) to coordinate the efforts of grass-roots organizations which felt that the establishment was not vigorous in its defense of Soviet Jewry; it helped stimulate such ecumenical efforts as the National Inter-Religious Task Force on Soviet Jewry (1972); and, in the late 1960s, it also manifested itself in the radical right-wing Jewish Defense League, although the JDL was strongly condemned and ostracized by the mainstream of the movement.

The movement for Jewish emigration which developed in the U.S.S.R.—particularly after the 1967 Middle East War, when official anti-Zionism and anti-Semitism caused many Russian Jews to reach the conclusion that their only hope was emigration—overlapped to some degree with the human rights movement in the U.S.S.R., but each movement remained distinct. The former had lost all hope in the possibility of change, while the latter was grounded in the hope that change was possible.[28] Similarly, while there was some overlap in those who supported Soviet Jewry and those who supported East European and Soviet dissidents, Soviet Jewry groups and Soviet Jews both were afraid that too close an identification with the cause of groups in the Soviet Union demanding nationalist autonomy (e.g., the Georgians, the Ukrainians, the Crimean Tatars) or other persecuted religious groups (e.g., the Baptists) would cause the Soviet authorities to halt Jewish emigration.[29] Thus, they often pursued strategies independently of each other.

This review suggests that a large number of organizations, both

[28] Joshua Rubenstein, *Soviet Dissidents: Their Struggle for Human Rights* (Boston, 1980), especially chap. 5, "Zionists and Democrats."

[29] Ibid. When the authors visited the Soviet Union in the summer of 1979 and talked with both dissidents and refuseniks (as well as with a variety of groups in the U.S. before the Moscow visit), it was clear that this tension continued. Yet many Russian Jews were involved in the Soviet human rights movement and many dissidents supported the Jews' right to emigration. Most people agreed, however, that a prime reason why the Soviets were so harsh in their sentencing of Anatoly Scharansky in July 1978 was that he formed a bridge between the two movements. And, consequently, many Soviet Jewry groups discouraged Soviet Jews from too close an association with other nationalists, persecuted religious minorities, or dissidents.

in the United States and abroad, were concerned with the protection of human rights in the early 1970s. Nonetheless, there has been a dramatic expansion in the human rights universe over the past ten years, and there are some distinctive features of NGO activity that differentiate it from the earlier period, particularly in the United States context.

The Development and Characteristics of the NGO Universe

In examining the growth of NGO human rights activity during the past several years, some of the most significant features have been: the increased visibility, scope of activity, and sophistication of universal human rights groups; the increased involvement of churches in human rights work, often (as with the National Council of Churches in the United States) establishing special human rights offices or committees;[30] the heightened sensitivity and involvement of professional associations in human rights work, especially scientific[31] and lawyers,[32] associations (manifested either in the estab-

---

[30] On the international level, Protestant involvement has been particularly evident since the Nairobi Assembly of the World Council of Churches in 1975, when the WCC dedicated itself to the search for "a just, participatory, and sustainable society," a conceptualization which in part grew out of a consultation on "Human Rights and Christian Responsibility" which it had organized the previous year. Catholic commitment is associated with Vatican I and Vatican II, which led to the creation of the Pontifical Commission of Justice and Peace and to national Justice and Peace commissions in many countries. The role of the churches in Latin America's human rights struggles has already received considerable attention; see, e.g., Brian H. Smith, S.J., "Churches and Human Rights in Latin America: Recent Trends in the Sub-continent," *Journal of Interamerican Studies and World Affairs* 21, no. 1 (February 1979): 89–127.

[31] In addition to the human rights responsibilities assumed by the NAS and the AAAS noted below, we have also seen the creation of such specifically focused organizations as Scientists for Orlov and Scharansky (SOS): the Medical Capacity Committee of Amnesty International-USA; and the Committee to Examine the Abuse of Psychiatry for Political Purposes, established by the World Psychiatric Association after its 1977 Honolulu Congress.

[32] The American legal profession traditionally has been not only conservative but hostile toward efforts to impose international human rights standards on the U.S.—demonstrated most notoriously in the American Bar Association

lishment of new organizations—such as the International Human Rights Law Group or the Lawyers Committee for International Human Rights—or the assumption by an established organization of specific human rights functions, as with the creation of the Clearinghouse on Science and Human Rights by the American Association for the Advancement of Science); the growth of support groups or groups with a special geographic focus (as with the Washington Office on Latin America or Transafrica), often rising and falling in the contexts of specific crises in Iran, Nicaragua, Bolivia, Taiwan, or the U.S.S.R.;[33] the development of groups with special interests (religious freedom,[34] the rights of indigenous peoples,[35] the rights of migrant workers or refugees);[36] the emergence of a large number

---

support of the Bricker Amendment battle of the 1950s. In recent years, however, the ABA has openly come out in support of the ratification of the major international human rights instruments. Furthermore, a large number of lawyers' groups, both in the U.S. and worldwide, have become active in the human rights struggle. Thus, there are now seven U.S. city bar associations that have international human rights committees, and at least a half dozen new lawyers' groups have arisen in the U.S. with a specific international human rights concern. Internationally, there is not only the International Commission of Jurists (with its recently created Center for the Independence of Judges and Lawyers) and its Marxist counterpart, the International Association of Democratic Lawyers, but also the Emergency Committee of the International Bar Association, the International Association of Young Lawyers, International Union of Lawyers, the Human Rights Committee of the Pan-African Union of Lawyers (created in Dakar in the summer of 1980), and the Centre for Human Rights of the Paris Bar, to name a few.

[33] While the Washington Office on Latin America, Transafrica, the Washington Office on Africa, and the Council on Hemispheric Affairs have a broad regional sweep and have become "established" human rights organizations, many support committees—such as the multiplicity of groups which existed in the U.S. during the Iranian and Nicaraguan crisis—are ad hoc responses to the crisis and dissolve when the crisis ends. A fairly comprehensive listing of Soviet Jewry groups in the U.S. has been compiled by Sheldon Benjamin, *Compendium on Soviet Dissent*, 1, *Soviet Jewish Studies, a Guide to Periodical Resources* (Cincinnati, 1979), pp. 25–26.

[34] For example, Freedom of Faith (New York), Appeal of Conscience Foundation (New York), Council on Religion and International Affairs (New York).

[35] For example, Cultural Survival (USA), Survival International (UK), International Work Group for Indigenous Affairs (Denmark).

[36] For example, Alien Rights Law Group (US) or Action Group on Immigration and Nationality (UK).

of groups concerned with the enforcement of international human rights standards, especially the Helsinki Final Act (both in Eastern Europe and in the West to support these Helsinki monitors);[37] the refocusing of many American-ethnic groups, particularly those concerned with Eastern Europe, on more explicitly human rights concerns; the emergence of centers for both research and teaching on human rights;[38] and, in the United States, an increased orientation of NGOs concerned with the defense of human rights to Congress, the Executive, and even the judiciary. An elaboration on this last point is necessary.

It is important to recall that in the years immediately following World War II, despite the descent of the Iron Curtain and the onset of the Cold War, the United States government—particularly under the dynamic leadership of Eleanor Roosevelt, who served as chairman of the United Nations Committee which drafted the Universal Declaration of Human Rights[39]—was in the forefront of attempts to codify international human rights standards. Then, in 1952, with the infamous compromise negotiated by Secretary of State John Foster Dulles on the Bricker Amendment,[40] all possi-

[37] Rubenstein, *Soviet Dissidents*, chap. 7, "The Helsinki Watch Groups" on the Soviet Helsinki monitoring groups; Commission on Security and Cooperation in Europe, *Profiles: The Helsinki Monitors* (Washington, D.C., Revised December 10, 1979) contains sketches of the individuals in many of these groups; *The Right to Know, the Right to Act*, also compiled by CSEC (May 1978) contains material on the Charter 77 Movement in Czechoslovakia, the dissident movement in Poland, and the Helsinki monitors in Rumania, in addition to the U.S.S.R.; and numerous hearings and documents of CSCE. Perhaps the best review of the day-to-day activities of organizations in Western Europe to support the East European dissidents is the *Help and Action Newsletter*, published by the French Help and Action Coordination Committee since 1977.

[38] In the U.S., for example, we have seen the development of the Center for the Study of Human Rights at Columbia University and the Urban Morgan Institute for Human Rights in Cincinnati; and also the emergence of the journal *Universal Human Rights*, based at the University of Maryland.

[39] See, e.g., A. Glenn Mower, Jr., *The United States, the United Nations and Human Rights: The Eleanor Roosevelt and Jimmy Carter Eras* (Westport, Conn., 1979).

[40] Thomas Buergenthal and Judith V. Torney, *International Human Rights and International Education* (Washington, D.C., 1976), chap. 5, "The United States and International Human Rights," especially pp. 87-91.

bility disappeared of Senate ratification of the Genocide Convention (signed by President Truman in 1949 and pending before the Senate ever since); the same held true for all other international human rights instruments.[41] While this did not mean that the United States executive would cease to be concerned about United Nations declarations or treaties on human rights drafted by the United Nations or other international organizations, the United States abdicated its leadership in those arenas. Furthermore, those concerned with the enforcement of international human rights standards, whether in the United States or abroad, expected little from Congress. Thus, universalistic human rights NGOs and others committed to the promotion and protection of human rights (e.g., the Women's Division of the Board of Global Ministries of the United Methodist Church or the Commission to Study the Organization of Peace), directed almost all of their attention to Turtle Bay or to public education, not to lobbying on the Hill.[42] And until the very end of the 1960s, the United Nations itself was almost totally absorbed in drafting international human rights standards, not with enforcing them.

In Western Europe, the twenty-fifth anniversary of the Universal Declaration of Human Rights in 1973 produced a considerable mobilization of human rights NGOs and political interest groups around the human rights issue. In Britain, for example, the Human Rights Network—a loose grouping of more than fifty British organizations concerned with human rights—emerged from that event to carry on projects initiated for the anniversary.[43] The same was not the case in the United States, where the event passed largely

---

[41] To this date the U.S. has not yet ratified the Genocide Convention, the United Nations Covenants or the Optional Protocol, the American Convention on Human Rights, and most other international agreements. For a recent discussion of the problem, see David Weissbrodt, "United States Ratification of the Human Rights Covenants," *Minnesota Law Review* 63, no. 1 (November 1978): 35–78.

[42] Peggy Billings, *Paradox and Promise in Human Rights* (New York, 1979), p. 6, notes the interest of the Methodist Church. The Commission was founded in 1939 as a research body to consider the reorganization or replacement of the League of Nations. For the past four decades, it has made the international promotion and protection of human rights one of its primary concerns.

[43] *HRI Newsletter* 3, no. 1 (September 1977): 3.

unnoticed—perhaps because attention was deflected by the Vietnam War, the Ellsberg trial, Watergate, and the overthrow of Allende, all of which occurred during that eventful year. Yet 1973 is taken as the benchmark year marking the beginning of a reawakened American concern for human rights. And one of two events is considered the milestone. For William Goodfellow, the historic Cambodia bombing amendment of July 1973—prohibiting further direct United States military involvement in Indochina—marks the start of "the liberal interregnum" in American foreign policy,[44] an interregnum whose end has already been signaled by the Iranian crisis and the United States reaction to the Soviet invasion of Afghanistan. For others, it is the hearings which Congressman Donald Fraser initiated the following month, as chairman of the House Subcommittee on International Organizations and Movements: the first systematic hearings on United States foreign policy and human rights across a broad sweep of countries and cases.[45]

Starting in 1973 and under the trauma of Chile, the American left began to identify human rights as their issue and began to recognize Congress as a significant mechanism for influencing the status of human rights in countries that were United States allies and the recipients of American military or economic assistance. Yet the milestone hearings were not the result of lobbying by the antiwar movement, by the old established human rights NGOs, or even by the Soviet Jewry groups, which at that time were already being drawn into the struggle over the Jackson-Vanik Amendment. Fraser, a Democrat from Minnesota, had been awakened to human rights during the Bangladesh crisis of 1971 and had, undoubtedly, also been affected by the discovery of tiger cages on Con Son Island by Tom Harkin (then a House staff member) and others a year earlier. Fraser was further sensitized to human rights by his participation in the Inter-Parliamentary Union, and in late 1972 he was part of

[44] William Goodfellow, "Human Rights as a Foreign Policy Tool: A Preliminary Assessment," paper presented at the 1980 annual meeting of the American Political Science Association, Washington, D.C., August 29, 1980.

[45] *International Protection of Human Rights: The Work of International Organizations and the Role of U.S. Foreign Policy*, Hearings before the Subcommittee on International Organizations and Movements of the Committee on Foreign Affairs, House of Representatives, 93d Cong., 1st sess. (Washington, D.C., 1974).

a study mission to the U.S.S.R. which, in the context of "tension and détente," examined the question of Soviet Jewry.[46]

The idea of using his Subcommittee to spotlight human rights violations throughout the world, and the role the United States might play in ameliorating the situation, was his own.[47] From the outset, Fraser was to be assisted by the extremely able staffer John Salzberg,[48] who was largely responsible for putting together Fraser's 1973 and subsequent hearings. In doing this, Salzberg was able to draw on his experience from 1971 to 1973 serving as executive secretary of the American Association for the International Commission of Jurists and representing the Geneva-based ICJ at U.N. headquarters in New York, then also the site of the United Nations Division of Human Rights.[49] He was also familiar with the professors of international law who dominated the academic field of human rights in the mid-1970s (Salzberg's 1973 doctorate from New York University focused on the role of the United Nations Subcommission on human rights).[50] Yet if both the human rights activists clustered around Turtle Bay and prestigious professors of international law were prepared to testify and provide evidence of

---

[46] Based on discussions with a staff member of the Congressman.

[47] Ibid. Confirmed by talks with many human rights activists.

[48] John Salzberg, who was at the time completing a Ph.D. at New York University, approached Fraser about a position when he heard of the congressman's interest in human rights; they also shared a common concern for Bangladesh. Fraser first took Salzberg onto his personal staff and, only six months later, Salzberg became part of the staff of the Committee of Foreign Affairs of the House although he had been doing committee work from the start.

[49] In 1976 the U.N. Division of Human Rights was moved from U.N. Headquarters in New York to Geneva, a move interpreted by many observers as an attempt by States to undercut the role of the U.N. Commission on Human Rights, and especially its Subcommission, in human rights protection. But until the late 1970s, meetings of the human rights bodies alternated each year between New York and Geneva.

[50] John P. Salzberg, "United Nations Sub-committee on Prevention of Discrimination and Protection of Minorities: A Functional Analysis of an Independent Expert Body Promoting Human Rights," Ph.D. diss., New York University, 1973. Salzberg's Master's thesis, also from NYU (in 1966) was "Human Rights Petition by Individuals Before the United Nations: Past and Prospective."

the violations throughout the world, neither group was oriented to the legislative arena.

The recommendations contained in the 1974 Report of the Subcommittee for United States action in the field of human rights and the early human rights legislation of 1973 and 1974 were primarily the result of independent Congressional initiatives.[51] (By *early* human rights legislation, we are referring to its congressional expression in the Foreign Assistance Act of 1973: The president should deny any economic or military assistance to the government of any foreign country "which practices the internment or imprisonment of that country's citizens for political purposes"; and section 502B of the Foreign Assistance Act of 1974, again stating that "except in extraordinary circumstances, the President shall substantially reduce or terminate security assistance to any government which engages in a consistent pattern of gross violations of internationally recognized human rights.")[52] Yet the Harkin Amendment of 1975—which was no longer merely a sense of Congress but "tied the hands of the Administration" by prohibiting the granting of economic assistance to gross violators unless it could be shown that such assistance was of "direct benefit" to "needy people"— was different. This amendment was largely drafted by two activists of the emerging anti-imperialist human rights community: Joseph Eldridge, a Methodist minister who had spent several years in Chile and who, in 1974, became director of a newly established Washington Office on Latin America; and Edward Snyder, a Yale Law School graduate from the class of 1951 and executive secretary of the Friends Committee on National Legislation, who was to serve as advisor to the new generation of human rights activists.[53]

---

[51] Human Rights and the World Community: A Call For U.S. Leadership, Report of the Subcommittee on International Organizations and Movements of the House Committee on Foreign Affairs, 93d Cong., 2d sess., 1974 (Washington, D.C., 1974).

[52] For a detailed treatment of this legislation, see David Weissbrodt, "Human Rights Legislation and United States Foreign Policy," *Georgia Journal of International and Comparative Law* 7 (1977): 231–87.

[53] Weissbrodt, in the article cited immediately above, is in error when he states that "nongovernmental organizations generally concerned with human rights devoted no significant attention to Congress during the critical

These activists were primarily drawn from the antiwar movement and from the civil rights movement before that.[54] But they eventually embraced people active in the antiapartheid movement; Latin Americanists and others concerned with the impact of United States policy in the hemisphere; as well as those who focused on repression in the Philippines, in Korea, and in other Asian countries where the dictatorial regimes were considered our staunch anti-Communist allies. If one examines the list of organizations which are members of the Coalition for a New Foreign and Military Policy, or the larger number of groups which participate in the Coalition's Human Rights Working Group (founded in 1976), there is strong participation of the progressive elements of Protestant churches and the Catholic Church as well as some involvement of the independent trade unions.[55] It was, therefore, perhaps a "natural" alliance that was forged between the left of the human rights community and those Congressmen who had also been active in the anti-Indochina war movement: Senators Hatfield, Oregon; Abourezk and McGovern, South Dakota; Kennedy, Massachusetts; and Cranston, California; and Representatives Fraser, Minnesota; Harkin, Iowa; Harrington, Massachusetts; and Solarz, New York. And it

---

formative period 1973 through 1975" and implies that they played no role in the passage of the Harkin Amendment. Human rights activists did become concerned when it was clear that the 1973 and 1974 "senses of Congress" were totally ineffectual, and they were particularly concerned by the enormous amounts of economic assistance still being funneled to Chile in 1975. Snyder and Eldridge drafted the legislation that was to become known as the Harkin Amendment and approached a number of Congressmen in search of a sponsor. Fraser, then involved in trying once again to restrict military assistance, was unwilling to take up a new issue. Nor did they have success with other congressmen they lobbied. Interestingly, neither Eldridge nor Snyder visited Harkin, and when they dropped a copy of their draft legislation off in his office, his key Administrative Assistant was absent. Yet, Harkin read the draft, liked it, and took it on himself.

[54] We refer, for example, to Jacqui Chagnon of Clergy and Laity Concerned, Brewster Rhodes of the Coalition for a New Foreign and Military Policy, Bruce Cameron of Americans for Democratic Action, Bill Goodfellow of the Center for International Policy, and Patricia Rengel formerly of the U.S. Catholic Conference and now with Amnesty International-USA.

[55] Scoble and Wiseberg, "The Human Rights Lobby in Washington," paper presented at the annual meeting of the American Political Science Association, New York, September 2, 1978.

was this alliance that reasserted the importance of Congress as an arena for curtailing United States government support to dictatorial, repressive, and corrupt regimes.

It is important to stress that this anti-imperialist-leaning segment of the human rights community had little direct interest in events internal to the Soviet Union or Eastern Europe. While it is hazardous to generalize across so wide a range of organizations and individuals—some of whom would identify themselves as Marxists, but many of whom would be traditional liberals—most could be characterized as opposing United States intervention in the Third World in the manner so typical of United States foreign policy from the 1950s to the 1970s. The Coalition for a New Foreign and Military Policy was concerned with United States–Soviet relations, but its concern was for dampening down the Cold War, halting the arms race, transferring funds from military procurement or R & D to meeting social domestic needs—not for supporting the human rights movement in the U.S.S.R. and Eastern Europe.

There seems, indeed, to have been an unwritten agreement among Coalition members not to deal with the issue of human rights in Communist Europe. This avoidance flowed logically from two sources. First, the Coalition dealt with human rights violations in areas in which those violations could be directly linked to United States foreign policy, especially military and economic assistance to the repressive regimes; this did not hold for violations in the U.S.S.R. and Eastern Europe. Second, to activate United States concern for East European repression might rekindle the Cold War, provide impetus to the arms race, and thereby strengthen the voices of the military-industrial-complex or of others who had a stake in undermining détente and the ongoing SALT negotiations. Therefore, Helsinki was applauded for its confidence-building measures and the moves to reduce arms and tension, not for Basket III's human rights provisions. In like manner, the Coalition did not attempt to open up discussion on the human rights violations of the Vietnamese government or the horrors that subsequently began to be told about Pol Pot's Cambodia.[56]

[56] The tendency of the Coalition to avoid the Vietnam-Cambodia human rights issue can be attributed in part to the feeling among many Coalition members that the U.S. must bear responsibility for that carnage. It is an issue which has, indeed, deeply split those who had been active in the peace

Meanwhile, another faction in Congress and another segment of the human rights community was concerned with the human rights violations in Eastern Europe and the U.S.S.R. It, too, was concerned with tying the hands of the administration, but from a very different ideological perspective. We are referring here to such Senators as "Scoop" Jackson (Washington), Hubert Humphrey (Minnesota), Jacob Javits (New York), and Abraham Ribicoff (Connecticut); to a coterie of perhaps a dozen or more big-city congressmen with significant Jewish populations in their constituencies; and to the Jewish establishment and Soviet Jewry organizations. It is commonly thought that Senator Jackson was responding to pressure initiated by "the American Jewish lobby," but in point of fact the Jackson-Vanik Amendment for which Jackson fought between 1972 and 1974 was the product of the Senator's own values—getting tough and staying tough on the Soviets—and his own motivation—his desire to run as the Democratic nominee for president in 1976.[57] Louis Rosenblum, chairman of the Union of Councils for Soviet Jewry, is credited with having first suggested that freedom of emigration be linked to trade concessions that the United States was considering granting to the Soviet Union, and he (together with Nathan Lewin of the National Center for Jewish Policy Studies) drew up legislation on this in 1971. However, the proposed amendment to the Export Administration Act of 1969 found no sponsor, and there was no personal contact between them and Jackson or his staff.

Paula Stern notes that when Jackson introduced his famous amendment on October 4, 1972, the idea of linking trade and emigration had been circulated for about six months to a few Senate offices by the more militant activists in the Jewish community. But many of the established well-known Jewish groups and leaders were

---

movement: Joan Baez leads a faction which demands that Americans should speak out and provide humanitarian assistance to refugees, while the others imply that the U.S. should remain silent because it has done enough harm, or that it should first fulfill its promises to provide economic assistance to Vietnam. Another highly divisive issue—and one which the Coalition has also failed to address—is the question of human rights violations in the territories occupied by Israel.

[57] Paula Stern, *Water's Edge: Domestic Politics and the Making of American Foreign Policy* (Westport, Conn., 1979).

opposed to the manipulation of Soviet-American trade for the sake of Soviet Jews. Thus, the Jackson Amendment "was more an initiative than a response. On his own, Senator Jackson embraced the motion of linking trade and emigration even before the Jewish lobby did. This is an important distinction as it contradicts strongly held myths about lobbyists in general and the 'Jewish lobby' in particular.... [That is,] there is an important distinction between a politician appealing to an interest group and a politician being pushed by a group to act, although a good politician admittedly anticipates constituents' desires."[58] This notwithstanding, over the next two years Jackson was able to rally both grass-roots and established Jewish groups behind him, and these groups subsequently lobbied on his behalf. He also was successful in bringing the AFL-CIO (especially George Meany, at least temporarily) into his pre-Convention coalition. Jewish groups alone were insufficient to cause "hundreds of Congressmen and three-quarters of the Senate" to cosponsor the Jackson Amendment; in its final version, Jackson's amendment—like a party platform—offered something for everybody and thus was supported by a wide spectrum of opinion. It included those genuinely concerned with the right of Soviet Jews to emigrate, people opposed to the limitation of strategic arms (SALT), those opposed to the liberalization of trade restrictions with the Soviet Union and Communist-bloc nations, and those who were pro-Israel and anti-Arab. Meanwhile, there is no evidence that the anti-imperialist human rights coalition took any genuine interest in, much less made any active opposition to, the Jackson-Vanik Amendment.

Midway between the anti-imperialist coalition and the Soviet Jewry/Eastern Europe–leaning coalition stood the more universalistic human rights NGOs: groups such as Amnesty International, USA, the American Association for the International Commission of Jurists, and the International League for Human Rights. While in the early 1970s they had begun to broaden their scope to include a concern for Congress as well as the United Nations, the leadership of these organizations was always more reserved and more cautious than "left" or "right." In particular, it was sensitive to the dangers of becoming too closely identified with one cause and with partisan

[58] Ibid., p. 21.

politics. Perhaps protective of its turf as well as its integrity, this leadership maintained some distance from both camps.[59] This was clearly demonstrated in the abortive 1977 attempt to build a "National Leadership Conference" of human rights NGOs to be discussed later.

The Impact of Carter on the NGOs and the Impact of the NGOs on Carter

Most observers think that the Carter administration's human rights policy, if not in fact "accidental," at least was certainly not thought out in advance—apart from any other collective or private interests being served.[60] Nevertheless, it did inspire enthusiasm among preexisting human rights organizations and also lent legitimacy to them and to others about to be formed. In the same vein, the Carter policy made it possible to talk seriously about human rights issues in intergovernmental arenas.

It should be remembered that in 1975 the signing of the Helsinki Final Act stimulated interest and group formation around human rights issues in both East and West Europe. In addition, in the year after Helsinki (1976) the two international covenants codifying the Universal Declaration of Human Rights gained the requisite number of ratifications to go into effect, as did the Optional Protocol to the United Nations Covenant on Civil and Political Rights. In this context the Carter administration's stance on human rights was part of a world trend, perhaps reaching its apex in the award of the Nobel Peace Prize to Amnesty International in December 1977. Nonetheless, the new attention to human rights provided neither a unification of groups in the domestic and international constituencies, an overarching ideology, nor a guiding strategy for goal-achievement.

---

[59] Thus, for example, none of the established universal human rights NGOs wanted to be closely associated with the effort of Ted Jacqueney and others to establish "Democracy International" in 1979 (perceived as being too right-wing); and while they cooperate with it, they will not be too closely associated with the Coalition for a New Foreign Policy (perceived as being too left-wing).

[60] Elizabeth Drew, "A Reporter at Large—Human Rights," *New Yorker*, July 18, 1977, pp. 36–62.

The Role of the NGOs

The continued fragmentation of the human rights community, the persisting ideological conflicts, and the lack of agreement on strategy or tactics are all illustrated by the failure of the amateurish attempt to create a "National Leadership Conference" on human rights in the United States that would embrace not only both extremes of the international human rights lobbies but also the domestic civil rights organizations. This occurred in October 1977, when a call was publicized at the initiative of Bayard Rustin—president of the A. Philip Randolph Institute, and regarded by many as one of the key strategists of the civil rights movement—to assemble the organizational components of a potential national leadership conference on international human rights, based on the model of the 1950s–1960s National Leadership Conference on Civil Rights. (The latter umbrella organization had brought together some 125 domestic organizations into an effective steering committee and lobbying coalition.) Although funded by the Ford Foundation and a call to *all* organizations concerned with effecting a more humane world and domestic order, the meeting was clearly dominated by the AFL-CIO, Jewish establishment organizations, East European émigré groups, and long-standing human rights organizations noted for a Cold War bias. In certain respects the meeting was dominated by the New York "Old Boy network"; the universalistic human rights NGOs (such as the International League for Human Rights), however, maintained a circumspect distance and subsequently dissociated themselves completely from this effort. Meanwhile, members of the Human Rights Working Group of the Coalition for a New Foreign and Military Policy (with the exception of Americans for Democratic Action) were invited only at the eleventh hour, after many protests of deliberate exclusion reached the Ford Foundation funders. (Of particular significance is the fact that the director of the Human Rights Office of the National Council of Churches, the American Friends Service Committee, and the Mennonites were all invited belatedly, a few days before the convocation.) It is possible, perhaps, that Bayard Rustin was so ill-informed about internationally focused human rights organizations that he was oblivious to the existence of the Human Rights Working Group, the churches, and other actors on the left. This does not, however explain the absence of any representatives of the American Indian movement and the Chicano communities or the fact that women, youth, and minorities were severely underrepresented on the panels.[61]

Moreover, suspicions that the conference was an attempt by the right to capture control of the human rights issue were reinforced: Speaker after speaker rose to condemn the violations of human rights in Eastern Europe, while glossing lightly over the violations of right-wing dictatorships. The Conference Draft Statement prepared by the organizers did little to bring unity to the ranks. In its emphasis on a Western conceptualization of civil and political rights over social, economic, and cultural ones, it served rather to widen the chasm between differing ideological perspectives. Given this tension, it is not hard to understand why Amnesty International, the International Commission of Jurists, as well as the International League backed away from all suggestions to institutionalize such a leadership conference. One might also assume that these seasoned activists must have felt some resentment toward a Johnny-come-lately to the international human rights struggle, with aspirations for a leading strategizing role.

Other forums in which diverse human rights NGOs were brought together revealed a similar inability to unify or produce an ideology or strategy. For example, in February 1978 the newly elevated Bureau of Human Rights and Humanitarian Affairs held its first NGO Conference, both to brief and to receive policy-relevant suggestions from some five hundred representatives of the human rights community. Yet when given a chance to voice their concerns to policymakers, few of the participants could see beyond their own particular interests or could generalize their concerns. Thus, the litany intoned was: What is the United States doing to achieve the independence of "Cossackstan"? To make it possible for Jews to emigrate from the Soviet Union? To effect a parole-visa program for Chileans? To terminate our assistance to Park in Korea? Each of these questions has internal validity. But, if there is to be a coalitional human rights movement, then there must be some ordering of priorities, some agreement on strategy if not a consensus of tactics. Such cohesion has been achieved only within limited ranges of the total spectrum of human rights groups: within the Human Rights Working Group of the Coalition, the ecumenical church

---

[61] The authors participated in this meeting, and this interpretation is based both on their observations and discussions with others.

efforts occasioned by repression in Latin America, or the movement to aid Soviet Jewry.[62]

As a consequence, it is possible to generalize only in a limited way about the impact of the Carter administration on these human rights groups or about their effect on its policies. In some real ways Carter was confronted with the human rights issue and its implicit threat to fracture even further the decaying Democratic presidential coalition, just as John Kennedy had been faced with similar threats from the domestic civil rights movement. However, if Kennedy was relatively successful in capturing, containing, and exploiting the civil rights issue, Carter bungled it.[63] Vogelgesang suggests that after strongly condemning Ford's refusal to meet the exiled Solzhenitsyn, Carter "had little choice but to respond promptly and publicly" to a letter from Sakharov that arrived eight days after his inauguration and to meet with Bukovsky early that year.[64] By doing this, Carter escalated the rhetoric of human rights to its apogee, even before the administration had appraised either its priorities or the practical steps that might be taken.

Thus, by March of 1977, when Carter made a series of proposals and personal commitments on human rights in his United Nations address—including the submission of four international human rights conventions to the United States Senate, for the speedy rati-

[62] From a sociological point of view, a movement must meet three criteria: (1) there must be an articulated ideology that the movement ascribes to; (2) there must be two or more specifically organized forms directed toward the achievement of one or more of the policy goals explicit in that ideology; and (3) there must be people who do not consider themselves members of any organization who nonetheless are committed to the implementation of that ideology. Thus, one may talk of *a number* of human rights movements in the U.S., but not of *one* movement comparable to the peace movement of the 1960s, the civil rights movement of the 1950s and 1960s, the labor movement of the 1930s, the woman's suffrage movement of the 19th century, or the abolitionist movement in American politics.

[63] Bruce Miroff, *Pragmatic Illusions: The Presidential Politics of John F. Kennedy* (New York, 1976). See especially chap. 6, " 'Listen, Mr. Kennedy': The Civil Rights Struggle"; and Harry M. Scoble, "Interdisciplinary Perspectives on Poverty: The View from Political Science," in Alvin Magid and Thomas Weaver, eds., *Perspectives on Poverty* (San Francisco, 1970), chap. 6.

[64] Vogelsang, *American Dream*, pp. 103–4.

fication of which he promised to work—he raised unrealistic expectations that he has been unwilling or unable to fulfill. His rhetoric frightened European allies, who were concerned about eroding the understanding emerging from discussion on Cooperation and Security in Europe (CSCE); his administration consistently opposed the attempts of the left to terminate or reduce assistance to right-wing dictatorships; its dramaturgy scared that portion of the American left concerned with détente and disarmament and also frightened business-as-usual businessmen seeking trade with the U.S.S.R.; and the universal human rights NGOs have become disillusioned with the administration's placing the covenants on a back burner for the single major achievement of the Panama Canal Treaties. Thus, while all members of the human rights community have been pleased by the Carter administration's promotion of human rights in the abstract, no one of them has been satsified with his implementation effort on the issue of their particular concern. Needless to say, in the context of the 1980 election the Carter administration has also managed to alienate many sectors of American society that have no interest in human rights.

Since the human rights lobbies are so fragmented, there has been no consistent and singular impact of the NGOs on Carter and the administration, except on a few marginal issues upon which there has been across-the-board agreement. For example, all groups have agreed that embassies should be required to report on human rights conditions in the host countries; all groups have wanted to see improvement in the quality of the 502B country status reports; all groups have agreed that the Bureau of Human Rights should gain institutionalization, legitimacy, and influence. But on any specific human rights issue—such as continuing scientific exchanges with the Soviet Union, terminating economic assistance to the Philippines, raising the issue of human rights violations in the People's Republic of China, opposing the investment of multinational corporations in South Africa, providing economic assistance to the Sandinista regime in Nicaragua—there is little agreement. What one finds is a replication of the situation evident with respect to much of United States foreign policy: two small and vehemently opposed minorities, with most of the other human rights groups indifferent. And, again, the totality of human rights organizations is but a small slice of all those engaged in American foreign policy.

Human Rights NGOs and Soviet-American Relations

Soviet-American relations in the near past and for the 1980s center on: preventing a nuclear war; controlling the proliferation of nuclear technology; avoiding an arms race; maintaining access to, if not control over, vital raw materials, particularly energy supplies; and preserving each superpower's self-proclaimed sphere of influence from challenges from each other or from Third World upstarts or dissenting allies. The question of whether United States concern for human rights has influenced any of the above issues has been hotly debated both inside and outside the country.

Within the United States, the right has repeatedly raised the claim that an official human rights policy lost both Iran and Nicaragua, echoing the charges of the McCarthyite 1950s, that the Democrats lost China. At the other extreme, the peace and disarmament lobbies have publicized their fears that excessive concern about Soviet violations of the human rights of dissidents and ethnic minorities is undercutting détente and especially SALT II; for these lobbies, avoidance of nuclear holocaust takes precedence over all else. Meanwhile, American businessmen unwilling to criticize themselves have termed human rights a policy of "exporting morality" which sacrifices export markets and trade.

In each of these instances it is difficult, if not impossible, to demonstrate a linkage between the activities of human rights NGOs and Carter's policy and between Carter's policy and the alleged outcome. With respect to Iran, Carter supported the shah until his downfall, and there is no evidence to suggest that human rights groups working to get the United States to dissociate itself from the shah had any significant impact. Similarly, in Nicaragua the United States bolstered Somoza until the final hour despite pressures from human rights NGOs. While one may argue that antishah and anti-Somoza forces took some courage from Carter's rhetoric about human rights, it is sheer nonsense to suggest that the revolutions in those countries were related causally to Carter's pronouncements or to the human rights NGOs which championed the struggles—even if one leaves aside the question of whether Iran or Nicaragua were ours to win or lose.

With respect to bilateral trade, there is no doubt that the passage of the Jackson-Vanik Amendment severely restricted American perception of opportunities for trading with the Soviet Union. But as we have previously shown, both the initiation and the passage of that amendment occurred primarily outside of the interests and actions of the human rights lobbies. Those concerned with liberalizing Jewish emigration from the U.S.S.R. were as much manipulated as they were manipulators, in a contest between traditional anti-Communists and the military-industrial interests versus free-trading American-based multi-nationals.[65] Meanwhile, those genuinely concerned with the issue of emigration by Soviet Jews have come to question the efficacy of explicit and public linkage of trade and political concessions.[66]

The argument of the peace and disarmament lobbies is both more substantial and more sophisticated. There is weight to the claim that the Soviets have as deep an interest as the United States in halting an escalating arms race that can destabilize the nuclear balance, limiting the proliferation of nuclear technology, and mutually reducing conventional forces in Europe; nonetheless, the climate in which such negotiations take place remains a significant factor. If the Soviets perceive the human rights issue as demanding a thorough restructuring of their political system and thus constituting a threat to Communist party power, protecting and defending their power interests will take precedence over disarmament and tension-reduction concerns. Furthermore, whatever threat-perception (or target of opportunity) motivated the Soviet invasion of Afghanistan, that event itself—coming on top of the free-floating emotions loosed in America by the Iranian hostage situation—contributed far more to the demise of détente than did either the efforts of the domestic human rights lobbies or the largely

---

[65] This unifactor explanation for the economic deterioration of America conveniently overlooks a host of causal factors, such as the success of the Marshall Plan in rebuilding the economic base of Western Europe; the aging and obsolescence of the machine tool stock in the U.S. (as measured by the five-year surveys of McGraw-Hill); unwillingness or inability of American management aggressively to seek export markets on the Japanese model; the extent to which the Overseas Private Investment Corporation has facilitated the shift of basic manufacture by U.S. multinationals into Third World locales, to cite just a few.

[66] Stern, *Water's Edge*, pp. 210–11.

symbolic gestures toward Russian dissidents by President Carter and his administration.

Yet it seems that human rights lobbyists must learn to be more subtle and more experimental in their tactics if they are to achieve substantive improvements in the human rights situation in Eastern Europe. At the same time they must recreate and preserve that relaxed attitude of genuine détente that is a necessary precondition to human rights gains. It is possible that the progression from the near disaster at Belgrade through Bonn in 1978 to the 1980 Hamburg Scientific Forum illustrates the range of tactics and strategies.

In terms of achieving substantive gains on human rights, the Belgrade Review of 1977 was a failure. The major role played by human rights NGOs in that process was that of providing factual information. A total of fifty-six witnesses testified before the Commission on Security and Cooperation in Europe, which held fourteen hearings between January and June of 1977. But the style of United States behavior was set by the head of the United States delegation to Belgrade: the abrasive style of a confrontational and prosecutorial attack set by Arthur Goldberg.[67] The two "victories" salvaged from Belgrade were the agreement for a further review session in Madrid in 1980 and the tacit acceptance by the U.S.S.R. that how a country treats its citizens is not simply a matter of "domestic jurisdiction."[68]

Between Belgrade and Madrid, the CSCE process called for "a meeting of leading personalities in science from the participating states to discuss interrelated problems of common interest concerning current and future developments in science, and to promote the expansion of contacts, communications, and the exchange of information between scientific institutions and among scientists." This involved a preparatory meeting in Bonn in June–July 1978 to set the agenda and procedures for the Scientific Forum in Hamburg, February–March 1980. These preparatory talks were stalled for a week when the British delegation, speaking for the member nations of the EEC, protested the Soviet trial of Aleksandr Ginzburg and

[67] Albert W. Sherer, Jr., "Helsinki's Child: Goldberg's Variations," *Foreign Policy*, no. 39 (Summer 1980), pp. 154–59.

[68] Dante B. Fascell, "Did Human Rights Survive Belgrade?" *Foreign Policy*, no. 31 (1978), pp. 104–18.

Anatoly Shcharansky, and the American delegation made its own separate protest. More notable than the temporary disruption in the proceedings, however, was the refusal of the United States delegation to be included in the British-EEC protest statement after having been urged to do so. Even so, the Bonn meeting succeeded in tying up organizational details for Hamburg.

The Scientific Forum opened just seven weeks after Afghanistan and the subsequent internal exile of Andrei Sakharov to the closed city of Gorky. Consequently, the level of indignation and outrage among Western scientists ran high. Yet in the view of many the Hamburg meeting was a relative success in balancing the interests of détente and human rights. In the emotional context of the times there were proposals by individual scientists, by informal and formal organizations of scientists, and by factions within Congress to institute a boycott of Hamburg and completely sever the mechanisms for scientific exchange patiently built up over the last twenty-one years. At the other extreme, one suspects that the bureaucratic scientists and many members of the American scientific establishment would have preferred business as usual or, at best, quiet diplomacy and an urging of discretion upon their Soviet counterparts in one-on-one private cocktail discussions. The position which won out, represented by such groups as the Human Rights Committee of the National Academy of Sciences and the Clearinghouse for Science and Human Rights of the American Association for the Advancement of Science, was to go to Hamburg but to talk about human rights, coordinating American criticism with that of Western allies, at the same time that the value of scientific exchange was equally emphasized. Indeed, both the HAS and the AAAS seem now to have accepted the multiple-strategy suggestion (i.e., encouraging individual boycotts based upon conscience so long as these are publicized, while at the same time maintaining associational contacts) put forth by Jeremy Stone of the Federation of American Scientists[69] and by the Brtish Council for Science and So-

---

[69] Jeremy J. Stone, "Scientific Freedom in the International Arena: Status Reports and Prospects," paper delivered at meeting of the American Political Science Association, Houston, Texas, January 1979; see also Robert W. Kates, "Human Rights Issues in Human Rights: The Experience of the Committee on Human Rights of the National Academy of Sciences," *Science* 201 (August 11, 1978): 502–6.

ciety in conjunction with the British Institute for Human Rights.[70] This is also the position advocated by many human rights activists who are members of professional associations which sometimes hold international congresses in countries with highly repressive regimes.[71]

Whether this measured approach will guide American behavior at Madrid is open to question. It is disturbing that the two cochairmen chosen by the Administration, Griffin Bell and Max Kampelman, both lack a track record in international human rights and in international affairs in general. Also, most of the public members designated seem to have gained patronage awards from the White House for past Democratic party activities and contributions. As before Belgrade, the human rights NGOs have played a major role in providing CSCE and other congressional bodies with written and oral testimony about human rights violations in Eastern Europe; but there is very little evidence to suggest that they will be anything more than observers at the Madrid meeting.[72] Once again, even so structured a situation—with a definable target date and a limited agenda—reveals little coordination, agreement, or impact across the array of domestically based human rights organizations. And with Soviet troops still in Afghanistan and the reemergence of Cold War mentalities in the United States, it is difficult to see what human rights NGOs will contribute to United States foreign policy or Soviet-American relations.

As with those who analyze American power in the world and shift from the optimism of omnipotence to the pessimism of impotence, so it is equally simplistic to judge the human rights NGOs as being either highly influential or powerless. They are only one set of factors in the complex interactions that determine American foreign policy. Far more important is the public mood: When it is

[70] *Scholarly Freedom and Human Rights: The Problem of Persecution and Oppression of Science and Scientists* (London, 1977).

[71] Scoble and Wiseberg, A Report on the XIth World Congress of the International Political Science Association (IPSA), Moscow, USSR, August 12-18, 1979; see also note 3.

[72] David A. Andelman, "The Road to Madrid," *Foreign Policy*, no. 39 (Summer 1980), pp. 159-72. For a rundown on what human rights NGOs are planning for Madrid, see *Human Rights Internet Reporter* 6, no. 1 (September-October 1980) and forthcoming and previous issues of the *HRI Newsletter*.

favorable to human rights the NGOs can reinforce policymakers and help shape specific policies; when it is unfavorable, they can hope to keep the issues alive through their research and activities.

Elsewhere in our research we,[73] as well as others,[74] have stressed the critical role that human rights NGOs play in countering both national and transnational forces of repression. We have enumerated six key and interrelated functions they perform: (1) information gathering, evaluation, and dissemination, which are their prime functions; without information on the status of human rights observance and on the nature and context of human rights violations, there is little hope for the protection of these rights; (2) advocacy (in legal terminology) or witnessing (in religious language), which means actively taking up the case of those whose rights are violated; (3) legal assistance and humanitarian relief—engagement of legal defense, provision of cocounsel, filing of amicus curiae briefs, sending legally trained foreign-national observers to public trials, publicizing (or counter publicizing) "political show trials"— on behalf of individuals accused of such vague political crimes as "conspiracy," "subversion," and "slander of the State"; and also other forms of assistance for victims and their families; (4) building solidarity among the oppressed and internationalizing and legitimating "local" concerns; (5) moral condemnation of human rights violators—"the mobilization of shame"—which may be effective because no government, even the most repressive, is totally insensitive to moral condemnation; and (6) lobbying national and international authorities, which may or may not alter the policies of governments or intergovernmental organizations but which, at the very least, keeps the issue of human rights alive in a variety of public forums. When these functions are examined in their interrelated-

---

[73] See especially Wiseberg and Scoble, "Transnational Actors in the Promotion and Protection of Human Rights: An Analysis of the Role and Impact of Non-governmental Organizations," paper presented at the XIth World Congress of the International Political Science Association, Moscow, USSR, August 11–18, 1979.

[74] Jerome J. Shestack, "Sisyphus Endures: The International Human Rights NGO," *New York Law School Law Review* 24, no. 1 (1978): 89–123; and David Weissbrodt, "The Role of International Non-governmental Organizations in the Implementation of Human Rights," *Texas International Law Journal* 12, nos. 2 & 3 (Spring/Summer 1977): 293–320.

ness, the role of the human rights NGO is that of assuring that human rights violations will not be perpetrated behind a veil of silence, that those struggling against oppression in their own societies will have their concerns echoed in international arenas, and that a range of pressures may be brought to bear upon offending regimes. No research, however, suggests that the activities of human rights NGOs can in any way fundamentally alter superpower relations, including the policies that the superpowers direct toward each other.

A *Neo-Con*sensus?
American Foreign Policy
in the 1980s

Richard A. Melanson

I

FOR a democratic polity to sustain a coherent foreign policy, a relatively broad and stable domestic consensus is essential. A democratic consensus can impart authority and legitimacy to foreign policy by sharing and supporting its premises, purposes, and values. While such a consensus cannot guarantee enlightened diplomacy, an effective foreign policy is probably impossible without it.

Revisionist historians have long argued that American foreign policy has been characterized by a remarkably consistent domestic consensus devoted to the protection and expansion of liberal capitalist values. This consensus, they assert, enabled the United States to conduct a brilliantly successful foreign policy (at least until Vietnam) based on the principles of informal or Open Door imperialism. To skeptics who point to the periodic "great debates" which have convulsed our domestic politics and paralyzed our foreign relations, the revisionists reply that these episodes should be understood as tactical disagreements carried on within the prevailing consensus.

In one sense, of course, Williams, Kolko, Gardner, and other revisionists are correct, insofar as the vast majority of Americans have not been anticapitalist, pro-Communist, or illiberal. Yet to identify a domestic consensus that is vaguely liberal, capitalist, and anti-Communist does not tell us a great deal about America or American foreign policy. And to write off the 1899 annexations controversy, the Versailles Treaty debate, and the Vietnam War unrest as insignificant tactical squabbles requires a truly Olympian perspective.

On the contrary, because of the vagaries, unruliness, and complexity of democratic life it should be unsurprising to discover that American foreign policy consensus has been relatively fragile, often limited in scope, and occasionally absent altogether.

II

There have been two periods of consensus in the post–World War II era of American foreign policy. The first, loosely termed *containment*, began to form in 1947, was fully operative by 1954, flourished until the mid 1960s, and was moribund by 1968. The second epoch, even more loosely dubbed *détente*, emerged between Nixon's "silent majority" speech of November 1969 and the last great antiwar march in May 1971, prevailed from mid-1971 until late 1973, and was floundering by early 1975. While dissimilar in several respects, each consensus was characterized by a focus on Soviet-American relations, specific diagnoses of Soviet capabilities and intentions, and relatively clear prescriptions for American responses to Moscow. What helped to give the earlier consensus much greater longevity was the presence of a remarkably cohesive, articulate elite responsible for shaping, sustaining, and ultimately destroying it.

Godfrey Hodgson is probably correct when he claims that an Establishment may be a permanent feature of American diplomacy.[1] Constitutional requirements, general public passivity, and the recondite nature of foreign policy expertise combine to render participatory democracy unworkable in America's international relations. A reasonably accessible establishment, lodged in the executive branch, which articulates policy, educates (and listens to) the attentive public, builds consensus, and avoids major foreign policy disasters is the most to which America can realistically aspire. In other words, an American foreign policy establishment is more or less inevitable. What remains to be determined are the nature of its membership and the quality of its performance.

The identity and axioms of the Establishment, which molded and maintained the Cold War, or containment consensus, have been

[1] *Foreign Policy*, no. 10 (Spring 1973), p. 40.

discussed at length by Hodgson.[2] Here we will only highlight his argument and offer a few modifications.

Although a disproportionate number of Establishment figures (particularly among the older generation) came from privileged East Coast backgrounds featuring Harvard and Yale educations, the Establishment "is defined not by sociology or education, and still less by genealogy; but by a history, a policy, an aspiration, an instinct, and a technique."[3] The origins of this Establishment can be traced back to the small group of advisers that Colonel House gathered around him at Versailles. After the treaty was defeated in 1920, these businessmen and academics—joined by a handful of international bankers and their lawyers—continued to struggle against a resurgent isolationism, largely through the newly formed Council on Foreign Relations in New York. But it was clearly World War II (and thus the "lessons" of Munich) which crystallized the Cold War Establishment of New York lawyers, bankers, and corporation executives; federal officials; and scholars. Specifically, the common experience of OSS service imparted to these youngish men a sense of power, accomplishment, destiny, and international involvement which would survive the Axis surrender. And when Soviet Communism replaced Fascism as America's chief adversary, these men returned to Washington to construct the new policy soon known as containment.

What was the outlook of this nascent Establishment? Conceived as bipartisan counterweights to an anticipated revitalized isolationism (particularly in Congress), members of the Establishment called themselves "liberal internationalists." They were convinced that America's reluctance to exert its power during the interwar years had helped to bring on World War II; thus, these men were determined to employ the presidency to build an internationalist consensus at home. Certain that the United States possessed the material resources to achieve world leadership, the Establishment believed that it had to supply the missing moral and spiritual ingredients necessary to transform crude power into international authority. Though they themselves rarely stood for election, these men had an instinct for the political center—an instinct that but-

[2] Ibid., pp. 3–40.
[3] Ibid, p. 8.

tressed their aspiration to serve as educators to an America whose traditional tendency was to vacillate dangerously between self-righteous isolation and indiscriminate intervention. Finally, while members of this Establishment feared international Communism as a mortal threat to Western values and institutions, they were unsympathetic to those who wished to ferret out domestic "subversives."

Thus far, the picture of the Cold War Establishment does not differ significantly from the revisionist characterization of a liberal, capitalist, anti-Communist consensus. Yet the revisionists ignore (and Hodgson does not explore) important disagreements and ambiguities within the Establishment and the consensus it solidified, especially between 1947 and 1950.

For many years commentators have noted a tension among the cornerstones of containment: the universalist implications of the Truman Doctrine, the more modest proposals of Mr. "X"—made even more so by George Kennan's subsequent disavowals—and the regional and economic foci of the Marshall Plan. Deep policy divisions persisted within the Truman administration even after the firing of Henry Wallace, as is made clear by reviewing the recently declassified memoranda and follow-up papers circulated by the Policy Planning Staff, the National Security Council, and the Joint Chiefs of Staff between 1947 and 1950.[4] Such a review exposes significant differences over issues like the nature of Soviet capabilities and intentions, the character of international Communism, the consequences of Mao's triumph in China, and the limits, if any, of America's security interests. Indeed, it is no exaggeration to argue that the policy centerpiece of the Cold War consensus, containment, remained an ambiguous and much debated notion until after the outbreak of the Korean War. These disagreements can, perhaps, be expressed most vividly by juxtaposing the views of George Kennan and Paul Nitze, Kennan's successor as the head of the Policy Planning Staff.

Reconstruction of Kennan's views of the late 1940s is complicated by the apparent disjunction between his public utterances

[4] See Thomas H. Etzold and John Lewis Gaddis, eds., *Containment: Documents on American Policy and Strategy, 1945–1950* (New York, 1978); Fred M. Kaplan, "Our Cold-War Policy, circa '50," *New York Times Magazine*, May 18, 1980, pp. 34, 88–94.

and his more private words. Critics such as Charles Gati[5] and Eduard Mark[6] have suggested that Mr. "X" faithfully reflected Kennan's contemporary outlook. But the analysis offered by John Lewis Gaddis[7] in this regard seems more persuasive, because it seeks to understand the complexity of Kennan's thought by focusing on his most comprehensive statements. According to Gaddis's account, Kennan believed that the chief danger of the Soviet Union was the psychological malaise which afflicted the states bordering Russia— not the Soviet military threat or the appeal of international Communism. Accordingly, Kennan's strategy of containment was primarily psychological. As a first step toward creating a stable and hospitable international environment, he asserted that the self-confidence of those borderlands, particularly the European ones, had to be restored. It was essential that America lend economic and political support—but not military commitments—to help these threatened states improve their psychological well being. After self-confidence had been restored and after the Soviets had suffered a consequent loss of influence in these areas, the West could expect, over a period of years, Moscow gradually to modify its approach to international relations so that negotiations might become feasible. The ultimate goal of Kennan's containment was not a Pax Americana but the reemergence of independent power centers in Europe and Japan, the eventual domestication of Soviet power, and the growth to maturity of American diplomacy.

In short, Kennan's strategy was more or less traditional (though he feared that the United States was an untraditional power), and it had to deal with a world temporarily dislocated by World War II. This strategy—which rejected permanent and global alliances, massive military commitments, and a preoccupation with ideology in favor of recreating an international order based on diplomacy, limit, and balance—was challenged by many in the Truman Administration, including Clark Clifford and Paul Nitze. Events like the Berlin blockade, the Czech coup, the successful Soviet testing

---

[5] Gati, ed., *Caging the Bear: Containment and the Cold War* (Indianapolis, 1974).

[6] "Mr. 'X' Was Inconsistent and Wrong," in Martin F. Herz, ed., *Decline of the West? George F. Kennan and the Critics* (Washington, D.C., 1979).

[7] Etzold and Gaddis, *Containment*, pp. 25-37.

A Neo-Consensus?

of the atomic bomb, and Chiang's defeat in China provided additional evidence for those in the administration who suspected that the Soviet Union was a dangerous, revolutionary state bent on world domination and was the director of a unified, international Communist movement. In addition, a series of bureaucratic changes and maneuvers during 1949 and 1950 gradually encouraged the emergence of a more ambitious strategy of containment, finally articulated in NSC–68. It was this more extensive notion of containment which prevailed and which provided the foreign policy Establishment with its raison d'être until the late 1960s. And it was *this* Containment, anticipated in the ringing words of the Truman Doctrine, which received public ratification in the form of the Cold War consensus.

The bureaucratic shifts which included the "retirement" of Kennan, the transfer of State Department Counsellor Charles E. Bohlen to Paris, and the resignation of Secretary of Defense Louis Johnson have been nicely summarized in a recent article by Fred M. Kaplan.[8] Kaplan indicates that, despite the "shocks" of 1948, the Truman administration was extremely reluctant to respond militarily to Soviet expansionism. Truman "had set an arbitrary $15 billion ceiling on defense spending, and a blue-ribbon panel declared in 1948 that even the proposed $14.2 billion budget for fiscal 1950 was 'unduly high,' given 'the ability of the economy to sustain' such high costs."[9] This more cautious conception of containment was not unanimously shared by Truman's advisers, as can be sensed by reading "Measures Required to Achieve U.S. Objectives with Respect to the U.S.S.R.," a top secret NSC paper, completed on March 30, 1949.[10] Among its ten major recommendations were a sharp escalation of the defense budget, significant increases in Western force levels, a global propaganda campaign, and an economic policy which would encourage domestic dissent in the Soviet Union.

This document, which anticipated the major thrust of NSC–68,

[8] Kaplan, "Our Cold-War Policy."

[9] Ibid., p. 88.

[10] U.S., Department of State, *Foreign Relations of the United States, 1949*, Diplomatic Papers, vol. 1, *National Security Affairs; Foreign Economic Policy*, (Washington, D.C., 1976), pp. 271–77.

was attacked, not surprisingly, by Bohlen and Kennan as "hysterical"[11] and "dangerous."[12] But as the "shocks" of 1948 were replaced by those of 1949, Bohlen, Kennan, and Johnson increasingly found themselves part of a losing coalition. Kaplan makes clear that their defeat was assured by the replacement of Edwin Nourse, a fiscal conservative, by the Keynesian, Leon Keyserling, as Chairman of the Council of Economic Advisers and by the creation of close ties, over Johnson's objections, between State Department officials and planners in the Department of Defense. These bureaucratic maneuvers made a more ambitious interpretation of containment appear both economically feasible and strategically necessary.

Soon after Kennan stepped down as Director of the Policy Planning Staff, the new secretary of state, Dean Acheson, recommended the Presidential creation of a special joint committee to study American objectives and strategic plans in light of the Soviet atomic test. This committee, officially known as the State-Defense Policy Review Group took advantage of Kennan's presence in Latin America to draft a report during February and March 1950 that eventually became NSC–68. It is interesting to note that during its deliberations this group called in only one outside witness, James B. Conant, who questioned the report's basic assumptions. Furthermore, Secretary of Defense Johnson was "deliberately kept out of the picture"[13] until the document was virtually complete.

Authored mostly by Paul Nitze, NSC–68 was melodramatically written in stark contrast to the more measured and calm prose of his immediate predecessor at the PPS. But perhaps the rhetoric was appropriate, for it had to support a set of recommendations that sharply escalated America's responses to the Soviet Union. By now the substance of NSC–68 is rather well known. It agreed with Kennan that the Soviet Union was basically unsatisfiable, but it perceived Russia as indistinguishable from a worldwide Communist revolutionary movement, newly capable of initiating a war against the West and intent on world domination. To counter this global threat to our security and values, Nitze and his associates counselled "a rapid build-up of political, economic, and military

---

[11] Bohlen memorandum, April 14, 1949, ibid., pp. 277–78.
[12] Kennan to Acheson, April 14, 1949, ibid., p. 282.
[13] Kaplan, "Our Cold-War Policy," p. 91.

strength in the Free World."[14] While no specific budget figures were suggested, Kaplan claims that "State Department officials were privately tossing around figures like $40 billion"[15] at a time when plans were being made for a fiscal 1951 defense budget of $13.2 billion.

NSC–68 was presented to President Truman on April 7, 1950. Although he seemed impressed with the diagnosis provided by the report, lingering "doubts about the fiscal wisdom of massive boosts in defense spending persisted."[16] These doubts were shared by others in the administration, including William Schaub of the Budget Bureau, but the outbreak of the Korean War in June gave to NSC–68 the psychological impetus needed to gain its acceptance.[17] Finally, fiscal opponents of NSC–68 were muted by a December 1950 memorandum by Leon Keyserling which argued that the American economy could easily support significantly higher defense spending.[18]

These two versions of containment, Kennan's and Nitze's, formed the parameters within which the Cold War consensus crystallized. Foreign policy debates, particularly after 1954, fell increasingly within the limits set by these two variants of Containment. Interestingly, the limits of discourse were particularly rigid within the ranks of the foreign policy Establishment. While fringes of the wider public (and Congress) might long for a new Henry Wallace or for a policy to "roll back" the Russians from Eastern Europe, Establishment debates (such as they were) occurred within a much narrower framework.

But it would not be correct to argue, as Kaplan does, that the NSC–68 version of Containment simply replaced Kennan's as the prevailing Cold War strategy. While the principles of NSC–68, emphasizing ideology, credibility, dominoes, globalism, and militarism, were generally embraced by the Establishment after 1950,

---

[14] U.S., Department of State, *Foreign Relations of the United States, 1950*, Diplomatic Papers, vol. 1, *National Security Affairs; Foreign Economic Policy*, (Washington, D.C., 1977), p. 432.

[15] Ibid., p. 92.

[16] Ibid., p. 93.

[17] December 14, 1950, ibid., pp. 468–69.

[18] December 8, 1950, ibid., pp. 427–31.

Kennan's diagnoses and prescriptions were never completely discredited. In particular, the so-called left wing of the Establishment was periodically supportive of this earlier and now recessive strain of containment.[19] Kennan's version, which stressed concepts like nationalism, regional autonomy, diplomacy, and a non-zero-sum view of the world, remained dormant for most of the 1950s but became increasingly influential as America's involvement in Vietnam deepened.

Both variants of containment, but particularly the more ambitious one, argued implicitly for the necessity of a domestic consensus. Containment theorists perceived a world full of conflict and danger and called on Americans to respond to these challenges with discipline, patience, vigilance, toughness, and absolute loyalty. For containment a domestic consensus was both prudent and moral.

However, the strength and resiliency of the prevailing Cold War consensus should not be exaggerated, for it depended on a number of rather unusual conditions. First, the defense outlays anticipated by NSC–68 required a domestic economy healthy enough to support both domestic welfare spending and a large defense budget. The unprecedented prosperity of most of the 1950s and 1960s, plus the Eisenhower administration's decision to save money through its massive retaliation doctrine, meant that "guns and butter" were provided without chronic inflation until the mid-1960s. In retrospect, it is also clear that cheap and abundant energy, America's technological supremacy, and the temporary weakness of other industrial economies gave to this prosperity an illusion of permanence which tended to institutionalize the otherwise tenuous assumptions of NSC–68. Second, although NSC–68's definition of American security interests fathered a series of bilateral and multilateral defense arrangements (e.g., ANZUS, Japan, SEATO, Baghdad Pact, and CENTO), they remained essentially putative until Vietnam. As long as they existed as "paper" promises which did not require expensive United States commitments (except NATO), these alliances enjoyed general domestic support. But when SEATO was activated to help justify our Vietnam involve-

---

[19] For example, Chester Bowles, George Ball, John McNaughton, John Kenneth Galbraith, Allen S. Whiting, and Adam Yarmolinsky.

ment, they became a good deal less popular. Third, many of the victories achieved by the United States during these years (e.g., in Iran, Guatemala, Lebanon, and the Congo) were obtained "on the cheap" through reliance on covert foreign policy instruments. Until Vietnam, the depth and resiliency of the Cold War consensus had never been seriously tested.

This realization leads us to the final circumstance: the Korean War. Why did this war not fragment the foreign policy Establishment and destroy the domestic consensus? The answer involves several unusual factors. First, Acheson and others suspected that the North Korean attack was a prelude to a Soviet assault on the West. Thus, the heart region of containment, Europe, could be invoked as an important reason to intervene in Korea. Second, that the United Nations had authorized and supported Washington's protection of the Rhee government gave our actions additional important legitimacy. And third, the generally enthusiastic assistance from Western allies made our actions in Korea appear even less unilateral. Yet despite all of these favorable circumstances, the public attitude toward the war was more grudging toleration than enthusiastic support. And while the Establishment did back Truman on Korea, the same cannot be said of Congress, in which important Republican voices urged "unleashing" Chiang and crossing the Yalu.

This controversy highlighted a more fundamental problem with the bipartisan Cold War consensus. Both versions of containment had always featured a certain ambiguity about the character of American security interests in Asia. It is important to remember that the Establishment was comprised of men who considered themselves "Europeanists" in varying degrees.[20] That is, they presumed that for a combination of strategic, historical, cultural, economic, political, and psychological reasons Western Europe should not be allowed to fall under Soviet domination. Kennan was very clear on this point: He considered the Rhine Valley and Great Britain to be two of the world's five strategically crucial areas (the others being Japan, the Soviet Union, and the United States). The rest of the Establishment agreed with Kennan's appreciation of the im-

[20] Especially in the State Department.

portance of Western Europe. Indeed, this region was deemed so vital to American interests that it was cited as a primary reason for the Korean intervention. The problem was that many in Congress, especially conservative Republicans, deeply resented containment's implicit subordination of Asia to Europe. Disgusted by the allegedly immoral and disastrous history of European diplomacy, these men perceived Asia as a potentially rich and friendly area in need of American political and religious values.

This struggle between the Europeanists of the Establishment and the "Asia Firsters" at the extreme fringes of the Cold War consensus tended to fade in importance after 1955, but it had much to do with the gradual "de-Europeanization" of the Establishment in the late 1950s and early 1960s. In other words, the primacy given to European defense and Russian aggression by Kennan and the more ambiguous roles given to these concepts by Acheson and Nitze largely were discarded by Rusk and Rostow. Johnson's lieutenants were neither Europeanists nor Asia Firsters but globalists who acted as if the entire world was of equal strategic value to the United States.

By defining America's interests in this interdependent and undiscriminating manner and by redefining China as the chief target of containment, the foreign policy Establishment of the 1960s pushed the Cold War consensus beyond its limits. Instead of providing something for everyone (the crediblity argument for the Europeanists and the SEATO rationale for the Asianists), this third version of containment (a logical, if not necessary, extension of NSC–68) shattered the domestic consensus. And without a consensus to support it, the foreign policy Establishment fractured along a fault line which ran from Walt Rostow to Daniel Ellsberg.

III

The second period of domestic consensus in postwar American foreign policy was even more fragile, limited, and short-lived than its predecessor. Constructed on the policy of détente by Nixon and Kissinger, this consensus prevailed for less than four years and was unable either to attract the unanimous support of the old Establishment or to produce a new foreign policy elite capable of cultivating a deeper domestic consensus.

Let us begin with the last point. The Vietnam War had so discredited large segments of the Cold War Establishment that it could no longer fulfill its earlier educative and advisory functions. In general, Nixon and Kissinger constructed détente without the assistance of this older Establishment. Occasionally, parts of it were mobilized by Kissinger for specific purposes, as in the case of opposition to the Mansfield amendment, but its influence had drastically waned and largely was confined to European issues. At the same time, Nixon and Kissinger were both unwilling and unable to encourage the emergence of a new and younger elite. Nixon's distrust of intellectuals and the eastern establishment, his penchant for secrecy, and his almost exclusive reliance on Kissinger meant that presidential support was lacking for the growth of a détente Establishment as the successor to the Cold War Establishment. Kissinger, who shared many of Nixon's biases, attempted to sell détente almost single-handedly with the help of a temporarily enthralled national press. Without a coherent foreign policy elite to institutionalize, legitimate, and refine it, détente gradually became a media buzzword subject to all the benefits and liabilities of journalstic infatuation. With the old Establishment discredited and in disarray and with so many potential members of a new foreign policy elite forsaking diplomacy in favor of environmentalism, consumerism, and neo-isolationism, perhaps Kissinger had no choice but to indulge in showmanship to popularize détente. But it is clear that these tactics ultimately did détente a disservice by politicizing and vulgarizing it.

The rather shallow and short-lived consensus that did emerge to support détente was further weakened by the substance of the policy. Most importantly, because détente described a process whereby tension was to be reduced between America and Russia, the Cold War concepts of discipline, sacrifice, and patience that had given to the earlier consensus a powerful moral impetus were no longer applicable. The inner logic of détente tended to diminish the moral basis for a domestic consensus. At the same time the torrent of dissent unleashed by the Vietnam War could no longer be stemmed by appeals to Cold War exigencies.

Second, like containment, the consensus spawned by détente was weakened by geographical limitations. That is, even though détente placed the Soviet-American relationship at the center of world affairs and derived all other relationships from it, Kissinger had difficulty in fitting Vietnam, the Third World, and Western Europe into this essentially bilateral framework. But whereas the Establishment supporters of containment had encountered only the opposition of the Asia Firsters until the late 1950s, in the early and mid 1970s détente was attacked by a variety of leftist critics who claimed that Kissinger's preoccupation with the Soviet Union had made him oblivious to areas and issues like Europe, the Third World, human rights, and economic justice. On the political right Kissinger was criticized not for making the Soviet Union the central focus of his policy but for disastrously underestimating the Soviet military threat. Kissinger was quite successful in containing these domestic dissenters until he and Nixon began to oversell détente to shore up an administration crippled by Watergate. Finally, Congress, which had provided almost unflagging bipartisan support for American foreign policy during the earlier era of consensus, dramatically reasserted itself in the wake of Vietnam and Watergate. Despite strenuous presidential objections, such measures as the War Powers Act, the Jackson-Vanik Amendment, the Stevenson Amendment, and the Clark Amendment were passed by a Congress intent on regulating a wide variety of foreign policy activities. Symptomatic of this remarkable shift was the new attitude of the old Establishment (or at least parts of it) toward Congress. Alternately tolerated and patronized by the Establishment during the Cold War as the seat of parochialism, chauvinism, and dim-wittedness, by the early 1970s Congress found itself being wooed and petitioned by those in the Establishment who had been disillusioned by the Vietnam War and by Nixon's apparent inability to end it.

In sum, the Cold War consensus that had been characterized by a confident presidency, an articulate and unified Establishment, a docile Congress, and an ideology that extolled the virtues of discipline, sacrifice, and patience was succeeded by a consensus vitiated by a disgraced president, a weak and quarrelsome Establishment, a rebellious Congress, and a policy that encouraged high expectations and justified dissent. By 1976 the second era of postwar consensus had disappeared under the double blows of Ronald Reagan and Jimmy Carter.

IV

There is no foreign policy consensus in the United States today, and the Carter and Reagan administrations' inability to shape one explains much of America's incoherent behavior in the world since 1977.

In retrospect it can be seen that Carter and his fellow refugees from the Trilateral Commission attempted to build such a consensus as soon as they assumed office. Yet the kind of consensus they aimed at was essentially negative: one that tapped discontent with Kissinger without providing a set of conceptual alternatives. While remaining rhetorically committed to a poorly articulated notion of détente, Carter chastized Kissinger for neglecting our democratic allies, human rights, and the Third World. Carter replaced Kissinger's alleged Soviet obsession with the idea, borrowed from the Trilateralists, of a more balanced American policy attending more or less equally to Russia, Europe, Japan, and the Third World. And from civil rights activists, opponents of détente on the left and the right, and those who possess what Robert W. Tucker has called the "new political sensibility,"[21] Carter adopted a perspective that emphasized human rights as a prime concern of American foreign policy.

This unlikely coalition of people and outlooks provided an election consensus that temporarily unified the Democratic party against Henry Kissinger, but it barely survived the inauguration of Jimmy Carter. The reasons for its quick demise are obvious. First, most of the Trilateralists with whom Carter packed his foreign policy apparatus were members of the old Cold War Establishment who had been singed by Vietnam and exiled by Henry Kissinger. Although chastened by their failures in the late 1960s, these men nevertheless remained practitioners of what they saw

[21] *The Inequality of Nations* (New York, 1977).

as realpolitik. Not surprisingly, these traditionalists were frequently annoyed by "new politics" congressmen who insisted on taking very seriously Carter's human rights rhetoric and other administration officials like Patricia Derian, whose priorities seemed to them dangerously naive.

Second, and even more damaging to Carter's efforts to build a new consensus, was his administration's inability to imbue its foreign policy with even the slightest shred of conceptual coherence. Compared to the ideational richness of Kennan and Kissinger or even the shrill consistency of Nitze, Dulles, and Rusk, the Carter foreign policy seemed confused and shallow. Directed by a president who lacked a comprehensive philosophy,[22] a secretary of state (until April 1980) whose forte was bargaining, and a national security adviser more famous for opportunism than conceptual clarity, Carter's diplomacy lacked unifying themes.

During 1977 and 1978 the Trilateral emphasis on the industrial democracies, the Soviet Union, and the Third World was blended uneasily with the issues of human rights, limited arms sales, and nuclear non-proliferation. Détente was no longer to possess the centrality of the Kissinger years but was to be supplemented by compelling interests in other issues and regions. The aim was, apparently, a foreign policy that would no longer subordinate everything to the Soviet connection but rather would recognize the seamless, interdependent nature of the contemporary world. Kissinger's allegedly anachronistic preoccupation with high politics would be balanced by a new (and more "American") attention to low politics and human rights. Because this highly ambitious goal was poorly articulated, seemingly devoid of guiding principles, and not supported by a vital and reunified foreign policy Establishment, the result was the very opposite of domestic consensus. Carter's confusion encouraged the further growth of special interest groups clamoring for a variety of favors concerning such issues as human rights, defense spending, arms sales, South Africa, and, of course, the Middle East. This patchwork of lobbies formed neither a consensus nor a reliable coalition of support for Carter's policies; it was, instead, a cacophony of single-issue groups frequently at war with one another. And Congress, which had provided

[22] "Carter Called Weak in Managerial Skills," *Baltimore Sun*, July 7, 1980, p. 1.

bipartisan support for the earlier Cold War consensus, proved to be a formidable foe of the Carter foreign policy. Panama, SALT II, the Cuban brigade, F-15s for the Saudis, and nuclear technology for India were but a few of the many confrontations which characterized executive-legislative relations.

Indeed, the only hint of a new domestic consensus during the Carter administration occurred in the aftermath of Iran and Afghanistan when a "rose garden" strategy was devised to portray Carter as a beleaguered, heroic statesman whose formerly optimistic perception of the world had been cruelly jolted by Brezhnev and Khomeini. The resulting flurry of White House activity—boycotts, embargoes, fact-finding missions, and an almost comic opera effort to build a wall of containment along the "arc of crisis"—was sufficiently impressive to help defeat Edward Kennedy in the early primaries. But when this frantic pace inevitably slowed during the spring and summer of 1980, no coherent, articulate policy toward the Soviet Union emerged to replace the piece-meal measures taken earlier in the year. Not surprisingly, public support for Carter's foreign policy threatened to return to pre-Iran and Afghanistan levels, and a new domestic consensus seemed no more likely than before the crises of late 1979.

V

Will a new foreign policy consensus take shape during the 1980s? If so, what sort of American foreign policy will this new consensus support? And to what degree might this policy and consensus focus on Soviet-American relations? Much depends on whether a new foreign policy Establishment emerges to transform vague and inchoate public moods into an articulate, consistent, conceptually rich foreign policy.

By far the most comprehensive recent study of public opinion and American foreign policy is the 1979 report prepared by the Chicago Council on Foreign Relations.[23] Although its surveys were completed a year before the crises in Iran and Afghanistan, the report's major findings have been confirmed in more selective polls

[23] John E. Rielly, ed., *American Public Opinion and U.S. Foreign Policy 1979*.

taken since late 1979.[24] The data indicate the growth of a national mood that increasingly rejects the introspective guilt of the post-Vietnam period and at the same time refuses to embrace the liberal internationalism of the Cold War years. This new disposition can perhaps best be characterized as "conservative nationalism," for it is informed by several defense-oriented, anti-interventionist tendencies. Higher defense budgets, more military (but not economic) aid, a willingness to defend NATO allies and Japan (but not Taiwan), more support for CIA covert activities, and a reluctance to intervene around the world to protect the Free World are responses which appear with higher frequency than in the Chicago Council's 1974 survey. No clear national consensus has yet emerged, but the trends "point to a mood of increasing insecurity in the American public. . . . The public shows an increasing attraction toward such conservative symbols as military power and anti-communism, but not toward extending our commitments abroad or renewing the tradition of Cold War interventionism. It is this defensive and self-interested quality that distinguishes the current mood from that of the Cold War."[25] Recent public attitudes about foreign policy reflect a sense of vulnerability, the desire for security, the preoccupation with Soviet military power, the disinclination for a global crusade, and the somewhat contradictory desires for American world leadership with reduced and restrained foreign commitments. But if the public trends and inclinations of the late 1970s are to form the core of a domestic consensus about American foreign policy in the 1980s, a new Establishment must emerge to translate the public mood into an articulate and coherent foreign policy.

The Carter administration was influenced and frequently served by a foreign policy elite of sorts. Drawn largely from the Trilateral Commission, this elite attempted to replace the balance-of-power East-West focus of Kissinger with a "world order" policy emphasizing North-South relations, economic interdependencies, and the growing disutility of military force. While it would be an exaggeration to call this elite a new foreign policy Establishment,

---

[24] *New York Times*, December 1, 1979, p. 1.

[25] William Schneider, "The Public and Foreign Policy," *Wall Street Journal*, November 7, 1979, p. 26.

as Carl Gershman has,[26] it does possess a more or less distinctive point of view. But its fumbling, often contradictory attempts to articulate this vision failed to encourage the reformation of a domestic consensus. Indeed, the human rights issue, which the administration had hoped would provide the moral impetus for a new consensus, proved so costly in terms of both alliance and adversary relations that it was all but abandoned by the end of 1978. Similarly, President Carter's early hopes that a more constructive approach to the Third World would encourage Southern moderation were dashed by Cambodia, Iran, and OPEC actions in the wake of the shah's overthrow. Almost by the process of elimination the Soviet Union (which helped this process by invading Afghanistan) emerged as the central focus of the Carter administration's foreign policy, and the public might justifiably be excused for responding with skepticism and confusion in November 1980.

In light of the trends in public opinion identified by the Chicago Council's study, it is extremely unlikely that Gershman's foreign policy Establishment will be able to construct a new domestic consensus in the 1980s. If such a consensus does emerge, it will probably do so in response to the efforts of another and quite different elite—the so-called neoconservatives. For it is surely they who better represent a public mood which we earlier referred to as "conservative nationalism."

Some members of this coterie prefer to be known as neo-liberals or new nationalists. However, the titular head of this group, Irving Kristol, has accepted "neoconservative" as an accurate description, and the name does seem as appropriate as any available alternative. There is no need here to attempt either a sociology or a history of neoconservatism.[27] Rather than engage in a comprehensive analysis

---

[26] "The Rise and Fall of the New Foreign Policy Establishment," *Commentary*, July 1980, pp. 13–24. Any analysis which attempts to include the disparate likes of Zbigniew Brzezinski, Cyrus Vance, Richard Falk, and Stanley Hoffmann in a unified, homogeneous Establishment must be questioned. Furthermore, even if it were possible to overlook the significant differences which separate these men, it would still be rash to call this group an "Establishment" if for no other reason than that it did not hold power long enough to institutionalize its views. In short, Gershman vastly overestimated the stability, cohesiveness, and longevity of this elite.

[27] George H. Nash, *The Conservative Intellectual Movement in America*

of neoconservatism—for this would entail an extensive examination of such figures as Kristol, Daniel Bell, Michael Novak, Edward Banfield, Robert Nisbet, Peter Berger, Ben Wattenberg, and Daniel Patrick Moynihan—this essay will concentrate on the foreign policy of neoconservatism. And to further simplify our discussion we will focus, at the cost of ignoring foreign policy writers like Walter Laqueur, Edward Luttwak, Michael Ledeen, P. T. Bauer, Carl Gershman, and Richard Pipes, on Norman Podhoretz and Robert W. Tucker.

Neoconservatism is not a monolithic ideology (though its adherents do share a number of general tenets), and Podhoretz and Tucker represent in several ways two of the movement's most prominent foreign policy wings. Norman Podhoretz, who considers himself more a New York intellectual than a foreign policy expert, was an anti-Communist liberal in the 1950s, a New Left fellow traveler in the 1960s, and a founding father of neoconservatism in the 1970s. Although as editor of *Commentary* Podhoretz had opened its pages to the likes of Paul Goodman and Norman O. Brown, he eventually became disgusted with the alleged excesses, hypocrisies, and stupidities of the New Left. Accordingly, after a period of painful reevaluation, Podhoretz dramatically steered *Commentary* to the right and made it an articulate spokesman for neoconservatism.[28]

One of the foreign policy analysts whom Podhoretz began to feature in *Commentary* (though not until 1975) was Robert W. Tucker, a political science professor at Johns Hopkins University. Originally trained by Hans Kelsen in international law and political philosophy, Tucker did not turn his attention fully to American foreign policy until the late 1960s. Since that time his political path has been almost as winding as that of Podhoretz, taking him from liberal Republicanism in the 1960s to McGovern's neighborhood in 1972 and (temporarily) into Reagan's camp in 1980.[29] The political odysseys of Podhoretz and Tucker should not, of course, be seen as prima facie evidence of inconsistency. Yet it should also

---

since 1945 (New York, 1976) and Peter Steinfels, *The Neo-Conservatives* (New York, 1979).

[28] *Breaking Ranks* (New York, 1979).

[29] "Reagan without Tears," *New Republic*, May 17, 1980, pp. 22–25.

be remembered that the self-assuredness now demonstrated in the employ of neoconservatism, particularly in the case of Podhoretz, has at other times served radically different causes.

Despite these similarities, however, even a casual reading of the works of these two men quickly reveals serious differences in temperament, priorities, and policy recommendations. Indeed, so significant are these differences that one may wonder whether both can live comfortably under the roof of neoconservatism. That they can do so stems primarily from the nearly identical diagnoses they offer regarding the contemporary condition of American foreign policy.

America, they and the other neoconservatives agree, is in decline and has been for well over a decade. The failure in Vietnam, the non-reciprocal nature of détente, Watergate and the subsequent crippling of the Presidency, the pathetic responses to OPEC and Third World radicalism, and, most importantly, our inability and unwillingness to counter the massive Soviet arms buildup are but the most dramatic examples of a profound and pervasive erosion of American power. This decline, neoconservatives like Berger and Wattenberg (who are students of American society) tell us, must be seen as part of a more general rotting of traditional liberal values. Employing moderate democrats (or republicans) like Madison and Tocqueville as benchmarks, they decry the excesses of blacks, women, homosexuals, and other minorities who seek more and more equality. The consequences of this "illiberal extremism" are painfully obvious: the fragmentation of the family, the eclipse of traditional religions, reverse discrimination, pornography, drugs, the spawning of a psychoanalytic elite, and the growth of a culture of appeasement. And if all this is not shocking enough, these radical ideas have been embraced by an erstwhile liberal elite (the domestic counterpart to Gershman's foreign policy Establishment) which has supervised this destruction of American values and institutions.

Instead of refurbishing a policy of containment to deal effectively with a now strategically superior Soviet Union, the United States, Podhoretz and Tucker argue, has responded with détente and virtual appeasement. The same elites who have accepted radicalism at home have likewise abandoned liberalism abroad. The result, Tucker asserts in *The Inequality of Nations*, is that these possessors of a "new political sensibility" have forgotten that the essential nature of international relations has been and continues to be one of inequality. Naively believing that the world has entered an age of global interdependence, this elite (which included Carter advisers like Joseph Nye of Harvard) contends that the nation-state is an increasingly obsolete institution which retards the redistribution of wealth and the protection of human rights. This view is naive, Tucker argues, because it presumes the disutility of military force, the exclusive usefulness of economic power, and the acceptance of these "truths" by Third World leaders. In fact, the West has voluntarily (and mistakenly) renounced military power, while Third World elites interpret redistribution as a traditional state-to-state process which has nothing to do with a new sensibility. Tucker concludes that interdependence will as likely lead to chaos as to order if not managed by the military power of the industrial democracies. Indeed, the paramount problem facing American foreign policy, the neoconservatives agree, is not the "world order" dialogue between North and South but the age-old confrontation of East and West,[30] and it is here that we have lost our will.

At this point, however, the neoconservative consensus begins to unravel. What is striking about this disagreement is the way in which it parallels the argument between George Kennan and Paul Nitze in the late 1940s about the proper definition of containment. In short, in contemporary neoconservatism there are two distinct prescriptions for dealing with the Soviets which correspond to the respective positions of Kennan and Nitze three decades ago. In the 1980s it is Robert W. Tucker who is urging a more limited version of containment remarkably similar to that proposed by Kennan at the Policy Planning Staff, while Normal Podhoretz's more grandiose vision seems to be a direct descendant of the one articulated by Nitze in NSC–68.

Indeed, the neoconservatives often claim that political circumstances of the late 1940s and of today are eerily similar. In the earlier period, they argue, an artificial and one-sided era of good feeling between the Soviet Union and the United States (World War II), encouraged by a well-intentioned but rather naive president, was cruelly ended by a series of Soviet political and military

---

[30] "Beyond Détente," *Commentary*, March 1977, pp. 42–45.

A Neo-Consensus?

advances in Europe, Asia, and the Middle East. The American left and its hero, Henry Wallace, had no plausible or persuasive explanation for Soviet behavior. As the country moved to the right, the parameters of the foreign policy debate were set by these two competing concepts of containment. In the contemporary situation a similarly artificial and one-sided era of good feeling between the Soviet Union and the United States (détente, 1972 version) was encouraged by a politically crippled President, and his well-intentioned but rather naive successors (especially Carter). As in the 1940s, this period of cooperation was ended abruptly by a series of Soviet military and political advances, this time in Africa, Southeast Asia, the Persian Gulf, and Afghanistan. Once again the American left, now in power because of the 1976 election, had no plausible or persuasive explanation for Soviet behavior.[31]

If the neoconservative rendering of this history is correct, and today's public mood would seem to accept large parts of it, then the foreign policy debate of the next few years probably will closely parallel that of the late 1940s. That is, it will occur within the parameters originally fixed by Kennan and Nitze and recently rediscovered by Tucker and Podhoretz. And as was true in the earlier case, even though some might denigrate this as just another in-house debate, its outcome will have significant consequences for American foreign policy in the 1980s.

Let us begin with Tucker's more modest, Kennanesque understanding of containment. According to it, Soviet behavior continues to be motivated by a combination of traditional and ideological interests. Regardless of the root causes, however, the inexorable and apparently unappeasable character of the Soviet military expansion has made the "Finlandization" of the West a distinct possibility. To counter this threat, the United States must construct a new policy of containment. Although he fails to acknowledge his intellectual debt to the early Kennan, Tucker is

[31] That the American left can provide no ready answers in the wake of Afganistan seems rather clear. Listen, for instance, to Stanley Hoffmann, one of the most articulate of neoconservatism's critics: "American foreign policy is faced with a protracted, often acrimonious crisis with its European allies, and stuck in a deadlock with its chief rival. And the choices that confront the US seem to be either more of the same, or far worse" ("The Crisis in the West," *New York Review of Books,* July 17, 1980, p. 41).

aware of the confusing legacy of containment: "From the very start, Containment carried with it an underlying ambiguity, since from the very start a narrower concept of security coexisted with a much broader concept and one that might readily be put to expansionist ends."[32] Hence he is critical of those who, on the basis of Vietnam, would renounce containment itself. But, Tucker asks, in a manner reminiscent of the early Kennan, "Why should the quintessential character of Containment be found in Vietnam rather than in Western Europe or Japan?"[33] It ought not to be so found, Tucker admonishes. "What may be argued is that containment was discredited at the margin, not at the center, where it has enjoyed a success that finds few historical parallels."[34] Indeed, "where Containment has failed is here, at the periphery. Certainly, this is where the larger purpose of Containment [i.e., preventing the emergence of Communist governments] has failed. It is also where the narrower purpose [i.e., maintaining a favorable power balance], with few notable exceptions, can and should be limited."[35] Therefore, it is really not a question of forsaking détente for the "old containment policy of the classic cold war," for the international environment is no longer conducive to such a policy. Because of these changed conditions, it is clear to Tucker that "Containment in the future will have to be characterized by more modest objectives than in the past."[36] And what are these objectives? Prevention of Soviet military superiority, defense of Western Europe and Japan, and guaranteed access to Persian Gulf oil. Tucker assures us that even in the 1980s America has the material resources to successfully manage such a containment policy. What we may be lacking is the will, for even this rather modest version of containment will demand sacrifice. But if the United States follows such a course, rewards should be forthcoming: "A great military power has emerged intent on altering the global status quo. Its position of military ascendancy may nevertheless prove to be quite transient,

[32] "Beyond Détente," p. 48.
[33] Ibid.
[34] Ibid.
[35] Ibid., p. 49.
[36] Ibid., p. 50.

since it does not have the material base to sustain the present advantageous position, should its principal rival—let alone its rival together with the rival's allies—determine to redress the military balance."[37]

Tucker's recommendations parallel in essential respects those made by George Kennan in the late 1940s. This new version of containment, like the old, is no global, Wilsonian crusade carried on in the name of moral absolutism, but a very traditional, state-centered policy that emphasizes diplomacy, limited interests, and power balances. And while Kennan thought containment would induce a collapse or a mellowing of the Soviet leadership, so Tucker hopes that containment, 1980s version, will force a new moderation on the Kremlin.

For Podhoretz, on the other hand, there has been but one kind of containment practiced by America since 1945, and its mood can best be captured by this call to arms: "The thoughtful observer of Russian-American relations will find no cause for complaint in the Kremlin's challenge to American society. He will rather experience a certain gratitude for a Providence which, by providing the American people with this implacable challenge, has made their entire security as a nation dependent on their pulling themselves together and accepting the responsibilities of moral and political leadership that history plainly intended them to bear."[38] The words, of course, belong to George Kennan—not the usually skeptical and circumspect Kennan, but the feverish Mr. "X"; it is significant that Podhoretz seeks to recapture the old Kennan with this passage, which seems much more akin to Nitze, Clifford, or Keyserling.

Containment, then, according to Podhoretz, was never ambiguous in its definition of American security interests. "No doubt," he

---

[37] "America in Decline: The Foreign Policy of Maturity," *America and the World 1979, Foreign Affairs* 58, no. 3 (1979): 484. It is over the issue of military power that Kennan and Tucker differ, for while Kennan was always hesitant to specify instances when America ought to employ military power, Tucker has no similar compunction. Indeed it was Tucker's willingness to consider the forcible interdiction of Persian Gulf oil fields in 1975 which first brought him a certain public notoriety.

[38] *The Present Danger* (New York, 1980), p. 22.

admits, "the 'counter-force' Kennan had in mind was not exclusively military,"[39] but "there can be even less doubt that the American interventions into Korea and Vietnam were entirely consistent with his formulations."[40] Yet as this essay earlier tried to show with the help of several recently declassified documents, it was not Kennan but rather his bureaucratic rivals who urged interventions "on the periphery." It was Kennan, after all, who, in an age of unprecedented American superiority, advised the United States to marshal its not unlimited resources in defense of Western Europe, Japan, and North America.[41] Apparently unaware of these circumstances, Podhoretz embraces the early Kennan as the father of *his* containment, fails even to mention NSC–68 and its much more ambitious programs, and then argues that the only choice for America in the 1980s is a continuation of "appeasement" or a return to "containment."

Which path will America choose? Podhoretz is cautiously optimistic that the "culture of appeasement" spawned by the legacy of Vietnam is being swept away by a "new nationalism." Podhoretz's friend, Irving Kristol, betrays an even more expansive mood when he claims that "what we are witnessing is a powerful nationalist revival in this nation, a revival that coincides with the twitching death-throes of an American foreign policy that has always regarded American nationalism more as a problem than as an ally."[42] But, Podhoretz tells us, despite several promising signs, "something is still missing from the new nationalism," because the response of grass-roots America to outrages like Iran and Afghanistan has been excessively informed by economic interests.[43] Before a new period of containment can emerge, "Communism" must be rediscovered as a term in our vocabulary. This rediscovery is essential, Podhoretz asserts, for only then we will recognize that our conflict with the Soviet Union is "a struggle for freedom and against Com-

---

[39] Ibid., p. 18.

[40] Ibid.

[41] See p. 190.

[42] "The Trilateral Commission Factor," *Wall Street Journal*, April 16, 1980, p. 24.

[43] *The Present Danger*, p. 90.

A Neo-Consensus?

munism,"[44] "for democracy and against totalitarianism."[45] And yet, and yet. Podhoretz detects in the current public mood the first stirrings of a "repressed strain of internationalist idealism"[46] which could launch this country on a new Wilsonian crusade to make the world of the 1980s safe for democracy.

The neoconservatives, however, claim not to be mere populists. Kristol, for example, warns that "precisely because it lacked intellectual guidance and articulation, popular sentiment on foreign affairs has frequently degenerated into a crude chauvinism, isolationism, or even downright paranoia."[47] To avoid these "democratic" excesses, America needs the services of a new foreign policy Establishment dedicated not to a "world order" ideology which shuns the use of force but rather committed to a nationalist perspective intent on reasserting American leadership.[48]

But where do the neoconservatives propose to find this new elite? Primarily, of course, they expect to draw members from their own ranks. Some, like Henry Jackson, Daniel Patrick Moynihan, and Jack Kemp, already hold political office. The neoconservatives realize, however, that before their views can have a significant, long-term impact, they must be institutionalized. In other words, the neoconservatives hope to build their new elite by winning the hearts and minds of the "new class." There is no need here to engage in a protracted discussion of this sociological phenomenon, for the "new class" has been analyzed endlessly in the popular and academic press. (Indeed, it even has had a journal named for it.) What is most striking about the new class is that in terms of education and income its members strongly resemble those of Gabriel Almond's "attentive public" identified three decades ago. Today's neoconservatives have given this 10 percent of the population a

[44] Ibid., p. 97.

[45] Ibid., p. 100.

[46] "The New Nationalism and the 1980 Elections," *Public Opinion*, February/March 1980, p. 5.

[47] "The Trilateral Commission Factor."

[48] It should be noted that Kristol and Podhoretz have their differences, for whereas Podhoretz wishes to tap Wilsonian idealism, Kristol invokes the memory of Theodore Roosevelt. Tucker would no doubt share Kristol's sentiments.

slight twist by endowing it with attitudes that embrace an "adversarial culture."[49] The task of the neoconservatives is to wean the new class away from the nihilistic, rad-lib works of Vidal, Mailer, Warhol, and others and replace them with authors, artists, and ideas that extol the virtues of traditional middle-class life. If this challenge can be met, the new class can be expected to sire a new, politically responsible, nationalistically oriented elite to manage America's foreign and domestic affairs.

VI

Can the neoconservative dream be realized? More precisely, will there emerge in the United States during the 1980s a new foreign policy consensus, articulated and guided by a new Establishment and dedicated to a "new nationalism" which constructs a revitalized policy of containment?

The answer is reasonably clear. As this essay has tried to show, within neoconservatism there are at least two significantly different understandings of containment. Even if the neoconservatives' sociological projections are correct (a large assumption), the foreign policy prescriptions of neoconservatism may be subverted by the fundamental ambiguity of its concepts. So long as the neoconservatives remain essentially a vocal and prolific counterelite blasting away at a common target—the hated status quo—these policy disagreements need not be paralyzing. But if in the 1980s neoconservatism becomes the prevailing ideology of America (the next "conventional wisdom"), serious practical difficulties may lie ahead.

Indeed, if neoconservatism wins the day, we might expect to see a new foreign policy debate reminiscent of the one that occurred in the Truman administration during the late 1940s. Once again the two variants of containment will fix the parameters of the debate. The more modest, balance-of-power proposals of Tucker, Kristol, and others will vie for supremacy with the more ambitious,

[49] Interview with Michael Novak, *U.S. News and World Report*, February 25, 1980, p. 69.

A Neo-Consensus?

ideological programs of Podhoretz, Moynihan, Elmo Zumwalt,[50] and their allies.

Which version of containment will triumph? Much, of course, depends on Soviet behavior. Nitze and his friends were no doubt helped in their bureaucratic battles in 1950 by the Russian atomic tests and the Korean War. But domestic circumstances will be, as in the earlier case, just as important. Remember that Leon Keyserling, with his neo-Keynesian faith in taxes, defense spending, and budget deficits, was a decisive factor in the struggle over NSC-68. In this regard the less grandiose containment of Tucker may be more consistent with the pronounced anti-Keynesian outlook of many neoconservatives.

It is possible that neither version of containment will prove persuasive enough to form the basis of a new domestic consensus. Tucker himself suggested in 1977 that "a domestic consensus on foreign policy of a kind even roughly comparable to the consensus of the pre-Vietnam period does not appear to be a meaningful possibility."[51] Recent public opinion surveys would seem to indicate, however, that some sort of consensus is now more likely.

If a new consensus does crystallize from the popular moods of today, one can only hope that it will ultimately support the (old) Kennan-Tucker version of containment. To reject it in favor of the Nitze-Podhoretz variant would invite disaster. The reduced margin the United States now possesses, compared to that of 1950, means that an NSC-68 policy would suffer frustration regardless of the "will" exercised by its supporters. This frustration could easily degenerate into a witch hunt for treasonous members of the adversarial culture, whether they be appeasers, homosexuals, or other provocateurs. Given the pugnacious and flamboyant character of Podhoretz's rhetoric, one does not need much imagination to suppose that an unsuccessful containment policy of the sort he proposes could rapidly lead to an indiscriminate search for scapegoats, not by neoconservatives, but by unscrupulous fear-mongers in search of enemies. If it did so the historical analogy proposed by

---

[50] See his glowing review of *The Present Danger*, "The Cold War Heats Up," *Washington Post Book World*, August 3, 1980, p. 9.

[51] "Beyond Détente," p. 50.

this essay would be complete, for the excesses of the 1950s were at least partially caused by the reaction to the failed promises of NSC–68.

Fortunately, the Tucker version of containment appears to have a better chance to serve as the core of a new consensus than did its predecessor in the late 1940s. In the earlier era the smashing victory of World War II, the temporary weakness of our allies, and the newness of the Soviet threat all combined to make Kennan's more traditional strategy appear almost bland. In the early 1980s, however, in the wake of Vietnam and Watergate, the growing multipolarity and interdependence of the world, and the decades-long resiliency of the Soviets, perhaps Americans will rally around the version of containment which their leaders so resoundingly rejected in 1950.

Perhaps.

Power and Prudence in Dealing with the U.S.S.R.

Seyom Brown

RECENT events are symptomatic of the anachronism of both the Cold War and détente-linkage approaches to United States–Soviet relations. Both approaches are based on assumptions that are no longer tenable about the leverage each superpower has over the other and about their respective capacities to control other countries. Yet the hallmark of an anachronism is its persistence beyond its period of constructive utility.

Just as the superpowers can ill afford to ignore the implications of seemingly peripheral developments, neither can they afford to base most of their foreign policies single-mindedly on the United States–Soviet equation. The Soviet Union's carrot-and-stick policies toward Japan, for example, are dictated as much by the Kremlin's economic desire for Japanese cooperation in Siberian development and political fear of a possible Tokyo-Peking axis as by Russian assessments of the strengths of American commitments and power in Northeast Asia. Within the larger United States/Soviet/Chinese /Japanese quadrangle, the U.S.S.R. is involved in three triangles— one with the United States and China, one with the United States and Japan, and one with China and Japan—and as many two-way relationships, each of which operates somewhat autonomously.

Or take the situation in the Middle East. In the principal disputes between Israel and the Arabs over Palestinian self-determination and the status of Jerusalem, American ambivalence flows in part from fear of Soviet exploitation of Arab grievances. But it flows just as much from the fear that the Arab oil producers will once again, as they did in the Yom Kippur War, use oil as a political weapon against the United States or any country that supports Israel's security. The Kremlin's attempts to polarize the region and engage in opportunistic power plays, especially if motivated increasingly by Russia's own growing appetite for Persian Gulf oil, can indeed threaten major United States interests. But as often as not, such Soviet efforts get tripped up by the tangled alignments and antagonisms of the area, regardless of what the United States does. On a variety of issues in the Middle East today—ranging from the Arab-Israeli conflict to the Iranian hostage situation, to the fight between Iraq and Iran, to the transfer of nuclear technologies to states in the region—both superpowers would be troubled by profound dilemmas even if they could forget about their own rivalry.

The list of situations is extensive in which policies designed primarily with reference to the United States—Soviet global equation of power can distort the formulation and implementation of policies germane to more proximate causes and consequences of local problems. The boiling crises in Namibia and the Republic of South Africa, the Moroccan-Algerian conflict over the Western Sahara, the epidemic of political instability in Central America and the Caribbean (including the Cuban refugee problem), the Vietnam-Thailand border conflict—each of these provides United States policymakers with plausible reasons to invoke, and make central to the issues at hand, the geopolitical relationship with the Soviet Union. But the fact that the Soviet Union has clients in each of these situations and will gain or lose influence depending upon specific outcomes is an insufficient basis for United States policies that subordinate other implicated interests to the interest of containing Soviet power. Indeed, the long-term prospects for containing Soviet power in many of these situations may be more promising if the United States makes its immediate decisions on whom and what to support primarily for reasons other than opposing whomever and whatever the Soviets are supporting.

To argue in 1980 against a preoccupation with Soviet activities around the globe may seem like a belated attempt to support the foreign policy concepts enunciated by the Carter administration during its first year in office—concepts that quickly came under attack as naively unresponsive to the Soviet military buildup and its increasingly displayed capacities and inclinations to project Soviet power beyond the confines of the Warsaw Pact. My argument is that such concepts, expressed most prominently (if somewhat sloppily) in the President's Notre Dame University speech of May 1977, were precisely what should have been implemented as the Russians began to flex their global muscular mobility. The Soviet Union having attained full status as a military superpower and having eroded United States superiority in strategic weapons and naval strength, now more than ever is the time to avoid policies of confrontation and direct leverage which make the military balance the most telling element of power. Furthermore, now that the Soviet Union has developed capacities for moving military forces (its own, through proxies, or in the form of arms shipments) across continents and oceans into remote lands, efforts by the United States to counter a new Soviet presence in an area by developing anti-Soviet military allies and political clients play right into the Kremlin strategy of developing new spheres of influence by polarizing regions or countries into left ("progressive") vs. right ("reactionary") forces. Why drive half a country or region into the Soviet camp when the Russians by their own efforts might have trouble gaining even a third?

The foreign policy which Carter enunciated at Notre Dame did not fail. It was scarcely tried, except in Rhodesia-Zimbabwe where, along with the British, the administration pursued a policy of helping to build a broadly based, black-led regime in which the Marxist "national liberation" movement would be allowed to play a prominent part. Paradoxically, focusing the strategy on the indigenous political requirements for a new Zimbabwe government rather than on the fact that the Soviets and the Cubans were providing material help to the militant liberationists had the effect of isolating the local black agents of Soviet expansion from the genuinely nationalist (albeit Marxist) black militants. By doing so, the strategy assured that the new Zimbabwe government would not be a Soviet satellite and would be favorably disposed to developing cooperative relationships with the United Kingdom and the United States. In other words, the most serious blow to Kremlin ambitions of establishing a Soviet sphere of influence in Southern Africa was struck not in the name of anticommunism or containment of the Soviet Union but in the name of black liberation. However, the Soviet invasion of Afghanistan, overlapping in time the denouement of the Zimbabwe liberation struggle, obscured the lessons the United States should have been learning in Southern Africa.

Unfortunately, those in the Carter administration who had been urging restraint (in dealings with foreign movements and leaders who had accepted Soviet help) and deference to broad-based indigenous political groups in the Third World—even those which might be overtly anti-American—were unable to capitalize on the Rhodesian model. The Soviet invasion of Afghanistan, coming on top of growing anger at the Iranians for holding the United States embassy personnel as hostages, upstaged the African situation and turned the President's ear to advisers who were ready to see each event as an expression of the global contest with the Soviet Union for geopolitical ascendancy. Concepts like the "arc of crisis" and the "indivisibility of détente" simply engulfed Vance's effort to focus on the unique particulars of each situation. Such broad-stroke generalizations provided the appearance of intellectual control over otherwise confusing and contradiction-laden events and a compelling rationale for machismo posturing that catered to the President's desire to counter domestic and foreign impressions that he was indecisive and timid.

The revival of Cold War heroics is romantic, and dangerously so, for it flies in the face of realities to which we need to adapt prudentially. It would recreate a role for the United States which is incompatible with essentially irreversible changes in the military balance of power, which ignores the way the Soviets structure their priorities, which is out of phase with systemic developments in the global political economy, and which affronts the self-concepts of the majority of the world's nations.

The Military Balance of Power

Now that the Soviets have made themselves our equal in overall strategic nuclear power, it would be an illusion to assume that they will allow the United States to regain a significant margin of superiority, no matter how much the Soviets might have to bleed their economy to prevent it. Similarly, no one worldly enough to reach a top leadership position in the U.S.S.R. will expect the United States to allow the Soviets to transform the essential equivalence of United States and Soviet strategic forces into a usable Soviet superiority in any key component of the strategic balance.

To liberally paraphrase a famous Kissinger question: "What, then, in God's name, is going on?" For the superpowers appear to be engaged in a new strategic arms race for superiority. Indeed, both sides are attempting to increase their capacity to knock out the other side's ICBMs while reducing the vulnerability of their own; to improve the range and accuracy of sub-launched strategic missiles while striving for breakthroughs in antisubmarine warfare; to develop new technologies, most prominently in the laser field, which can be applied in modes constituting, in effect, an antiballistic missile capability; and to upgrade their intermediate-range strategic forces affecting the balance in the European theater.

On each side the new programs are justified as insurance against the other side's presumed drive to obtain strategic superiority. Strategic sophisticates—whether Russian or American—no longer seriously attribute to each other the objective of being able, in an all-out attack, to *disarm* the other side's strategic retaliatory capability at the outset of a war. But they do attribute to each other the intention of having strategic "war-fighting" forces which could be used to severely *degrade* the other side's strategic forces and overall military power in the early phases of a war, while one's own massive society-destroying forces are held back as a continuing threat to deter a massive reprisal by the enemy.

Today's strategic wisdom has it that a *perception* that one side could prevail in an initial "counterforce" campaign—that is, could degrade the other's military capabilities more than its own would be degraded—could well be translated by the side perceived to be superior in this respect into a decisive edge in the overall balance of power, for the simple reason that one could then pose as being less afraid of strategic war than one's opponents. The jargon of the strategic experts provides a vivid warning of the implications: The side that has counterforce superiority will be able to dominate the usable top rungs of the escalation ladder and, by credibly threatening to ascend to these top rungs, can dominate conflicts at lower levels, even political confrontations that have not yet turned violent. According to former Secretary of Defense Harold Brown, it was to deny the Soviets this kind of military superiority that he recommended, and Carter approved in Presidential Directive no. 59, a revision of strategic doctrine that would strengthen American capabilities for controlled strategic attacks on military installations.

The main point I wish to make here is that both super-powers' absolute determination not to allow the other to gain strategic superiority now encompasses the "war-fighting" components of their strategic arsenals as well as the massive, society-destroying deterrent components of their arsenals. Consequently, neither side realistically can expect to gain a degree of strategic superiority over the other that can be translated into coercive diplomatic leverage, even as we move beyond the MAD (Mutual Assured Destruction) era in the balance of terror. Each understandably feels compelled to build new counterforce systems to prevent the other side from gaining such an edge, and each views the other's programs as indicative of an intention to gain such an edge; but any such edge is highly unlikely to materialize, let alone to be sustained for any length of time.

One hope has been that the counterforce modernization of strategic forces and the associated strategic "war-fighting" logic would restore the credibility of United States pledges to use strategic nuclear forces against the Soviet Union in a future war for the control of Central Europe, if NATO forces otherwise would be defeated by the Warsaw Pact forces. The premise is that NATO possession of effective strategic war-fighting capabilities will remove any confidence the Soviets might have had in the MAD-only era that they could bully the West Europeans without placing the Soviet homeland in jeopardy. (This is part of the rationale of NATO's plan to deploy in West Europe cruise missiles and extended-range Pershings capable of striking Soviet territory.) The new deployments may indeed reequalize the fear of the Soviet Union and the United States that any war in Europe could rapidly turn into World War III and that neither side can control the risks. To this extent, moving beyond MAD could help to reduce the political leverage the Soviets might have hoped to gain from maintaining local military superiority in the European theater while attaining parity with the United States in intercontinental strategic forces.

But the balance of terror nonetheless retains its stark implications: Even with its beefed-up capabilities in Europe and counterforce modernization of its intercontinental strategic arsenal, the United States probably could do no better than to fight the Soviet Union to a draw over Europe before facing a level of thermonuclear warfare that would be suicidal for both sides. Rather than reviving the credibility of a vigorous NATO response to Soviet provocations, the full integration into NATO war plans of capabilities that blur the distinction between local tactical war and strategic war may be more inhibiting on member countries than were previous configurations of the military balance.

The basic reality cannot be avoided. The Soviet Union's attainment of essential strategic equality with the United States has reduced dramatically the efficacy of United States policies that rely primarily on the military balance of power to contain Soviet imperial expansion. Of course, an across-the-board military balance vis-à-vis the Soviet Union must be maintained in order to limit the Soviets' opportunities to enlarge their international sphere of control simply by applying military muscle. But the military ballance will be insufficient to prevent *all* Soviet military aggression and woefully irrelevant to other forms of Soviet influence building.

Situations may emerge on the rimland regions of the vast Eurasian landmass—where the West historically has confronted and turned back Russian expansionary drives—in which the Soviet Union, by a combination of relatively easy overland access and new naval capabilities for interdicting sea-borne access by the West, can dominate rather decisively if the East-West military balance alone is the controlling factor. This should have been the main lesson of the Christmas 1979 invasion of Afghanistan, not the lesson that we should redress the military balance—the latter being implied in the quick-fix responses by the Carter administration of procuring a Rapid Deployment Force, attempting to resurrect the moribund military alliance with Pakistan, negotiating new base agreements with countries on the Indian Ocean littoral, and threatening possible military action against the Russians if their actions indicate an effort to gain control over the Persian Gulf area. Nor can the United States attempt to regain an ability to affect Iran's internal political situation by augmenting United States military capabilities in and deployable to the Persian Gulf area. Such efforts only compound the errors in previous American policy toward Iran.

The most salient political movements and alignments in the Near East (in an area characterized by highly fluid and shifting alignments) are not those organized by the superpowers and treated as pawns in their global rivalry. Yet the previous status of Iran as the favorite United States client in the region and the shah as our Iranian hero (see Kissinger's almost worshipful paean to the shah in his *Memoirs*) was a function of Iran's weight and reliability as a military and political ally of the United States against Soviet attempts to penetrate the area militarily and politically, and of the shah's draconian determination to break the back of indigenous leftist movements. As it turned out, we were lucky that the vanguard of the revolution that overthrew the shah was not sponsored by and beholden to the Soviet Union. We may, however, still drive the revolution into the hands of its minority who are Marxists, and the even smaller minority who are pro-Soviet, if by continuing to threaten the Iranians on the hostage issue, or by seeming to tilt toward Baghdad in the Iraqi-Iranian conflict, we confirm the propaganda of the Marxists that the United States remains the main "imperialist" enemy. Indeed, that might already have happened were it not for the Iranian outrage at the Soviet Union's invasion of Afghanistan and their subsequent anger at the Kremlin for acquiescing in, if not abetting, Iraq's September 1980 military attack on Iran.

The best that the United States can hope for internationally from most of the countries in the Middle East is a determined posture of nonalignment with either superpower. But even this hope may crash in any country if domestic chaos produces such confusion that a disciplined group of pro-Soviet militants (even if a small minority) is able to establish enclaves of control with Soviet covert help and then convert these into a larger, perhaps even dominating, Soviet presence, under everyone's noses. It is highly implausible that the Russians, once in, could be backed out (as they were from Iran in 1946) by implicit or explicit United States military threats. Nor are the United States efforts to create new military allies in the region, to fill the regional power vacuum left by Iran's defection from the United States security system, likely to reduce the chances of these worst-case internal developments. On the contrary, they are more likely to exacerbate the virulence of anti-Americanism among Muslim nationalists of various ideological persuasions.

Our frustrations in the Iran and Afghanistan situations and our paltry leverage in the war between Iraq and Iran are the product of having to learn over and over again, ever since the Suez crisis of 1956, that tending to the East-West balance of military power, while necessary in and of itself, will not give us the wherewithal to tend effectively to our interests in the Middle East—commercial access to the region's oil supplies, the security of Israel, *and* the containment of Soviet imperial expansion. Military logistical factors, which are still importantly determined by geography, put the United States at a disadvantage in attempting to compete directly with the Soviet Union in capabilities that these powers could use against each other in war for control of the region; and a competition for military allies to play the Kremlin's preferred game of polarizing the region and making its clients even more completely dependent upon the Soviet Union. Nixon and Kissinger eventually learned that the best way to have the Russians thrown out of Egypt was not for the United States to attempt to do it, but to let Sadat do it for his own reasons. They did not, however, apply what they had learned to Africa. Carter and Brzezinski, except for Zimbabwe, appear to have been extraordinarily slow learners in analogous situations. And the Reagan team seems determined to reinstitute a foreign policy based on a view of the world as basically bipolar, with Moscow and Washington the only relevant poles of attraction, and with the essence of their power being military—leading to policies based on the premise that in an arms race with the Soviet Union, the United States will be able to regain its lost status as the preeminent global power. But surely this is romanticism, not realism.

The Dangers of Military Confrontation and the Search for Other Levers on Soviet Behavior

Top United States policymakers had quite accurate views of the Kremlin's international priorities starting about 1946, when the containment policy was formulated, to the Cuban Missile crisis of 1962, up through the Nixon-Kissinger initiatives for détente with the U.S.S.R. and normalization of relations with China in 1972. The Soviet leaders, it was understood, were interested primarily in securing their own power base against a world perceived as hostile to the Marxist-Leninist experiment in Russia. The doctrine that there had to be "socialism in one country" first—that immediate priority should be given to securing the Soviet state, from which the world revolution subsequently could be directed and supported—was correctly seen by the United States government's

Sovietologists as engendering a basically cautious international policy by the Soviet Union: foreign adventures, international revolutionary zeal that would substantially raise the risks of the survival of the U.S.S.R. itself, would have to be deferred. The Soviets might probe for power vacuums, for weak spots beyond the periphery of their satellite empire in Eastern Europe, but if they struck steel they would push no further, and they might even retreat if confronted with the prospects of counteraction threatening the security of the U.S.S.R.

Given these Soviet priorities and calculations, the policy of containing the Soviet Union within its existing sphere of control principally by manipulating the military components of power would make sense as long as the United States held the high cards for any major military confrontation. The Kremlin could be deterred, and a war would not have to be fought. The Soviet Union could be pushed into abandoning its belt of satellite states in Eastern Europe only over new millions of dead bodies, however, for the Russians regarded this security-belt dividend from World War II as essential to their own survival.

The Soviets could be dissuaded relatively easily from expansionary moves, whether motivated by traditional Russian imperialist drives or by Bolshevik messianic impulses, if the West and in particular the United States had the will to engage in countermoves that carried a high risk of nuclear war if the Kremlin dared to take up the challenge. Even in the city of Berlin, where the Western presence 110 miles into communist East Germany was a persisting embarrassment to the Soviets and where massive local Soviet and East German forces could overwhelm the token deployments of United States and West German forces, Stalin in 1948–1949 and then Khrushchev in 1958 and 1961 were turned back from their probes to test the West's determination. The Soviets backed off because the United States made credible its willingness to fight to sustain the Western sectors of the city and strongly suggested by its deployments and its rhetoric that the fight would not be confined to Berlin and its environs but would rapidly expand to threaten the Soviet homeland itself.

However, the Russians have not been deterred from applying major military force against insurrectionary movements in East Germany in 1953, Hungary in 1956, and Czechoslovakia in 1968, or from erecting a wall through the city of Berlin in 1961 to keep discontented Easterners from escaping to the West. In each of these cases, effective United States countermoves were precluded by assumptions about priority Soviet security interests in Eastern Europe and by the fear, probably warranted, that the Russians would fight desperately to sustain them.

In short, the policy of deterring Soviet aggressive moves has worked only where the targets of Kremlin international power plays have been of secondary interest to the Soviets—that is, not crucial for the survival of the Soviet state in Russia. It has not worked, even in the era of American strategic nuclear superiority, where the Kremlin has attempted to maintain control over areas and situations essential (in its view) to the security of the U.S.S.R.

The basic Soviet priorities have not changed. But the requirements one can deduce from them for an effective and prudent United States foreign policy are not the same as they were in the period when the United States held a decisive advantage in the global military balance of power because of its strategic nuclear superiority.

Where it can be credibly held that vital United States security interests are at stake and the Soviets are pursuing only secondary interests, attempts to contain Soviet expansion by threats of military counteraction may still make sense. Certainly, the United States should maintain military forces for such situations, even though effective diplomacy would make it unnecessary to employ these forces in actual battle. Especially problematic are situations in which there is a clash of secondary interests between the United States and the Soviet Union. It is here that the changed military balance does bear heavily on mutual assessments of the will to sustain one's position if it comes to a confrontation. Such situations carry great risks of the kinds of miscalculations that could spark World War III.

When the United States had obvious military superiority (at least at the top rungs of the escalation ladder), it had the luxury of inflating its secondary interests when they were threatened into primary ones—repelling the invasion of South Korea by the Soviet Union's allies; securing the political status of West Berlin against Soviet attempts to make the East Germans the authorizing power for Western access to and activities in the city—by directly engaging American prestige. The Russians had sense enough not to lock themselves into a confrontation sequence with the Americans in such circumstances by engaging their own prestige beyond what was appropriate for secondary interests. Now, however, with the United States having lost the military wherewithal to dominate the top of the escalation ladder, the Soviets may not want to acquiesce in the kind of one-sided interest-inflation stratagems it allowed the United States to get away with in the past. The Soviets too may be tempted to inflate their secondary interests into primary ones by engaging their prestige, by making unequivocal public statements of commitment, or by putting Russian bodies on the line, say, in a confrontation on the Berlin Autobahn or at the Strait of Hormuz controlling access to the Persian Gulf, under the assumption that, given essential strategic equality, the Americans must be bluffing.

In other words, more than at any time in the sixty-three years of the United States–Soviet relationship, conditions are now ripe for terrible games of chicken, in which both sides have committed themselves to incompatible objectives so heavily and visibly that neither can back down without great humiliation; therefore, each becomes all the more determined to demonstrate an irrevocable commitment to persist toward its objective, in the hope that the certainty of a head-on collision will convince the *other* side to swerve out of the way first.

The Soviet leadership now gives a higher priority than ever before to maintaining the image of equality with the United States as a global superpower. In the past, yielding in a confrontation over a peripheral objective could be justified as elementary Bolshevik realism in light of the "correlation of forces." Today, under the changed correlation of forces, the United States should be equally ready to yield; therefore, the Soviet leadership is more likely than before to regard backing down under pressure as un-Bolshevik. A superpower worthy of the name must demonstrate steadfastness on behalf of those who have accepted its protection, or else be humiliated in front of the world as not having the courage to match its attained power.

The détente policies of Kissinger were in part an attempt to find benign channels for this new Kremlin determination to be regarded by the world as a superpower coequal with the United

States. Negotiation rather than confrontation would be a saner approach to dealing with the Soviet leaders, given their changed perception of the correlation of forces. Thus the Nixon-Brezhnev Declaration of Principles signed at the 1972 Moscow Summit, wherein both sides affirmed that "in the nuclear age there is no alternative to conducting their mutual relations on the basis of peaceful coexistence," pledged to develop relations with each other "based on the principles of sovereignty, equality, non-interference in internal affairs and mutual advantage," and to refrain from "efforts to obtain unilateral advantage at the expense of the other, directly or indirectly."

Kissinger at the time took all this coexistence verbiage very seriously, as a necessary part of the realpolitik imperative of committing the revolutionary power to principles of legitimacy at the moment when its continued paranoid pursuit of absolute security, coupled with its attainment of full strategic nuclear equality vis-à-vis those who would counter its aggressive moves, could plunge the world into a total holocaust. Coequal political status and a visible consultative relationship with the United States were one set of inducements in the package of incentives offered to the Kremlin to pursue a moderate foreign policy.

Another set of incentives working upon the Soviets to pursue benign policies toward the capitalist West was created in the Kremlin itself in the late 1960s when it abandoned the policy of providing for the Soviet Union's economic well-being primarily *within* the "Socialist Commonwealth" through specialization of production and trade among the member countries. Henceforth, or at least for the next few five-year planning periods, the U.S.S.R. would attempt to take advantage of the specialization of production within the global market by actively expanding its commerce with the United States and other non-socialist countries.

To be allowed to buy and sell in the global market on an equal basis with the capitalists, to qualify for "Most Favored Nation" trading status in the United States and for government-sponsored credits, the Soviets would have to show themselves to be not only reliable commercial partners but also constructive participants in the existing international system—not the leaders of a worldwide revolutionary conspiracy determined to smash the existing system. In the first time since 1947, when Stalin in rejecting the Marshall

Plan made it clear he had no intention of participating in the capitalist-run system according to its rules, the Soviet leaders in the late 1960s were indicating a willingness to accept such a moderation of the role of the U.S.S.R.

Nixon and Kissinger were willing to credit the Brezhnev regime with a sincere intention to adhere to the rules of the Western state system. They faced a Congress determined to limit the war powers of the presidency and other foreign policy prerogatives of the executive branch which for three decades had sustained the role of the United States as policeman against Soviet aggressive expansion. In the late 1960s and early 1970s the Congress, reflecting growing popular sentiments, was in a mood to trim the defense budget as well—not only to prevent further Vietnams but also to devote more of the nation's resources to improving conditions at home instead of attempting to do good in an ungrateful world.

Détente was supposed to be a grand bargain struck between the superpowers: You refrain from exploiting your enlarged military prowess to take advantage of us in our post-Vietnam retrenchment from overseas involvements and we will help you out in your drive to modernize your economy and to attain international respectability. A cooperative approach was essential to the ability of each power to implement its basic policies without embarrassment. Moreover, if both sides adhered to the bargain, the prospects for successfully negotiating SALT and other arms-limitation agreements were enhanced; neither would expect to have to rely on its military arsenal for coercing the other to refrain from intolerable moves.

The Sino-Soviet conflict, meanwhile, provided another powerful lever the United States could apply to the Kremlin: United States–Chinese negotiations which implied possible help to China in building power in Asia against the Russians. The Kremlin presumably would compete with Peking to be in the good graces of the United States and accordingly, in addition to other accommodationist policies, would bring pressure on the North Vietnamese to negotiate a compromise peace with the Americans.

As it turned out, neither the expansion of American-Soviet commerce nor the United States–China connection provided as much levering power on the Kremlin as expected. The prospects for a sufficient interlinking of the American and Soviet economies to give the Kremlin a material interest in détente were undercut severely by the conditions Congress imposed (especially Soviet liberalization of their restrictions of Jewish emigration) on extending to the U.S.S.R. Most Favored Nation trading privileges and Export-Import Bank credits. Kissinger argued in vain against congressional attempts to get a controlling grip on the commercial lever and to use it on matters the Russians considered under their total sovereign control. Suggestions that such leverage might be used to dissuade the Soviets from their intervention with the Cubans in Angola were met with jeers from Brezhnev and his associates. They perceived that in the one area in which United States-Soviet commerce had expanded appreciably—grain shipments—the American farmers would now act as a lobby for the Kremlin to assure no major constrictions in the flow. In other fields of high interest to Soviet economic planners, such as advanced computers, electronics, and oil-drilling technology, the Russians told their potential American suppliers that although they preferred the United States technologies, they would satisfy their needs in Japan and Western Europe if the American government tried to make them pay a "political price" over and above the normal market price for such purchases. Here too, the Kremlin was able to create lobbies in behalf of fair trading with the Russians in the American government (especially in the Commerce Department) and in powerful elements of the business community. Experience with the economic side of détente quickly showed that any attempt to use commerce directly as a one-sided lever on Soviet political policy was bound to be neutralized by the essential structure of the economic relationships, which characteristically involved a *mutual* interest.

But even the more modest hope that United States-Soviet commerce would provide restraints on hawkish elements within each country has turned out to be mostly illusion. Less than one-tenth of 1 percent of the GNP of each country is involved in United States-Soviet trade—hardly a level of "interdependence" that could not be dispensed with for higher reasons of state. Perhaps the incentives for continuing and expanding commerce on both sides could deter the two countries from getting into bitter confrontations over tertiary objectives; but for the secondary yet highly significant interests of each—for example, access to the petroleum resources and militarily important locales in the Persian Gulf area—the "opportunity costs" of aggressive behavior, in the sense of sacrificing some of the economic benefits of détente, apparently have not weighed heavily in the choice of strategies in Moscow or Washington.

The China connection too has been found wanting as a lever on Soviet behavior once the initial impact had been registered in the early 1970s. When revealed dramatically in the first visits to China of Kissinger and Nixon, it probably did operate as a powerful goad to the Russians to strengthen their own détente relationship with the Americans. That the connection as first unveiled in the 1972 Shanghai communique was very loose but had the potential of enlargement and solidification, was supposed to provide leverage on the Soviets. Presumably the Kremlin would have great fear that the limited economic and technological cooperation discussed by the Chinese and the Americans in 1972 could provide the scaffolding for an American-sponsored military buildup of China as a counterweight to the U.S.S.R. in Asia and even, at some time in the future, a Sino-American alliance. Yet Moscow's fear of a growth and solidification of the United States–China connection has been difficult for Washington to exploit. One problem has been that during the Carter administration the Americans appear to have lost control over the timetable for the elaboration of the connection with China. Peking clearly was the pacesetter in the move to have full diplomatic recognition coincide with China's military incursion into Vietnam to punish it for bullying China's allies in Cambodia. At the time the United States government was not particularly anxious to create the impression that it was endorsing the Chinese military incursion; yet this unavoidably was the impression created, and the Chinese surely must have anticipated and relished this effect.

United States and Chinese interests simply do not coincide on the degree of hostility each has for the Soviet Union and on how best to articulate, in rhetoric and concrete acts, the Sino-American side of this triangle in dealings with the Russians. Chinese and American interests are even less likely to be fully congruent in Asia, especially with respect to other large countries in the region, particularly Japan and Indonesia—not to mention Taiwan or South Korea. Thus, the United States cannot afford to regard the China connection only as a function of its own relationship with the

U.S.S.R. It must be elaborated carefully with respect to the myriad of intersecting American and Chinese interests, some of them antagonistic, not only in Asia, but also in Africa, the Middle East, and even Europe. It would be imprudent, to say the least, to hold United States diplomacy toward China hostage to the heating and cooling of our relationship with the U.S.S.R. The Russians themselves have begun to realize how constrained we are in actually using the China lever (or card, if you must); and this has further reduced its effectiveness.

The United States–Soviet Rivalry in a Pluralistic World

The dangers of the Cold War approach to dealing with the U.S.S.R. and the ineptitude of the détente-linkage approach emanate from a central premise they both share: that the world is still essentially bipolar. There are a number of empirical and philosophical confusions at the root of the persistence of this false premise. One is the equation in international relations of military power with political power. Another is the confusion of the gross power of a country with its polar attractiveness to other countries. Still another is the tendency to regard what is most dramatic in a situation as its essence.

If military power is measured by the capacity to inflict physical destruction, then in the military realm surely the United States and the Soviet Union are superpowers and the others are of lesser account. Only the United States and the Soviet Union can convincingly balance each other's military power, and thus if any other state gets itself into an all-out military confrontation with either of the superpowers, the only hope the smaller state has of defending itself is to accept the protection of the rival superpower. The implication is that either superpower can push around any other country in the system if it chooses to unless it is countered by the other superpower. And if force continues to be the *ultima ratio* of international politics, then what's all this nonsense about the end of bipolarity?

The main problem with the above chain of reasoning, which leads to the conclusion that military bipolarity still prevails in the world and, by extension, that the world is essentially bipolar, is the reductionist fallacy that all or most international politics operates at its ultimate level, where who can destroy whom the worst determines the bargaining. In fact, the real stuff of most international politics involves assessments of who can do what to whom—negatively and positively—well below the *ultima ratio* of the global balance of military power. More often than not, the substance of what lesser powers want from each other and from the superpowers and the relative values placed on different objectives are the immediate and sufficient determinants of who gets what in international relations. Any so-called superpower that is not well tuned into and responsive to the rather mundane values and objectives of those it hopes to influence will find itself isolated and ultimately impotent in the normal, everyday realm of politics. And it is by effectiveness in this normal realm that friends are made and alliances forged for even some of the more extreme confrontations.

The states that constitute real poles of attraction are thus those with foreign policies, resources, and diplomats capable of relating positively to the needs of other societies. On such a scale of attractiveness, the world of 1980 is far from bipolar.

This is not an academic quibble over the semantics of discourse. Rather, it is a warning against the consequences of the conceptual traps that have closed the minds of many policymakers and their advisers to the requirements and opportunities for effectively conducting this country's rivalry with the Soviet Union for influence in an increasingly pluralistic world system.

If the world were still indeed as bipolar as it was during the first fifteen years or so after World War II, then attempts to contain Soviet expansionism primarily by influencing the Soviet leadership's perceptions of what the United States could do directly to them (or *for* them) could be regarded as an effective and efficient foreign policy. But today there are very few situations in which Soviet incentives to enlarge upon their current global presence or to engage in coercive power plays can be altered significantly by our threats or promises to give or withhold anything from the Soviet Union itself. In most situations the Kremlin will calculate the advantages and disadvantages of particular moves in terms of the acceptability of or resistance to them within the countries that are the targets of their moves. In most circumstances, the United States itself will be a target of Soviet moves only in the remotest sense. And the Soviets are likely to be unimpressed by efforts to appoint ourselves as the real targets.

A more effective and efficient general strategy of containing Soviet expansion in the 1980s would be based on the assumption that the most prudent means of limiting Soviet power and influence is to help other people to attain what they value through means that enlarge their pride in themselves as capable of determining their own way of life. The United States should not just tolerate East-West nonalignment as a legitimate foreign policy stance for most countries today, but should positively endorse it. Similarly, with respect to the complexion of regimes within some states, it would not be the province of the United States to insist that they must choose to be either Marxist or non-Marxist, socialist or capitalist, or what have you. Rather, the United States would once again invoke the traditional support for the notion that we do indeed stand for the right of each nation to determine its own form of government according to what it decides suits it best—the only proviso being that the elemental human right of individuals to be protected against brutal treatment by private parties or governments should be maintained in all societies.

Such a policy would also mean putting the tangible resources and talents of this country where our rhetoric is when it comes to the attempt to do good works abroad. The worthiness of a foreign partner for help in putting advanced technologies to work, for a concessionary loan to finance local development efforts, for scientific and cultural exchange programs, would not be determined on the basis of a loyalty test on whom he would stand with in some future conflict between the United States and the Soviet Union. His stance would be expected to emerge later, if it ever becomes important to decide, from the productive relationships he develops now, rather than the other way around.

The East-West loyalty test is too simple a criterion, yet it remains tempting for policy planners and bureaucrats as a neat and easy way out of the more difficult (and often more controversial) task of deriving criteria for allocating scarce resources among foreign clients. Such criteria, which often must be applied and marginally revised on a case-by-case basis, are more difficult to explain to congressional committees, to sell to the public, and to represent in negotiations with other countries. But such an approach to the conduct of foreign relations ought to cut across the grain of this country's domestic pluralistic style and our pre–World War II traditions of international nonalignment less than it would contradict the fundamental tenets and style of the Soviet Union's politics.

If the United States has a natural comparative advantage in the competition with the U.S.S.R. for global influence, it lies precisely here—in the respective capacities of the two to relate their own normal ways of conducting the more mundane business of life to the variety of ways of life attempting to coexist in the contemporary world. To conceive of and run our global competition with the Soviets primarily in terms of the military ingredients of power is to concede the Soviets, now pretty much our military equals, more influence than they deserve. No less foolish is the effort to reduce Soviet influence by attempting to persuade them by direct inducements not to compete against us in the world with those very instruments of power in which they are our equals. Our job is to work more with the other countries—the potential Soviet targets—rather than on the Russians.

This is not to suggest that we give short shrift to preventing the Soviet Union from gaining military superiority, especially in the strategic weapons field, or give up on attempting to plug the gaps in the ability of the United States in conjunction with our allies to defeat militarily any local Soviet military aggression beyond their current sphere of physical control. Soviet attempts to exploit their newfound military prowess must, of course, be kept to a minimum.

I am, however, arguing against the revival of the idea that because force is the only thing the Russians understand, a military containment policy is not only necessary but sufficient. We may have had the luxury of making that fallacious deduction in the past. It was never our *best* way of dealing with the Russians; and today, when increasingly the best way to deal with the Russians is to deal first with the rest of the world, it is pitifully quixotic.

How does my approach relate to some of the other ideas in this volume? First, with reference to the general objective of containing Soviet power and expansion, I believe that containment must continue to be a basic objective, but specific American foreign policies need not always parade under an anti-Soviet, let alone anti-Communist, banner. Emphasis should be put on the proximate factors of containment—namely, the ability and will of countries in the expansionary path of the U.S.S.R. to resist Soviet power plays. The power equation between the Soviet Union and such potential targets of its expansion is in the first instance a measure of the ability of the Soviet Union to provide or deny what these countries want at the mundane levels of economics, technology, and military hardware, not at the *ultima ratio* level of the Soviet Union's ability to overpower such countries in military conflict. It is important, therefore, for potential targets of Soviet power plays to be able to get what they want elsewhere and, better yet, to deny to the U.S.S.R. what the Kremlin wants. In other words, such countries should be encouraged to reduce their dependence on the U.S.S.R. and to increase the dependence of the U.S.S.R. on *them*, not necessarily the United States.

This suggests a United States policy of containment similar to George Kennan's prescriptions of the late 1940s for strengthening the economic and political fiber of societies, in contrast to a reliance primarily on a military balance of power organized by the United States. And it is similar to Kennan's underlying assumption that Russia's actual use of its ultimate capacity to smash such countries militarily is not credible in most of the cases we will be encountering. Afghanistan should be regarded as the exception rather than the typical case.

Second, in terms of the distinction developed by Gaddis, my approach would be a type of *nonsymmetrical*, as opposed to symmetrical, containment. It is not an attempt to match Soviet power region by region, country by country. Rather, it seeks to relate United States capacities to other countries' wants on a case-by-case basis according to the timetable that emerges out of the particular bilateral relationships, not primarily as a reaction to heightened Soviet involvement.

Third, my approach does not rule out the activation of balances of power—global and regional—to contain the hegemonal impulses of the Soviet Union. But such balances of power should be allowed to form for the most part spontaneously rather than as a result of a systematic grand strategy to form a New Coalition (including China), as proposed by Thomas Robinson.

Fourth, my approach is consistent with a positive exploitation of the opportunities for economic and technological cooperation across ideological lines, pointed to in the Asian region by Allen Whiting. Some of the large-scale cooperative ventures should involve the U.S.S.R.—not as a part of a crude leverage-linkage strategy, but rather because the vast Eurasian continent is ripe for development, and the dynamic energies of the U.S.S.R. are better loosed on this immense and dramatic task than on acts of domestic repression and international machismo.

Fifth, on the handling of the human rights problems my position is that a fundamental and durable expansion of human rights in a repressive country is more likely to result from basic socioeconomic and political development than from other countries or international organizations making human rights reforms a condition for dealing with that country. The best hope for a more open society in the Soviet Union lies in its emergence from its historic isolation and paranoid fear of the outside world. Perhaps the only hope for the U.S.S.R. breaking out of the cruel historical dialectic recounted by Yanov—Russia's oscillation between tentative liberalization and draconian repression—lies in a solid commitment by the government and party leadership to economic and technological modernization that will require, unavoidably, long-term interaction with the economies and centers of technological innovation in the West. However, by making such interaction a reward for liberalization and by holding it back punitively when liberalization is stalled, we may simply strengthen the hands of the illiberal, xenophobic forces in Soviet society which want to prevent any penetration of the U.S.S.R. by carriers of the idea of greater freedom.

Contributors

Index

Contributors

SEYOM BROWN is Professor of Politics at Brandeis University. He has been Director of the U.S.-Soviet Relations Program at the Carnegie Endowment for International Peace, a Senior Fellow at the Brookings Institution, and a social scientist at the Rand Corporation. He has also been a consultant to the Department of State and the Department of Defense. He is the author of *New Forces in World Politics* and other works.

JOHN LEWIS GADDIS is Professor of History at Ohio University. He has also taught at the U.S. Naval War College (1975–77) and at the University of Helsinki (1980–81). He is the author of *The United States and the Origins of the Cold War* (1972), *Russia, the Soviet Union, and the United States: An Interpretive History* (1978), and *From Kennan to Kissinger: The Idea of Containment in Postwar American Strategy and Diplomacy* (forthcoming 1982).

RICHARD A. MELANSON, Coleader of this conference and Director of the Public Affairs Conference Center in 1979–80, is an Assistant Professor of Political Science at Kenyon College. He received his Ph.D. from Johns Hopkins University in 1974 and taught previously at UCLA. He is the author of several articles on American foreign policy. Dr. Melanson, currently an NEH Fellow, is working on a book entitled "Writing History and Making Policy: The Cold War, Vietnam, and American Diplomacy."

THOMAS W. ROBINSON is Professor of International Relations at the National War College, National Defense University. A student of Chinese and Soviet domestic politics and foreign policies, international relations, and national security studies, he has held posts at the Rand Corporation and the Council on Foreign Relations and has taught at a number of universities, including Columbia, Dartmouth, Princeton, UCLA, and Washington. He has published widely in these fields, has edited and coauthored a number of books, and is preparing studies of Chinese foreign policy, Soviet Asian policy, and Chinese political biography.

MYRON RUSH is Professor of Government at Cornell University. For ten years, before coming to Cornell, he was a Senior Staff Member of the Rand Corporation. He has been awarded research fellowships by the National Humanities Foundation, the Research Institute on Communist Affairs, Columbia University, and the Social Science Research Council. He is the author of the following books: *How Communist States Change Their Rulers; Political Succession in the USSR; The Rise of Khrushchev*; and *Strategic Power and Soviet Foreign Policy* (coauthor).

KENNETH W. THOMPSON is Director of the White Burkett Miller Center of Public Affairs, Distinguished Professor at the University of Virginia, and former Vice President of the Rockefeller Foundation. His books include *Political Realism; Understanding World Politics; Ethics, Functionalism and Power in International Politics; American Diplomacy; Christian Ethics and the Dilemmas of Foreign Policy; The Moral Issue in Statecraft; Foreign Assistance; Interpreters and Critics of the Cold War; Foreign Policy and the Democratic Process*; and most recently *Masters of International Thought*; and *Morality and Foreign Policy*.

ALLEN S. WHITING is Professor of Political Science at the University of Michigan where he teaches courses on China and Sino-Soviet relations. Mr. Whiting, who received his Ph.D. from Columbia University in 1952, has written widely on international relations. Among his many works are *China Crosses the Yalu; China's Future*; and *China and the United States: What Next?*, and, in 1981, *Siberian Development and East Asia: Threat or Promise?*

LAURIE S. WISEBERG is Executive Director of the Human Rights Internet and Coeditor of the *Human Rights Internet Reporter*. A political scientist and a graduate of UCLA, the University of London, and McGill, she has taught at the University of Illinois, Ahmadu Eello University (Nigeria), and the University of Wales and is the author of numerous articles on international human rights.

ALEXANDER YANOV is a Research Associate at the Institute of International Studies, University of California, Berkeley. He received his M.A. in history from Moscow State University and his Ph.D. in philosophy at the Plekhanov Institute of National Economy in Moscow. For 20 years he had been a free-lance political writer in Moscow until exiled in 1974. Since then he has been taught at the University of Texas at Austin, Queens College, and Berkeley, and has been a Fellow of the National Endowment for the Humanities. He is the author of *Détente after Brezhnev; The Russian New Right*; and *The Origin of Autocracy*.

Index

Acheson, Dean, 192, 195, 196
Afghanistan, 15–16, 24–25, 217–18, 221–22
Almond, Gabriel, 211
Amnesty International, 173, 174
Arms race, 17
Autocracy, in Russian history, 45–50

Binyon, Michael, 36–37, 38
Bohlen, Charles E., 191, 192
Brezhnev, Leonid I.: Afghanistan 38, 87; Soviet economic growth, 40; military expenditures, 40–41; de-Stalinization, 61–66; Establishment Right, 65–66; succession question, 69–89; 26th Party Congress, 70; Secretariat, 70, 79–80; Politburo, 70–72; five-year plans, 71, 85, 227; transfer of power, 73–75; candidates for succession of, 75–77; institutional competition for succession of, 78–80; new leadership generation, 80–83; domestic heritage, 84–86; foreign policy heritage, 87–88; détente, 87–88, 227
Brown, Harold, 219
Brzezinski, Zbigniew, 41, 135
Burke, Edmund, 142
Butterfield, Herbert, 143

Caddell, Patrick, 134
Carter administration: approach to the Soviet Union, 11, 22, 216–18; revision of strategic doctrine, 219–20; and Persian Gulf, 221–22; Iran, 221, 222; *see also* Détente, Containment, Human rights, Foreign policy establishment, *and* Foreign policy consensus, U.S.
Catherine the Great, Tsarina, 44
Chernenko, K. U., 75–76, 77
Chicago Council on Foreign Relations, 201, 202
Chou En-lai, 93
Clausewitz, Carl von, 23, 24
Clifford, Clark, 190, 209

Coalition for a New Foreign and Military Policy, 170, 171
Cold War: reasons for durability, 1–4; responsibility for, 4–7; reappearance of in late 1970s, 112–15, 218
Cold War revisionism, 186, 189
Containment: history of, 8–11; symmetrical and asymmetrical styles, 8–11; in the 1980s, 18–21, 25–33; and "friction," 23–25; and détente, 32; as a grand, anti-Soviet coalition, 113–19, 122–27; and domestic consensus, 187–96; versions of Kennan and Nitze, 189–94; and Vietnam, 194; versions of Tucker and Podhoretz, 207–14
Council on Foreign Relations, 215

Daniel, Yuri, 158
Denisevich, Ivan, 36
Derian, Patt, 147, 200
De-Stalinization: in Russian history, 37, 45, 47, 50; in the Soviet Union, 53–66
Détente: and Nixon administration, 10, 11–16, 223, 228–29; and Ford administration, 10; and Carter administration, 11, 22; Soviet perception of, 18–19; deficiencies in U.S. approach, 12–14; and domestic consensus, 187, 196–99; and Vietnam War, 197; and "linkage," 21
Dulles, John Foster, 9, 144, 165

Economic interdependence, 32, 229–30
Eisenhower Doctrine, 24
Ellsberg, Daniel, 196
Energy dependence, U.S., 18, 25, 28–29, 32, 222–23

Foreign policy consensus, U.S.: during Cold War, 187–96; and détente, 196–99; prospects for the 1980s, 201–14; and Carter administration, 199–201

Foreign policy establishment, U.S.: during Cold War, 187–96; and Korean War, 195; and Asia, 195–96; and détente, 196–99; "new" Establishment, 199–200, 202–3, 212
Fraser, Donald, 167–68

Galanskov, Yuri, 159
Gershman, Carl, 203, 204
Ginzburg, Alexandr, 159, 181
Goldberg, Arthur, 35, 181
Golitsyn, Vasilii, 38
Gromyko, Andrei A., 72, 88

Hammer, Armand, 151
Harkin, Tom, 167, 169
Hodgson, Godfrey, 187, 188, 189
Hough, Jerry, 42, 53
Howard, Michael, 149–50
Human rights: and Soviet-American relations, 134–50, 179–83; and Carter administration, 26, 30, 134–37, 145–47, 177–79, 200; and emigration of Soviet Jews, 134; and moralism, 137–38, 145–48; and cynicism, 137, 140–45; and moral reasoning, 138, 148–50; *see also* Human rights organizations
Human rights organizations, 155–85; and Eastern Europe, 158; and the Soviet Union, 158–60; and Soviet Jewry, 161–62, 172; and Latin America, 157, 167; and Helsinki Agreements, 160, 165, 171, 174, 181, 183; and the United Nations, 165–67, 168; and Southeast Asia, 167, 171; and U.S. Congress, 167–69; attempts to build coalition of, 174, 175–77; appropriate role of NGOs, 184–85

International system: transformation of, 128–33; accommodation to Soviet power, 121–24; and bipolarity, 215–20
Iran, 2, 3, 20, 203, 216
Ivan the Terrible, 44, 45, 46, 49, 67

Jackson, Henry, 21, 134, 172, 211
Jackson-Vanik amendment, 21, 153, 167, 172–73, 180, 198
Johnson, Louis, 191, 192

Kaplan, Fred M., 191, 193
Kennan, Edward L., 142
Kennan, George F., 3, 8, 24, 144, 189–92, 195–96, 206, 207, 213, 235
Kennedy administration, 9–10, 16
Keynes, John Maynard, 138
Keyserling, Leon, 192, 193
Khrushchev, Nikita S., 11, 34, 36, 52, 58, 59–61, 77, 78, 224
Kirilenko, A. P., 70, 75, 76–77, 79, 86
Kissinger, Henry A.: and détente, 11–16, 196–99, 223–24, 228–29; and human rights, 135, 198; and nuclear weapons, 218; and Iran 221–22; *see also* Détente *and* Containment
Kosygin, Alexei, 63, 64, 79, 93
Kristol, Irving, 210, 211, 212

Lenin, V. I., 34

Malenkov, G. M., 58, 59–61, 63, 64, 77
Mannheim, Karl, 143
Mao Tse-tung, 25, 92
Military power: limits to its use in the 1980s, 25, 216, 231–35; and strategic balance, 27, 218–23; and conventional balance, 27–28; and terrorist groups, 28; and Soviet priorities, 223–26; and Persian Gulf, 226; *see also* Containment
Moynihan, Daniel Patrick, 42, 211, 213

Nekipelov, Viktor, 35, 48
Nekrasov, Viktor, 36
Neo-conservatism, and American foreign policy, 203–14
Niebuhr, Reinhold, 135, 138, 139
Nitze, Paul, 189, 192, 196, 200, 206, 207, 213
Nixon administration, *see* Détente, Foreign policy consensus, *and* human rights
Nixon Doctrine, 10

Index

NSC–68, 8, 9, 191–94, 206, 210, 213, 214

Paul, Tsar, 49
Peter I, Tsar, 37, 44, 46
Podhoretz, Norman, 204, 207, 209–11, 213

Reagan, Ronald, 199, 223
Rossiter, Clinton, 143–44
Rostow, Walt, 35, 196
Rusk, Dean, 196, 200
Rustin, Bayard, 175

Sakharov, Andrei, 21, 146, 160, 182
SALT, 13, 21, 27, 30, 31, 145, 147
Salzberg, John, 168
Shcharansky, Anatoly, 182
Sino-American relations, 106–11, 125–26; and arms sales, 107; and "parallel strategic interests," 108, 230–31; future of, 132–33
Sino-Soviet relations, 90–111; prospects for war, 92–97; Ussuri River clash, 92, 94; and Cultural Revolution, 94; and nuclear weapons, 95; and Vietnam, 96–97; prospects for peace, 97–104; and Taiwan, 102–3; and Siberia, 104–6, 109–11; and Japan, 106, 109–11; and the U.S., 106–11, 228–29; *see also* Containment
Solzhenitsyn, Alexander, 177
Stalin, Josef, 5–6, 44, 46, 67, 89, 224, 227–28
Stalinization, 45; and Establishment Right, 51–53; and Brezhnev, 65–66; *see also* Autocracy
Stern, Paula, 172
Suslov, M. A., 75, 76

Toqueville, Alexis de, 139, 205
Trilateral Commission, 199, 200
Truman Doctrine, 191
Truman, Harry S., 191, 193, 195
Tucker, Robert W., 199, 204–6, 207–9, 212, 213, 214
Turner, Stansfield, 39

Ustinov, D. F., 72, 76

Vance, Cyrus, 21, 146–47
Vogelgesang, Sandra, 154, 177

Wilson, Woodrow, 137

Zimbabwe, 24, 217, 223
Zinov'ev, Alexander, 48